CHOP FRY WATCH LEARN

切　炒　觀　學

Fu Pei-mei on the set of her best-known television cooking program, *Fu Pei-mei Time* (*Fu Pei-mei shijian*), in 1994. Fu taught Chinese cooking on television for more than forty years, from the start of broadcasting in Taiwan in 1962 until her retirement in 2002.

CHOP 切

FRY 炒

WATCH 觀

LEARN 學

FU PEI-MEI AND THE
MAKING OF MODERN
CHINESE FOOD

Michelle T. King

W. W. NORTON & COMPANY
Independent Publishers Since 1923

Portions of Chapters 1, 2, 3, 5, and 8 were previously published in "The Julia Child of Chinese Cooking, or the Fu Pei-mei of French Food?: Comparative Contexts of Female Culinary Celebrity," in *Gastronomica: The Journal of Critical Food Studies* 18, no. 1 (February 2018): 15–26.

Portions of Chapter 4 were previously published in "What is 'Chinese' Food? Historicizing the Concept of Culinary Regionalism," in *Global Food History* 6, no. 2 (Summer 2020): 89–109. The article is available online: www.tandfonline.com/doi/full/10.1080/20549547.2020.1736427.

Portions of Chapter 6 were previously published in "A Cookbook in Search of a Country: Fu Pei-mei and the Conundrum of Chinese Culinary Nationalism," in *Culinary Nationalism in Asia*, ed. Michelle T. King (Bloomsbury Academic, 2019), 56–72. Bloomsbury Academic is an imprint of Bloomsbury Publishing plc.

For information about permission to reproduce selections from this book, write to Permissions, W. W. Norton & Company, Inc., 500 Fifth Avenue, New York, NY 10110

For information about special discounts for bulk purchases, please contact W. W. Norton Special Sales at specialsales@wwnorton.com or 800-233-4830

Manufacturing by Lakeside Book Company
Book design by Daniel Lagin
Production manager: Louise Mattarelliano

Library of Congress Cataloging-in-Publication Data Available

ISBN 978-1-324-02128-5

W. W. Norton & Company, Inc.
500 Fifth Avenue, New York, N.Y. 10110
www.wwnorton.com

W. W. Norton & Company Ltd.
15 Carlisle Street, London W1D 3BS

1 2 3 4 5 6 7 8 9 0

To Ma and Ba,
for all the meals of my childhood.

To Ian, Penelope, and Hamish,
for all the meals yet to come.

Contents

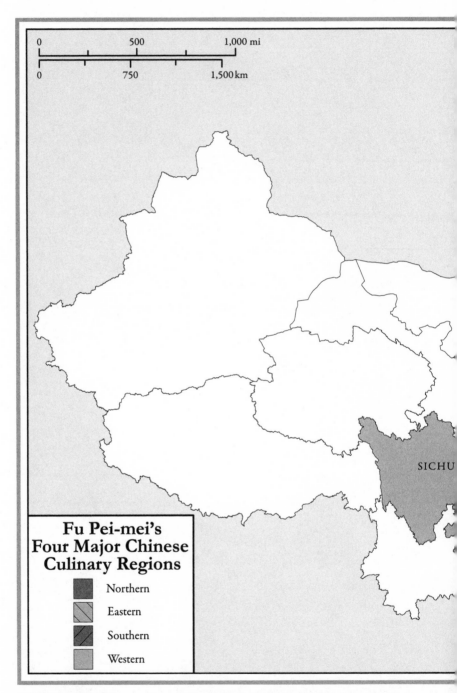

China's four major culinary regions, as delineated by Fu Pei-mei in the first volume of her best-selling, bilingual Chinese-English cookbook, *Pei Mei's Chinese Cook Book*, Vol. I (1969), superimposed on a current map of the People's Republic of China.

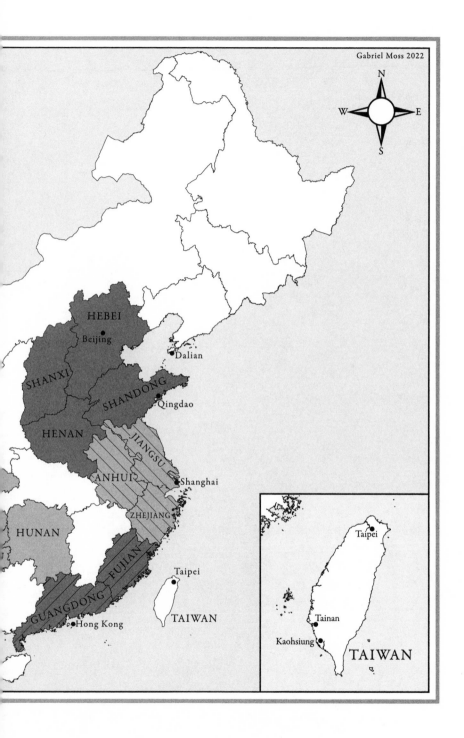

Gabriel Moss 2022

N
W   E
S

HEBEI
●Beijing
●Dalian

SHANXI

SHANDONG
●Qingdao

HENAN

JIANGSU

ANHUI
●Shanghai

ZHEJIANG

HUNAN

FUJIAN

GUANGDONG

●Hong Kong

Taipei

TAIWAN

Taipei

Tainan

Kaohsiung

TAIWAN

Introduction

IN THE FREEZER, READY TO EAT

"In the Freezer, Ready to Eat Food" list, handwritten in Chinese and English by the author's mother, Ellen Huang King (January 6, 2019).

W HEN I WAS A CHILD, I WOULD SOMETIMES TAKE my mother's copy of *Pei Mei's Chinese Cook Book* (1969) off the shelf, lie on the floor, and idly flip through its pages. I would puzzle over the odd, technicolor photographs of food and stilted renderings of recipes in English, ignoring the original versions of the same recipes in Chinese on the facing pages because I couldn't read them at the time. My parents had emigrated from Taiwan almost two decades earlier and we lived in the middle of Michigan. I had no idea that Fu's cookbook was a best-seller in Taiwan or that Fu was a television celebrity there with her own long-running cooking show. All I knew was that Fu's cookbook sat alongside *The Joy of Cooking* on our bookshelf, just as a battered old Tatung rice cooker sat next to the Cuisinart on our kitchen countertop. Much later, when I was living on my own, I asked my mother how to make some dishes we had eaten growing up. She suggested that if I wanted to learn how to cook Chinese food, I could start by borrowing her copy of Fu's cookbook. I tried my hand at a few of the recipes—the directions were minimal and the use of oil copious—but didn't think much more about it.

My family, like so many other immigrant families, speaks the language of food (in our case, in the dialect of dumplings). Several years ago, when my mother and father came for an extended visit, they packed my freezer with home-cooked Chinese dishes, ready to defrost and eat. This was nothing unusual—whenever my mother visits, I look forward to eating my favorite Chinese dishes and then savoring the bounty with several more weeks of home-cooked meals stored in the freezer. This time, though, my mother also left behind a three-page handwritten inventory of all the dishes they had made, in both Chinese and English. Beyond the tofu (meat)balls, beef with onions, scallion pancakes, radish cakes, *mushu* pork, *mapo* tofu, five-spice dried tofu with pork and pickled greens, braised pork, braised fried tofu puffs, tea eggs, and stewed eggs, they also prepared specific ingredients with the idea that I would cook them later. Item 10 was frozen bass fillets and chopped scallions, awaiting only the addition of chopped ginger and garlic, wine, soy sauce, and oil, before a few minutes of cooking time in the microwave, according to my mother's explicit instructions. (I am to add a little *doubanjiang*, or fermented bean sauce, if I like, she appends in a final note.) More than any other document I possess, this list—at once maternal, bilingual, and centered on food—explains my motives for writing this book. It is not just about the contents of my freezer, but about the continual efforts of my mother to fill it, all to ensure that my husband, children, and I get tasty, home-cooked meals despite our frazzled and busy lives.

I have always thought of my mother as a great Chinese home cook, but this was not always the case. She only learned how to cook as a matter of necessity, after she came to the United States from Taiwan as a graduate student in 1963, two years before Fu Pei-mei published her first cookbook. It was in America that my mother had her first banana split, at Marshall Field's in Chicago (she was aghast that anyone could eat that much ice cream), and it was from an American girl that she learned what it meant to go on a diet (she was aghast that anyone could eat cottage cheese, which tasted like soap to her). Throughout my mother's childhood, she had been encouraged to focus on school and never spent much time in the kitchen. Moving into a rooming house in Minneapolis at age twenty-three marked the first time she ever had to look after herself. My mother subsisted on a diet of hard-boiled eggs, peanut butter, and apples—all cheap sources of nutrition requiring little preparation. She only cobbled together the skills to cook Chinese food over the course of many years by leafing through the occasional cookbook, like Fu's, and tasting dishes that other Chinese mothers brought to potlucks. The fact that she cooked almost every day and our family rarely went out to eat also imposed the regime of daily practice.

How did this transformation take place, from non-cook to home cook, not only for my mother, but for countless other twentieth-century Chinese women of her generation, in Taiwan, in the United States, and around the world? How did they take on the task of feeding their families, and how did they manage to juggle these domestic duties with their careers? I ask myself these questions constantly after giving birth to my own two children. I know exactly what good home-cooked food is and how I want to feed my kids. I want to provide them with a tangible—and delicious—sense of family and identity, as my Chinese immigrant parents did for me. My own taste buds have been trained over the years with every hand-folded potsticker, steamed and fried with lacy crisps to my father's exacting standards, and with every bowl of my mother's hot and sour soup, overflowing with my favorite combination of wood ear fungus, dried lily buds, shredded pork, tofu, bamboo shoots, mushrooms, and brined shrimp. I want my kids to have their own favorite dishes, ones they will dream about and ask me to make every time they come home from college. Yet the daily reality of making this happen seems out of reach for me.

My life as a college professor and working mom means that cooking dinner often falls through the cracks, between the endless juggling of teaching classes, attending meetings, and trying to squeeze in time to write a book, to say nothing of managing mundane routines of drop-offs, pick-ups, and doctor's appointments. We get takeout at least once a week, if not more often, requiring the constant weighing of speed and convenience against health and nutrition in my mental good-enough-mom calculations. But instead of fish fingers and chicken nuggets, our go-to version of a quick dinner is boiled frozen dumplings—and my kids eat *a lot* of dumplings. Although I consider myself an ardent feminist and every other aspect of homemaking has long since gone to the dogs, this desire to feed my family simple, unfussy, home-cooked Chinese meals is firmly lodged inside me.

And so I found myself flipping through Fu Pei-mei's cookbook once again, after my first child was born, looking for Chinese recipes that wouldn't make too many demands on my time or my limited cooking abilities. Suddenly, I see Fu's cookbook with new eyes. In the intervening decades, I have been trained as a gender historian of China and can now read Chinese. For the first time, I notice that alongside all the recipes and pictures of dishes, Fu's cookbook contains copies of newspaper clippings from her world travels, photographs of her shaking hands with VIPs or teaching different groups of international students. In 1969, the United States still had diplomatic relations exclusively with the Republic of China (ROC) on Taiwan and no ties at all with the People's Republic of China (PRC) on the mainland; the wife of the American ambassador to Taiwan even wrote the foreword to Fu's cookbook. In effect, the pages of Fu's cookbook provide a paper trail, the kind that a professional historian can track down and follow, like a bloodhound on the scent. No longer is Fu's cookbook just a curious, dusty relic of my parents' past—now I see it as a vivid portal into another time and place, a window onto still-tangled social questions about domesticity and feminism, as they emerged and transformed the shape of postwar Taiwan. Intrigued and excited, I set out to learn everything I can about Fu.

This book is the result of that journey, an intimate portrait of twentieth-century Chinese home cooking, animated by multiple generations of women preoccupied with the fundamental, everyday dilemma of what to make for dinner—and one impressive woman who made it seem possible. In these pages, you won't find the familiar images of Chinese food as seen in Chinese American restaurants, created for consumption by foreigners and festooned with red lanterns, takeout boxes, fortune cookies, and the chopsticks font. Instead, I offer a history of Chinese food from the inside, centered on the place where most Chinese actually eat it: at home around the family dinner table, made with love (and various degrees of culinary skill) by mom. When told in this way, with twentieth-century women's lives, homes, and families at the center, the story of Chinese food is transformed. It is no longer simply the hoary cultural inheritance of centuries of unchanging culinary tradition, but just as much a modern product of television, electric rice cookers, and trans-Pacific jetliners.

The story of Fu Pei-mei (1931–2004), Taiwan's beloved television cooking authority and cookbook author, is intimately bound up with the making of that post-World War II generation of middle-class female Chinese home cooks in Taiwan and around the world. Fu was just eighteen when she arrived in Taiwan in 1949 as a wartime refugee from mainland China. When she married two years later, Fu, like so many other women she would eventually teach, had no idea how to cook. Yet as a young housewife she launched a career as a television cooking instructor that would last four decades, entrancing millions of viewers who grew up watching her prepare thousands of delectable dishes with skill and verve. She authored dozens of best-selling cookbooks, led a flourishing cooking school in Taipei, and, as her fame grew, traveled beyond the borders of Taiwan, teaching the rest of the world as the Republic of China's most beloved ambassador of Chinese cooking. Fu's story reminds us that skilled home cooks—even Chinese ones—are made in the kitchen, not born through blood.

The circumstances of her birth and the timing of her culinary career gave Fu a front row seat to every major political and social event affecting modern Taiwan's history for more than seventy years. Through the pages of Fu's cookbooks and the story of her life, we come to understand not only the twists and turns of Taiwan's modern political history, but also the dynamic shift in women's roles during the postwar economic boom, when women began to leave kitchens and cooking behind for jobs in offices and factories. Fu appeared on television during its debut in Taiwan in the 1960s, saw the rise of the feminist movement in the 1970s, and navigated the shifting diplomatic fortunes of the Republic of China (Taiwan) in the international arena in the 1980s, particularly after the demise of its official diplomatic relations with the United States in favor of mainland China. These same decades saw the arrival of the electric rice cooker, refrigerator, and gas range in Taiwan's kitchens, as well as the rise of industrialized foods and a welter of new restaurants, including fast-food chains, which dramatically changed food preparation and consumption for women and their families. Women of Fu's generation in Taiwan turned to Fu because she methodically taught them how to cook an astounding range of unfamiliar Chinese regional dishes right on their television sets, in ways their own mothers and grandmothers never could.

The same culinary lessons absorbed by women in Taiwan also traveled around the world, as Fu's cookbooks were packed into suitcases of students going overseas to study, hankering for a taste of home. Fu's cookbooks would eventually become totems of culinary identity and cultural memory in the United States, Canada, and many other countries, as first-generation immigrant parents (like mine) passed them on to their second-generation children (like me). As a result, Fu's legacy spans Taiwan, Asia, and the globe, with multigenerational fans found wherever diasporic Chinese have landed. Some of their voices are included in this book in the form of what I call Kitchen Conversations, which are interviews with modern Chinese women, many of whom are relatives or family friends, conducted in order to understand how Fu's cookbooks fit into their real working lives.

I have also drawn upon an extensive range of other historical and contemporary sources in both Chinese and English in order to trace this story, including Fu's own autobiography, cookbooks, recipes, newspaper articles, women's magazines, essays and books by Chinese epicureans, short stories and novels, Taiwan's early equivalent of the *TV Guide*, print advertisements, photographs, maps, political posters and writings, radio and television broadcasts (including Fu's own cooking show), a fictionalized television series about Fu's life, YouTube videos, Instagram posts, blogs, and dozens of other interviews with cookbook authors, food writers, chefs, home cooks, and Fu's own family members.

The history of Chinese food as seen through Fu Pei-mei's life and career is not a story of timeless tradition, but one of modern transformation—of self and family, of cuisine and society. And no one embodied this modern transformation of Chinese cuisine in all its global, gendered, political, and technological dimensions better than Fu. That all these dramatic changes took shape in a Cold War climate foregrounds Taiwan's outsized role in shaping modern Chinese cuisine as we know it today. As it turns out, the oil-stained pages of my mother's copies of Fu's cookbooks contain more than just the recipes and photos of a delicious, beloved cuisine—they also reflect a tumultuous modern history, a social revolution for women, technological changes in the kitchen, and multiple generations of families, connected across oceans by an abiding love of Chinese food.

Notes on Terminology

Readers may wonder why I use the term "Chinese" instead of "Taiwanese" in the title and throughout this book, as well as using the former term to describe Fu Pei-mei and the style of home cooking she was attempting to master. Although Fu was born in mainland China, most of her adult life and her career took place on the island of Taiwan.

So why not call her Taiwanese? The short and simple answer is that I use the term "Chinese" because that is the term Fu herself used at the time. When Fu Pei-mei published the first volume of her best-selling bilingual cookbook series in 1969, she called it *Pei Mei's Chinese Cook Book* in English: this was the cuisine she claimed expertise in, the cuisine she wanted to share with the world. Yet the nuances of the complex political histories behind these identity labels of "Chinese" and "Taiwanese," and Fu's use of either term, require a much longer and involved explanation, one which develops over the course of this book.

Much more will be said about this issue in Chapter 8, but at the outset, I want to emphasize that I use the term "Chinese" throughout this book not as a narrow geopolitical reference to mainland China, but in its broadest possible cultural sense, as a way to highlight the ties that bind together people of Han descent all around the world. For me, the term also signals the connection to earlier generations and the vast repertoire of literary, cultural, and culinary traditions that existed well before the dichotomous contemporary political divide between mainland China and Taiwan. Chinese terms frequently used in Taiwan make this distinction clearer, indicating a difference between 中國 *Zhongguo*, or China-as-country, and 中華 *Zhonghua*, or Chinese-as-culture.

One of the themes of this book is that Chinese identities are complex, diverse, and above all else, not uniform. I have tried to remain true to common usage at any given historical moment and to each speaker's self-description. But readers should recognize that the meanings of these identity labels are not fixed, and their usage continues to evolve. This is true even in my own case: Although I've always called myself "Chinese American," after writing this book, I'm more inclined to introduce myself as "Chinese American by way of Taiwan" (others have used "Taiwanese Chinese American") in order to suggest to others more clearly the complexity of my family background.

Another term that has shifted historically is the name of the northern Chinese city known to us today as Beijing, the capital of China. The city's name changed multiple times in the early twentieth century, from Beijing (from 1644–1927, under the Qing dynasty and early Republic of China), to Beiping (between 1928 and 1949, under the Republic of China), back to Beijing (since 1949 after the establishment of the People's Republic of China). Throughout those same years, the anglicized name Peking was also used by foreigners. I have followed the usage of each individual writer, but readers should understand that Beiping, Peking, and Beijing all refer to the same northern Chinese city.

Most of the Chinese transliterations in this book are romanized using the *pinyin* system, adopted in mainland China. A few exceptions include names and places better known by other romanizations, such as Chiang Kai-shek (as opposed to the *pinyin* rendering of his name, *Jiang Jieshi*) or the KMT (abbreviation of the Kuomintang Party, or Nationalist Party, instead of *Guomindang*). Chinese characters appear in their traditional forms, as used in Taiwan.

CHOP FRY WATCH LEARN

切　炒　觀　學

1

EXILE AND ARRIVAL

Fu Pei-mei, at approximately age 19, riding her bike to work as a typist in Taipei
(ca. early 1950s).

I N 1949, WHEN FU PEI-MEI WAS ONLY EIGHTEEN, SHE LIN-gered at the door of a typewriting shop on a small side street in the northern Chinese city of Qingdao. She was on one of her extended jaunts around town, trying to spend as much time as possible outside every day because she was staying temporarily with distant relatives as an unwanted house guest. Inside the shop, typists sat working at their machines, but the sound they made was not a steady *tap-tap-tap*. Instead, it was a slower cadence: *ka-clunk* (pause) *ka-clunk* (pause) *ka-clunk* (pause). A Chinese typist had to search for the metal type-face of a single, backward, upside-down character among thousands of possibilities, one at a time. With her left hand, a typist pushed the han-dle of a heavy, flat, gliding tray filled with thousands of tiny blocks of metal type—pause. Once she found the correct character, she pressed the selector key firmly with the right index finger, which picked up the type to impress it onto the paper before dropping it back down onto the tray—*ka-clunk*.

Mustering her courage to go inside, Fu continued to watch, spell-bound. She soon found herself chatting with the owner, asking if she might learn the trade. She volunteered to assist the typists in their work, picking out individual character type to set in the trays or cleaning the tray beds. Gradually, she learned how each part of the type-writer functioned, and then eventually got the hang of typing itself. It took strength just to push the type tray back and forth. "Some of the machines were so old they could barely glide anymore," she recalled in her autobiography. "At the end of the day, your shoulders and back would be aching, and your right index finger, which struck the key, grew a callus." (Later, after getting married, she would discover the same callus on her husband's right index finger, but that, he told her with a laugh, was the result of playing so much mahjong.)

Fu's fledgling typing skills helped her land her first paid job when she arrived in Taiwan later that same year. At first the work was ago-nizingly slow. She had to scrutinize more than three thousand pieces of metal type, laid out in a 35-by-97 grid, arranged by Chinese char-acter components called radicals. The work was exhausting and dried out her eyes. But soon, the pause between each *ka-clunk* became shorter and shorter. "After a while," Fu wrote, "I no longer needed to use my eyes to search for radicals anymore; I could type from memory. My sense of the distance my hand needed to push the selector became more and more accurate." With determination and practice, Fu had trained her eyes and hands to work together. She had become a true typewriter girl—one of a new generation of young, unmarried Chinese women taking on office jobs in the twentieth century.

In Taiwan, Fu found a level of independence and freedom that she had not enjoyed on the mainland. Her work as a typist, first in a typing pool, then as a typing teacher, and eventually as an office lady in a local trading company in Taipei, allowed her to support not only herself, but also her father and older brother, with whom she had been reunited. They had emigrated to Taiwan the year before Fu did to search for work, but the aftermath of both World War II (1937–1945) and the Chinese Civil War (1945–1949) imposed a pinched existence on everyone. For men like Fu's father and older brother, everything in Taiwan after the war was flipped on its head, like the metal characters on a Chinese typewriter. They were frequently unemployed or underemployed, whereas Fu, still a young wisp of woman, managed to thrive.

In those early years in Taiwan, the closest Fu Pei-mei got to food preparation was during lunch at the local trading company where she worked. As the hour drew near, Fu would glance at the clock, waiting to hear the footsteps of the delivery boy coming up the stairs. Every day, her Shanghainese colleagues ordered six dishes and a soup from a nearby Jiangsu-Zhejiang style restaurant, which satisfied their Shanghainese tastes. Her workmates would set the table and call everyone over to eat. "I didn't know anything about cooking or cuisine at that time," recalled Fu, who was from the north and unfamiliar with southern dishes. "Every dish had its own particular qualities, and they all tasted delicious." Fu worked in the trading office for only ten months, but she always remembered those satisfying lunches— and that period of independence as a young, unmarried professional woman, riding her bike to and from work each day. Arriving in Taiwan in 1949 had been an adventure in itself, a time of grit and trial in her life that she never forgot.

●　●　●

Whenever Fu Pei-mei recalled the idyllic early years of her childhood, blushing pink cherry blossoms in full spring flower always came to mind. Her father's family lived in coastal Shandong Province, but as a teen he had followed an uncle across the Bohai Sea to the prosperous port city of Dalian, in Liaoning Province. Fu was born in Dalian in 1931, the oldest daughter and third child in a family of seven children. During elementary school her family moved to the countryside. Her father, a prosperous business owner, built a solid, Western-style house with glass windows—in contrast to the traditional, walled, northern Chinese courtyard house—that overlooked a fruit orchard with cherry, pear, and apple trees. There was a smaller Japanese-style living room downstairs for ordinary guests, with tatami mat flooring and sliding paper screen doors, and a second, private living room upstairs for just the family, complete with all the fine bourgeois trappings of "a piano, Tianjin carpet, and French velvet sofa." (World War I had disrupted supplies of imported rugs from Turkey and Iran, giving Tianjin the chance to emerge as a source of luxurious handwoven carpets made for the American export market.)

Fu's hometown, the northern port city of Dalian, and the Liaodong Peninsula upon which it sat, had been desirable trophies in the late nineteenth-century contest among foreign imperial powers for territory and influence in China. Britain, France, Germany, Russia, the United States, and Japan, as the Chinese saying went, were intent on carving up the country like a melon. The Russians, having coerced the weakened Qing dynasty to cede a twenty-five-year lease on the Liaodong Peninsula in 1898, had built a city there they called Dal'nii, to serve as its premier warm water port in Asia. (The Russian word meant "distant" or "remote," indicating its far-flung location in relation to the European heart of the Russian empire.) Yet by 1905, the Russians had themselves been defeated by the Japanese in the Russo-Japanese War, a conflict that served as a wake-up call to Europeans; they could no longer underestimate this Asian rival. The Japanese assumed control of the port city, which they renamed Dairen, or Dalian in Chinese. Dalian, which means "great connector," lived up to its name: it would serve as the southern terminus for the Manchurian Railway network and become the gateway for Japan's growing imperial ambitions in China.

For centuries China had been the dominant political power in East Asia, extending its cultural influence over both Japan and Korea. In relational terms, China regarded Japan as its less significant younger brother. But the family dynamic abruptly changed in the late nineteenth century, when Japan emerged as Asia's leading political, military, and industrial power. To avoid China's fate at the hands of superior Western firepower, a group of young, reform-minded leaders took control of Japan and proceeded to modernize the country's military, build its industries and infrastructure, and adopt new forms of constitutional governance in what would come to be known as the Meiji Restoration (1868–1912). Japan's rapid modernization efforts paid off. The younger brother gave the older brother a sound thrashing when Japan defeated China in the first Sino-Japanese War (1894–95), in a fight over control of the Korean Peninsula. As one of the spoils of that war, the Japanese acquired the island of Taiwan, which became its first colonial possession in 1895 and would remain a Japanese colony for another fifty years. Aggressive expansion of Japan's Asian empire, a yellow riposte to European and American imperial ambitions, soon followed. Japan annexed Korea in 1910 and in 1931 it invaded Manchuria on the Chinese mainland. Japanese incursions in northern China erupted into the full-fledged Second Sino-Japanese War in 1937, which would soon become engulfed in the larger global geopolitical conflict of World War II.

Growing up in Japanese-occupied Dalian, Fu's childhood love of cherry blossoms was thus more emblematic than she might have understood at the time. Although many Chinese deeply resented Japanese territorial expansion in the years leading up to World War II, Fu's father was a lifelong Japanophile, having developed a great number of contacts through his business, which imported European and American alcohol and canned goods via Japanese middlemen. (He would eventually move to Japan permanently in 1950 and remain there alone until his death eight years later.) He even sent Fu to a Japanese elementary school, where she was the only Chinese student. She became fluent in the language and developed a fondness for all things Japanese, an appreciation she would maintain for the rest of her life. One of the few times she went out to eat as a child with her father was to enjoy *oyakodon* (a dish that literally means "parent–child bowl" in Japanese, because it contains both chicken and eggs), a homey Japanese meal of simmered meat over rice. Decades later, when Fu hosted a Chinese cooking program on Fuji Television in the late 1970s, she would marvel at the efficiency and professionalism of the entire Japanese production team: Every single person was "conscientious, punctual, and collaborative, from first to last."

The petals of this cherry blossom idyll were quickly scattered. The defeat of the Japanese at the end of World War II in 1945 and the surrender of Dalian first to Soviet and then eventually to Chinese Communist control resulted in more instability in Fu's family life, not less. The rivalries among foreign imperial powers that had previously sundered China were now recast as an internal civil war between the Nationalist Party, under the leadership of Chiang Kai-shek, and the Communist Party, under the leadership of Mao Zedong. Although her father could still conduct business in Japanese-occupied Dalian throughout World War II, the retreat of the Japanese in its aftermath resulted in anxious uncertainty about the city's future. He soon left with his oldest son to look for new business opportunities elsewhere in northern China. Fu was also unhappy because schooling in Dalian under the new Communist regime had turned into a series of political self-criticisms and struggle sessions against other classmates, providing little in the way of actual learning. In 1946, when she was just fifteen, Fu left home with her oldest brother's wife, in an attempt to find her father and oldest brother, leaving behind her mother and other siblings.

Thus began Fu's three teenage "wandering years," as she and her sister-in-law tried to locate Fu's father and older brother, bunking with any family relations they could find along the way. In Yantai, on the Shandong Peninsula, they stayed with Fu's uncle, making ends meet through odd jobs. While at her uncle's house, Fu was mortified to have to stand on the street with her cousins, shouting to passersby to buy the family's few remaining precious possessions—a copper bell, vases, porcelain, a bead curtain. As her uncle had no money to hire workers and no longer owned a donkey, she and her cousins pushed a heavy millstone to grind corn for the family. The millstone weighed seventy or eighty pounds, and after pushing it around in a circle even a few times, "you felt dizzy enough to faint." Her sister-in-law couldn't stand it, but Fu was determined to press on: "Like the little donkey, I learned to close my eyes."

The worsening conditions during the civil war meant that by its end, in 1949, between one and two million refugees would flee with Chiang Kai-shek and the Nationalist Party to the island of Taiwan, while the Communist Party emerged victorious on the mainland under Mao Zedong. After their retreat from the mainland, Taiwan became the last stronghold of the Nationalist Party and endured as the sole remaining territory of the Republic of China. Chiang Kai-shek claimed that the setback would be only temporary, certain that American aid would soon flow to help them fight back against the Communists. The island had been a Japanese colony for fifty years (1895–1945) before it was handed back to the Nationalist Chinese government at the end of World War II. Fu's father and brother were among those who had headed to Taiwan in the waning years of the Civil War, and Fu and her sister-in-law were determined to follow them. It was during one leg of this last journey that they passed through Qingdao, where Fu lingered at the door of the fateful typewriter shop.

● ● ●

From the perspective of that typewriter shop door, Fu could not possibly have stood farther from the rarified elite world of Chinese cuisine, as it had been depicted by Chinese men for centuries. Chinese food writing prior to the twentieth century was an almost exclusively male affair with regard to authorship, readership, and the social worlds depicted. By and large, Chinese literati—who were by definition male—produced poems and essays about drinking and eating with male friends, for the vicarious pleasure of other male literati.

The eighteenth-century epicure Yuan Mei's (1715–1797) well-known culinary treatise, *Recipes from the Garden of Contentment* (*Suiyuan shidan*) (1792), for example, recounts the eating experience of the gentleman scholar, providing a series of buying and tasting notes with a plethora of do's and don'ts for like-minded connoisseurs. For Chinese male gourmets of the imperial era, food was something to be enjoyed, admired, and aesthetically judged—but not something which they themselves produced or cooked with their own two hands. Indeed, in the hierarchy of culinary activity, the gentleman's palate was valued more than the skilled hands of his cook.

Yuan Mei, for example, wrote an homage to his personal chef, Wang Xiaoyu, whom he admired not only for his exceptional culinary skills, but also for his sense of economy. Wang did not need fancy, rare, or expensive ingredients, Yuan Mei boasted, to make something taste delicious. Yuan Mei once asked Wang why he stayed with him when he could have commanded a much higher salary in a wealthier household. In response, Wang explained that what he appreciated most was Yuan Mei's refined palate: although it made him an exacting employer, working for Mei was the only way Wang could improve his cooking. "The ordinary hard-drinking revelers at a fashionable dinner-party would be equally happy to gulp down any stinking mess," Wang scoffed. "They may say what a wonderful cook I am, but in the service of such people my art can only decline.... You, on the contrary, continually criticize me, abuse me, fly into a rage with me, but on every such occasion make me aware of some real defect." Yuan Mei's encomium to his chef in other words, somehow ends up in admiration for his own refined sense of taste.

This characteristically gendered notion of the gentleman's palate guiding the hands of his uneducated male cook persisted well into the twentieth century. F. T. Cheng (1884–1970) served as the Republic of China's last ambassador in London in the late 1940s, before Great Britain reestablished diplomatic relations with the People's Republic of China on the mainland in 1950. At the encouragement of friends, Cheng published a short book, *Musings of a Chinese Gourmet* (1954). He prided himself on having "trained" at least two cooks, one in Peking and another in Nanjing (who would later work for the British foreign minister), as well as having "polished" another cook in London. For Cheng, there was no question of whose skills were more important in the relationship between the "man of taste" and his cook: "The latter is in general merely one who is able to prepare a meal of some sort, whereas the former, though he may not have done more cooking himself in his life than boiling an egg, knows what is good or bad." It was the gentleman's refinement and culinary knowledge that carried the day, raising the standards of Chinese cuisine to their glorified heights.

Chinese gourmets of the twentieth century like F. T. Cheng, however, had to contend with a wider world in which Chinese cultural superiority was no longer as assured as it had been in Yuan Mei's eighteenth century. Starting with the Opium War (1839–42) in the mid-nineteenth century, the repeated humiliations of decades of foreign imperialism had inspired a vigorous sense of Chinese nationalism by the first half of the twentieth century, in culinary as well as political realms. Modern Chinese gourmets like Cheng were convinced that Chinese cuisine offered the world the best measure of the country's glory, despite its widespread poverty, the weakness of its central government, and the country's general inability to defend itself against foreign predation. Lin Yutang (1895–1976), philosopher and bon vivant, celebrated the superiority of Chinese cuisine in numerous essays written in English for Western audiences. In his book, *My Country and My People* (1935), Lin wrote of his fellow countrymen, "If there is anything we are serious about, it is neither religion nor learning, but food. We openly acclaim eating as one of the few joys of this human life." To this, he added more pointedly, "In the cooking of ordinary things like vegetables and chickens, the Chinese have a rich store to hand to the West, when the West is ready and humble enough to learn it. This seems unlikely until China has built a few good gunboats and can punch the West in the jaw, when it will be admitted that we are unquestionably better cooks as a nation." In Lin's eyes, culinary influence was directly proportional to political and military power.

Other modern Chinese gourmets, such as Qi Rushan (1877–1962), playwright and scholar of Chinese opera, argued in 1956 for the superiority of Chinese cuisine on the basis of its two fundamental pillars of cooking technique. *Huohou* 火候 (literally, "fire-time") indicated the precise control of heat over time, essential for quick-cooking methods such as stir-frying, while *daogong* 刀功 (literally, "knife-skill") encompassed dozens of different types of cuts for various kinds of ingredients using just a single cleaver. An individual family chef had to master both *huohou* and *daogong,* whereas in large, professional Chinese restaurant kitchens, separate teams performed each skill. In Beiping before the war, Qi had frequented famous restaurants and often went to their kitchens to chat with the cooks. One set of chefs was entirely responsible for the cleaver work, cutting, and other prep, whereas another set was entirely responsible for manning the stove and adding all seasonings. In addition, a subset of prep chefs would be responsible for making all the northern flour-based foods, such as pancakes, noodles, dumplings, or buns. It was up to the cleaver man to decide which ingredients should be paired, how much of any given ingredient to cut, and what cutting techniques should be used. If the stove man did not use everything that the cleaver man had cut, Qi wrote, "the face of the one at the chopping board would be ugly to look at. This would count as not being able to get along, and the two of them would begin to fight."

Daogong was a culinary art in itself, with dozens of different ways to cut just one piece of meat or some scallions. The cicada wing cut, for example, described in a Tang dynasty (618–907) text, was so named because of the sheer thinness of the resulting slice. In Qi's opinion, Western chefs were not nearly so fastidious about knife skills. "They never pay attention to how thinly something is sliced, or how finely it is shredded," Qi grumbled. As a result, Western cooking was "a little closer to primitive times" because the kitchen did not do all the labor ahead of time for the diner. Western diners had to take responsibility for using their own knives and forks to cut up large pieces of meat at the table, such as roast beef. Meanwhile, Chinese food was "more evolved" because the work was completed entirely by the kitchen and diners could simply use an elegant pair of chopsticks to eat.

An even more impressive display of speed and precision came at the stove, where talented chefs honed their sense of *huohou* down to the second. As Qi recalled, the stove chefs never even looked at the condiments—oil, vinegar, soy sauce, and the like—let alone measured them, before tossing a dipperful into the wok while stir-frying. Another newspaper writer, Xia Chengying (1919–2002), described how his family's cook would use a steel spatula to "fry like mad" with one hand, while his other hand would "dip and spoon up all the seasonings one by one in rapid succession like a dragonfly flitting on the water." Nor did the chefs ever taste anything while they cooked. Qi once asked a restaurant chef why this was so. The chef scoffed and said, "Not only is there no time to taste, there's no time to even look to see if you have too much or too little of any condiment. If every scoopful needed to be glanced at, considered, and only then put into the wok, then the dish would be overcooked and not tasty." So precise was this sense of *huohou* that an experienced chef would even take into account the ambient room temperature and the distance the diner was sitting from the kitchen. "If it's farther away and a warm day, then you must make the *huohou* a bit more gentle," the chef explained to Qi. "That way, when it arrives at the table, it will be just perfect. In our kitchen lingo, we call this type of dish an 'eating fire-time dish' (吃火 候的菜 *chi huohou de cai*)."

Beyond the role of men as connoisseurs and chefs, the commensal pleasures of the table were also typically seen as part of a male social world, from the imperial age to the early twentieth century. F. T. Cheng recalled the "good old days of Peking," before the war, when the enjoyment of food had been a regular occasion to enjoy the company of other male friends. Such dining or drinking groups "met weekly or fortnightly or on the occasion of the birthday of one of the members, who played host in turn." The meetings were usually at a member's home, especially if one had a talented family chef, but occasionally they would meet at a restaurant. Sometimes these gatherings served as salons, with members sharing their latest painting or poem for others to critique; at other times good food served simply to promote "good fellowship and good understanding."

Only occasionally did any of these modern Chinese male gour-mets acknowledge the role of Chinese women in the kitchen, and even then, the gentleman's palate still held pride of place. Lin Yutang's wife and daughter, Lin (née Liao) Tsuifeng and Lin Hsiangju, for exam-ple, wrote two English-language Chinese cookbooks, *Cooking with the Chinese Flavor* (1956) and *Chinese Gastronomy* (1969). Lin Yutang recalled overhearing many intense mother–daughter discussions in the kitchen over proper techniques and tastes, while he sat in the liv-ing room. The women were detailed and precise in their exchanges, a pair of culinary scientists debating proper laboratory methods. "It was like a party recalling a hunting or fishing trip, or a trip to the Arc-tic," Lin wrote. Yet despite living with two exceptional home cooks, Lin had no qualms about claiming that "acting as a fastidious and dis-cerning critic" was his own "contribution to the excellent level of my household dinners.... The wine-taster still serves a valuable func-tion, even though he does not grow the vine himself."

Indeed, for Lin, eating and having no hand in the cooking was a man's rightful place. "When a man has driven himself to work all day, he has the right to look forward to a delightful supper at home, cooked with respect for the food and for its eater," he wrote. "Admittedly," he added, perhaps with the tiniest shadow of sheepishness, "this is

a man's point of view; he does not have to do the cooking himself."
Lin's chauvinist bluster, however, did not actually carry much weight
in his female-dominated household: this time around, the Chinese
male gourmet no longer had the last word. Lin confessed that often,
when "telling my friends about the secret of preparing certain dishes,
I often have to draw up sharp." His wife Tsuifeng would quickly
interject, chiding him, "No, no, Y.T. That is not the way." Tsuifeng,
the real kitchen genius, had no problem putting her husband in his
rightful place as the passive recipient of a meal, not its inventive and
knowledgeable creator.

● ● ●

Having arrived in Taiwan around 1949, Fu, like her fellow wartime
refugees, was a "mainlander" (*waishengren*), in contrast to the "native
provincials" (*benshengren*), ethnic Hokkien and Hakka descendants
whose ancestors had migrated from Fujian and Guangdong Provinces
starting from the seventeenth century onward. These early Chinese
migrants soon outnumbered the small percentage of indigenous Aus-
tronesian islanders. Together, all these groups experienced fifty years
under Japanese colonial rule (1895–1945), which is frequently highlighted as a distinct marker of Taiwan's collective identity, differen-
tiating its history from that of China. In the years leading up to and
shortly after the end of the Chinese Civil War in 1949, between one
and two million refugees and military personnel from the mainland
joined a total existing island population of six million. At the time,
the term "Taiwanese" (*Taiwanren*) referred explicitly to Hokkien and
Hakka descendants born on the island. Similarly, until very recently,
"Taiwanese" cuisine (*Taiwancai* or *Taicai*) has referred to the tastes
and dishes developed on the island of Taiwan itself, a style rooted
largely in Fujianese cuisine, but also influenced by Japanese culture
after fifty years of colonial rule. In the early postwar decades, the term
"Taiwanese cuisine" did not typically include the range of mainlander

regional cuisines, such as Sichuanese, Hunanese, Shanghainese, Cantonese, or Beijing cuisines, which were instead collectively called
"mainlander cuisines" (*waishengcai*). (The boundaries of these postwar identities have been softening in recent decades, however, as a
result of democratization efforts starting in the 1980s, described in
Chapter 8.)

Traditional Chinese regional food identities were shaped by geography and climate. Those from land-locked Sichuan and Hunan in
southwestern and central China enjoyed spicy, sour, earthy dishes,
often with smoked ingredients. Those from Guangdong and Fujian
along the southeastern coast enjoyed light, fresh dishes, featuring seafoods from their abundant coastlines, and emphasizing the natural
tastes of the ingredients. Guangdong (Cantonese) cuisine also incor-
porated foreign ingredients, as it was the site of China's first port open
to foreign traders. Migrants from Jiangsu and Zhejiang (often named
together as "Jiang-Zhe"), centered on the major metropolis of Shanghai on the eastern coast, along with the preeminent culinary cities of
Yangzhou, Hangzhou, and Suzhou, were known for their refined palates, with a preference for delicate, light tastes. They enjoyed sweeter,
intricately made dishes, featuring ingredients from the abundant riv-
ers and lakes in both provinces. Those from northern China, including Hebei, Henan, Shanxi, Shandong, Liaoning, and the city of Beijing,
did not eat rice-based diets; instead, they were well-known for their
wheat flour-based dishes—dumplings, noodles, buns, pancakes, all
stuffed with anything, and eaten with everything else—as well as saltier fare, flavored with scallions and garlic. Each of these provinces
could be considered a culinary region in its own right, while dozens of
other culinary regions were sandwiched in between.

Although the chaos of war had disrupted the lives of millions of
mainlander refugees and native Taiwanese, the mainlander exodus
would eventually transform the culinary landscape of Taiwan, con-
centrating an extraordinary variety of Chinese regional and ethnic

cuisines on a single, small island. A 1956 registry of the provincial origins of mainlanders arriving in Taiwan illustrates the tremendous diversity of the recent wartime migrants, who came from more than a dozen provinces and three major cities, all scattered across a map of China (Map 1). Fujian, the province directly across the Taiwan Strait, had the largest share of mainlander migrants (fifteen percent), but many came from the eastern provinces of Zhejiang (twelve percent) and Jiangsu (ten percent), the southern province of Guangdong (ten percent), and the northern province of Shandong (ten percent). Other migrants had arrived from Hunan (six percent) or Anhui (five percent), whereas still others came from Henan, Sichuan, Hubei, and Hebei (approximately four percent each). Another segment came directly from China's largest cities, including Beiping, Shanghai, and Nanjing (together totaling about four percent). Smaller numbers of migrants came from other provinces. Each of these places, large and small, had its own distinctive regional food culture, which homesick migrants brought to Taiwan with them.

Mainlander migrants were not only divided by region; gender and generational differences also brought dramatic changes in family and social structures. Male mainlanders outnumbered female mainlanders by almost three to one, and most arriving mainlander women were already married. Consequently, large numbers of mainlander men, particularly young, single, low-ranking military men with few resources, would never find a spouse and remained lifelong bachelors. Others were luckier and found local Taiwanese women to marry, often from poorer families willing to marry their daughters off to more privileged mainlanders. (For their part, local Taiwanese women often appreciated that they had no in-laws to care for if they married a mainlander and thus had fewer household duties.) Mainlander enlisted men with families lived in military dependents' villages (*juancun*), where they continued to preserve familiar regional food traditions. Taiwan's beloved beef noodle soup (*niuroumian*), for example, a spicy broth with noodles and large chunks of braised beef in it, has its roots in the *juancun*. The dish was most likely created by mainlander soldiers homesick for familiar tastes and eager to find a way to make a living by selling a bowl of noodles.

Multigenerational extended families found themselves divided across the Taiwan Strait. Younger family members often moved to Taiwan, while the older ones stayed behind on the mainland, refusing to leave the only homes they had ever known. Infants and young children were left behind too. When the time came to flee to Taiwan, my maternal grandfather's mother and younger brother, who lived in Fujian, refused to come along with my grandfather, who was an officer in the Nationalist Army. His family members were Fujianese farming folk and reluctant to leave behind their land and money. My maternal grandparents also contemplated leaving behind my mother's youngest sister, who had just been born in March 1949, until she was old enough to come to Taiwan. Luckily, they did bring her along. My aunt explained it this way: "They thought, 'If we go, what will happen to everything? They figured there was no way that there could be fighting for that much longer. The Japanese had left after eight years, and these were our own people.... No one thought that the rest of their lives would pass." Ultimately, Cold War hostilities divided family members living in mainland China from those in Taiwan for almost four decades, until 1987 when the travel ban between Taiwan and mainland China was finally lifted.

Although the arrival of so many mainlander migrants would eventually add a tremendous range of new tastes to Taiwan's foodscape, the abrupt transition to Nationalist rule for those already living on the island also had traumatic consequences. Many Taiwanese chafed at the impositions of corrupt Nationalist officials arriving after 1945 and the worsening conditions of hyperinflation, caused by a government deficit and flawed economic policies. Discontent boiled over in mass protests in what has come to be known as the February 28 Incident of

1947. The evening before that date, agents from the Tobacco Monopoly Bureau and police attempted to confiscate contraband cigarettes from a widow selling them near a teahouse in Taipei. One officer struck the woman on the head with his pistol when they tried to arrest her, and an angry crowd gathered. Another officer fired into the crowd and shot a bystander who died the next day, leading to mass unrest. In the weeks that followed, island-wide protests were brutally suppressed under the orders of the governor, Chen Yi. Though exact figures are unknown, some twenty thousand civilians may have been shot and killed, and many others arrested. Martial law would be imposed two years later and would last for nearly four decades until 1987. The law granted the Nationalist government the power to suppress political opponents (including both Taiwanese and mainlanders), during the period that came to be known as the "White Terror." Public discussion of the event was prohibited, and many mainlanders arriving in its aftermath had little idea of what had happened.

Meanwhile, mainlanders themselves had just endured their own wartime trauma and were preoccupied by their own sense of loss. Catherine Chen, a family friend of ours whose grandfather served as a minister in the Nationalist government, was eleven years old when her family left Nanjing for Taiwan in 1949. "We lost everything in China," she says. "When we moved out, we had a house by the lake. All we did was just close the door and go, leaving everything behind. You had no time to sell anything or negotiate a contract or whatever. Just close the door and leave. So, we left with just the suitcases that we could carry. That's all we had." In Fu Pei-mei's own family, although her father and older brother got to Taiwan first, and she and her sister-in-law arrived there in 1949, her mother and other siblings stayed behind on the mainland. After the People's Republic of China was established on the mainland, its citizens could not leave the country without special permission to travel abroad. Luckily, Fu's elderly mother and parents-in-law were allowed to leave mainland China in 1962, partially reuniting their families. By then, Fu had not seen her mother for sixteen years, during which time she had grown from a gangly teenager into a young mother with three of her own children. Throughout the 1950s, Fu had had no older female relatives to turn to for help with her young children or to teach her how to cook.

Settling down in Taiwan meant more than finding a place to live and a way to earn money. Food was an intimate and desperate matter: a simple bowl of noodles could take a yearning exile back to his or her home region of China, now forever lost. This elegiac mood was best captured in a 1971 short story by Pai Hsien-yung, Taiwan's foremost modern short story author. "Glory's by Blossom Bridge" is narrated by a noodle shop proprietress from Guilin, in Guangxi Province, who carries on the tradition of her grandfather's horsemeat and rice noodle shop by making her own version of the dish in Taipei. Many of her customers are single men from her home province, who have no wives or family in Taipei. As a result, they take all their meals at her shop, often for years at a time. For her favorite customer, a gentlemanly schoolteacher named Mr. Lu, she makes extra effort: "I always put something extra in Mr. Lu's order—beef, I'd give him the shank cut, pork, all lean meat. At least once a week I'd make him a piping-hot bowl of noodles with my own hands: braised beef liver and hundred-leaf tripe, sprinkled with parsley and sesame oil, and topped off with a handful of deep-fried peanuts." But Mr. Lu dreams of more care and connection than the occasional bowl of shop noodles can offer: he hopes to be reunited with his childhood sweetheart, who is still trapped back home in Guilin on the mainland. Yet no happy reunion occurs. Instead, he is cheated of his life savings in a botched attempt to bring his sweetheart to Taiwan and meets with his own tragic fate. When the narrator goes to his room at the end of the story, she finds it empty, except for a single photograph of a younger, more innocent Mr. Lu and his young love standing at Guilin's famous Blossom Bridge.

Coming to terms with permanent exile in Taiwan took years for the generation of adults most deeply affected by these personal and professional losses. Some wounds never healed. Pai Hsien-yung recognized that his father and mother had suffered "endless turmoil and anguish" in leaving everything and everyone behind in their homeland. But he also asserted in 1976 that the first generation of émigré writers to Taiwan, shook to the core by this "cultural cataclysm," had been "incapacitated by nostalgia" and "lacked the necessary perspective and courage to explore their new situation in all its complexity. To admit their banishment as permanent was beyond endurance." In comparison, Pai felt it was only his own second generation of writers who "attempted to explore with unflinching candor the reality of their historical situation" on Taiwan. It took time, in other words, for an entire generation of traumatized war refugees to come to grips with and accept their new situation—if they ever did.

But who could blame those who chose to look backward, instead of forward? What is nostalgia but a sense of loss tinged with regret? For the better part of a decade, Chiang Kai-shek had insisted that the Nationalists would fight their way back and defeat the Communist forces on the mainland. That, of course, never came to pass. Moreover, for almost four decades there was no direct communication or travel between Taiwan and the mainland. For those who had lived the most robust part of their adult lives in China before making the journey to Taiwan, to speak of the "good old days of Peking" was not merely to think back to the past, but to think back to a place that could now only exist in their dreams and memories. All those places—and many of the people they had known and loved—were now forever lost.

Decades after her wartime journey, Fu Pei-mei still recalled how, in the hold of the ship that brought her to Taiwan, a passenger had brought along a gigantic wok and a crock filled with *lu* sauce, a mixture of soy sauce, sugar, garlic, ginger, and unique blend of spices, used in all manner of braised dishes. The remains of each iteration of the sauce are used in the next batch, intensifying and deepening the flavor over many decades, much like a sourdough starter. The translator of one of Fu's bilingual cookbooks, Nicki Croghan, to whom Fu would later recount this story, remarked, "That's what impressed me most. Here you are running away for your life, you know, and what do you take with you from China? A food item, a sauce that's been passed on in your family for generations."

For a country and a people like China's—riven by decades of war, dislocation, upheaval, and migration throughout the twentieth century—the accumulation of family heirlooms will never be measured in furniture. Passing down large physical items—a grandfather clock, a chest of drawers, a table, a painting—is only possible when people have means and stay rooted in one place. Too many Chinese families caught in its mid-century wars had to drop everything and run, abandoning their homes, cherished possessions, and even loved ones. Maybe this is why food takes on such significance for so many Chinese. Food is eminently portable. If the memory of a dish lingers on your tongue and you know how to cook the dishes of your family, the taste of home is never farther than your kitchen, wherever you have landed in life. Yet in the same way, food is a fickle mistress: a poor approximation of a beloved dish may simply remind you of everything you have lost.

2

MAKING A HOME

Family photograph of Fu Pei-mei (right), her husband, Cheng Shao-ching (top left), and their three children, daughters Cheng An-chi (bottom left), Cheng Mei-chi (bottom middle), and son Cheng Hsien-hao (bottom right) (ca. late 1950s).

ARLY IN HER MARRIAGE, FU TRIED TO MAKE HER OWN
餃子 *jiaozi*—boiled dumplings that were a northern Chinese
staple and her husband's favorite dish, especially when filled
with prawns. Making *jiaozi* required mixing flour and cold water to
form a dough; rolling it out into thin, even, identical circles for the
wrappers; filling them with a balanced mixture of chopped prawns,
ground pork, scallions, yellow chives, ginger, salt, soy sauce, and sesame oil; and sealing the edges neatly with pinched folds to make rows
of plump, identical, standing soldiers. Fu's husband, Cheng Shao-
ching, had exacting tastes: the wrappers had to be thin and exquisitely
wrapped; the filling had to be generous, with a bit of juice. Moreover,
the filling could only be made with prawns, not shrimp, which had a
different flavor and texture that he did not care for. They were to be
boiled and served hot, with a dipping sauce. Fu tried to make them to
please her husband, but he never seemed satisfied. Finally, one day she
asked, "Were they good?" and he answered angrily, "How could anyone eat these *jiaozi*? Every single one is just a bag of water."

She looked at the plate, and indeed, the wrappers had opened at
the edges, allowing boiling water to get inside and dilute the taste of
the filling. "How could they have leaked?" she thought to herself. She

had taken care to pinch every fold tightly to seal in the filling. From that meal forward, Fu carefully inspected every *jiaozi* before serving them to her husband, setting aside all the burst ones to eat herself, while giving him only those which were still intact. Yet despite her meticulous efforts, some leaky *jiaozi* still managed to slip by. She had to watch as her husband would "take a bite and throw it aside." Once her husband got so angry that he flung aside his chopsticks and walked away from the table. Fu was mortified. "I felt my tears well up. I was so ashamed, but had no place to hide."

The next day Fu marched over to her neighbor's apartment, old Mrs. Liu's, to beg for help, bringing filling, wrappers, and all. Could Mrs. Liu please show her how to wrap *jiaozi* so they didn't burst when boiled? Mrs. Liu laughed, and said, "Hah, missy! How could you be this old and still not know how to wrap dumplings?" But Mrs. Liu agreed to help and watched Fu's technique. First, Fu put some filling in the center of a wrapper, then she used chopsticks to moisten the edge of the wrapper, then she folded it over into a half circle and pinched tight each layered fold. Wasn't that how it was done? "Not like that, not like that," tsked Mrs. Liu. "Why on earth are you using a chopstick to moisten the edge? It's all oily—it'll burst open just as soon as you boil it." As soon as Mrs. Liu spoke, it dawned on her: they were the same chopsticks she had used to mix the filling, which had a bit of oil in it. The dumpling wrappers, made of flour and water, might appear to be sealed before cooking, but once they hit boiling water, they would never stay closed. She felt like an idiot. "Something so simple, but I didn't know anything back then. Because of this I had endured so much resentment!" How many times had she inspected the cooked *jiaozi*, examining each one to ensure it had not leaked? How many times had she stood by, watching and worrying, counting how many *jiaozi* her husband would toss aside?

At the time of the *jiaozi* episode, Fu Pei-mei and her husband, Cheng Shao-ching, were living in Kaohsiung, a city in the far south of

Taiwan, in an apartment with a kitchen at the end of the hallway that was shared with five other families. The newlyweds had been introduced barely a year earlier, while Fu was working as a secretary in Taipei. Another colleague had invited her over for lunch, and afterward, three young men from her hometown of Dalian also turned up, one of whom was Cheng. Fu had no idea that it was a setup, meant to introduce her to a potential mate. Because she had not been told, she was naturally chatty and warm, instead of awkward and shy, and Cheng took immediate interest. For her part, Fu hoped to find a partner from her hometown of Dalian to make it easier to return to the mainland someday to see her mother and other siblings. Within a month, the two were engaged. Cheng and Fu were married in 1951, when Fu was twenty, only two short years after she had arrived in Taiwan.

Though he never wished for his wife to work outside the home, Cheng Shao-ching was the one who inadvertently pushed Fu toward a culinary career. Cheng had a gift for numbers and was trained as an accountant. He worked in the Kaohsiung office of a Hong Kong shipping company as a manager in the finance department before moving back to Taipei where he rose in the ranks to vice president of the company. In those early years, Cheng's office handled only two ships arriving in the docks every month. There was not much to do every day—except play mahjong. Thus Cheng's love for numbers took the form of mahjong tiles in the afterhours: he was so good that he earned himself the nickname, Master of the Tiles.

Cheng brought his workmates back to their apartment to play because he and Fu did not yet have any children to disrupt their game. At the time, the only thing that Fu could cook for their guests was fried rice or fried noodles, and even her versions of these were terrible. Cheng would grumble to Fu, "Can't you change it up a little, and make something tasty?" "What on earth have you cooked?" "Anyone could do better than you!" He was acutely embarrassed by appearing to be a cheap host because all the players chipped in each week to pay for food and cigarettes. On no account, he warned, should she skimp on spending for the food, lest they appear to be trying to stretch the money too far. Fu seethed inside and thought to herself, "I don't care a fig about your money! Better that you don't even take it out of your pockets anymore! Instead, I'll treat and you can all eat for free on me!"

Yet Fu neither confronted Cheng openly nor did she reject the notion that, as a housewife, she was responsible for cooking all the meals for her husband and his friends. She just kept quiet and strategized about how to become a better cook. In early 1950s Taiwan, there weren't many ways for a grown woman without nearby friends and family to learn how to cook, and formal cooking schools and cookbooks were still uncommon. Fu surreptitiously tried to watch various street food vendors—the rice noodle man near the market, an old Shandong lady making scallion pancakes near the bus stop—but it was haphazard and difficult to glean much. Luckily, she soon gave birth to their first child, and the mahjong players moved their game to another apartment, sparing her the indignity of having to cook badly for Cheng's friends for the next few years.

● ● ●

For Fu Pei-mei, there was no such thing as food for food's sake; cooking was always an act of energetic devotion to the family—whether or not they appreciated it. In a radio interview in the 1980s, after she had been teaching for more than two decades, Fu observed, "Cooking has to have some love in it. . . . Most women want to make good dishes for their husbands and children to eat to make their homes happier and cozier. I don't think there is anyone who doesn't have a family or doesn't have a sweetheart, whether a young lady or an older woman, who would think to learn how to cook just for herself. That's just not very likely."

Marriage and children gave Fu's life a shape and purpose, conferring upon her a well-recognized status in Chinese society. Tellingly, the first line of Fu's preface to her autobiography describes her family, not her culinary career: "I had a husband who loved me absolutely, and still have a filial son and two daughters devoted to me, a daughter-in-law, two sons-in-law, and seven adorable grandchildren." Fu's attitude toward cooking and the family stood in stark contrast to Julia Child, Fu's American counterpart and culinary contemporary. Child gushed and enthused about French food for American television audiences, but to her, children were more of a hinderance to the enjoyment of good food, not a motivation for making it. Julia married at age thirty-four; she and her husband Paul never had any children and didn't seem to regret it. Of her childlessness, Child only briefly remarked in her autobiography, "It was sad, but we didn't spend too much time thinking about it and never considered adoption. It was just one of those things." In the introduction to her classic *Mastering the Art of French Cooking* (1961), Child baldly wrote, "This is a book for the servantless American cook who can be unconcerned on occasion with budgets, waistlines, time schedules, children's meals, the parent-chauffeur-den mother syndrome or anything else which might interfere with the enjoyment of producing something wonderful to eat." Nor did the American public seem to care much about Child's childlessness. When Child appeared on the cover of *Time* magazine in 1966, the focus was solely on food, not family. Fu, on the other hand, never left behind her identity as a housewife and mother, even as her professional life flourished and her everyday reality was lived as a career woman.

Fu's attitudes (and her husband's expectations) toward family and a woman's role within it were not unusual at the time. They were influenced by a combination of long-standing Chinese views about gender roles, as well as a host of social circumstances that were unique to postwar Taiwan. Some of these societal shifts, such as the modern trend toward living in small family units, consisting only of parents and children, could already be observed in mainland China in the first half of the twentieth century. Other changes, however, resulted from the social dislocations and adjustments of mainlanders fleeing to Taiwan in 1949, with families divided and many older family members left behind. In the decades of postwar peace that followed, the ideal of the modern nuclear family took hold in Taiwan, centered on the figure of the housewife, who simultaneously served as the family manager, emotional center, and household drudge.

• • •

Confucian teachings had long prescribed the division of labor between the sexes as a complementary distinction between the "inner" (內 *nei*) and "outer" (外 *wai*) realms. While men were to make their way in the wider world, gaining money and glory for their families in public, women were to hold sway over the household and private life. In earlier centuries, women were described in Chinese solely by their family roles—daughter, sister, wife, mother, mother-in-law, sister-in-law, aunt, grandmother, concubine, servant—and only occasionally identified by their roles outside of the family (e.g., midwife, nun, prostitute). In the premodern era, there was no Chinese word for housewife to describe a woman whose specific job was to stay at home and care for the family because staying at home was the only socially acceptable role for most women. Instead, a woman's idealized role as the primary nurturing and guiding force in the home was captured in the four-character Chinese phrase, 賢妻良母 *xianqi liangmu*, meaning "virtuous wife and loving mother."

After marriage, family always meant a husband's family because a woman became part of her husband's lineage and went to live under the same roof as her husband and his relations. Beyond a woman's husband and their children, a wealthy joint household would include her husband's parents, her husband's brothers, their wives and children, any of her husband's unmarried sisters, plus any concubines and servants of all kinds. Ban Zhao's *Admonitions for Women* was an influential book of advice written by a well-known female historian during the Eastern Han dynasty (25–220 CE). Even in the first century, Ban Zhao had no illusions about the potential difficulty of a young married woman adjusting to living her life entirely within her husband's extended family: "There are times when love may lead to differences of opinion; there are times when duty may lead to disagreement.... Excepting only sages, few are able to be faultless." The only way for a woman to get along successfully under these conditions, according to Ban Zhao, was for her to be a paragon of humility: "Let a woman modestly yield to others; let her respect others; let her put others first, herself last." This was Ban Zhao's essential recommendation for dealing with every significant relationship in a woman's life, starting with serving her husband, obeying her parents-in-law, and gaining the good will of her brothers- and sisters-in-law.

While living in a large, extended family brought its own set of headaches, at least in one regard it was less burdensome—for elite women, in any case. In imperial China, the phrase "women's work" (女功 *nügong*) had never referred to housework. Instead, the term encompassed the tasks of spinning, weaving, embroidery, and sericulture (raising silkworms to produce silk), which were the preferred occupations for proper elite women. Elite women in the late imperial period could be seen as competent household managers and "virtuous wives/loving mothers" without undertaking the actual drudgery of housework or childcare. Caring for small children, cleaning, or cooking were tasks of manual labor that could be readily completed by a variety of household servants. Wang Xifeng, for example, an ambitious and omni-competent female character in the classic eighteenth-century Qing novel, *The Dream of the Red Chamber*, acts more like the household's CEO than its cleaning and cooking staff. She makes decisions about significant household expenditures and manages rent incomes, disciplines maid servants, and decides on menus, but she doesn't roll up her sleeves herself to cook or clean.

Apart from serving her husband and parents-in-law, a traditional Chinese woman's other major responsibility was to bear sons to continue her husband's lineage, and then to guide and educate her children. No Chinese mother was more celebrated in this regard than Mencius' mother. Mencius (372–289 BCE) was one of China's most famous philosophers after Confucius. His father died when he was three, and his widowed mother moved three times, away from a cemetery and away from a public market, before finally finding the most beneficial location for her son's education, near a school. One day, Mencius came home from school while his mother was weaving, which was her only way to support them. She asked how his studies were going, and he answered lackadaisically, "Same as usual." She beckoned him to come near her loom, and then (rather dramatically, it must be said) brandished a knife and cut the cloth in two so it fell to the ground. How would Mencius ever become a true gentleman with this attitude? Studying only half-heartedly was no better than weaving a cloth only halfway—both were worthless. Mencius, like any good Chinese son, took the lesson to heart and needed no more reminders.

For more than two millennia these fundamental family values and structures held sway, but they began to shatter under the pressure of immense political and social change in the early twentieth century, as China painfully forged a modern nation from an ancient empire. The last Chinese dynasty fell in 1911, and with it all the certainties of the old ways. Progressive Chinese social reformers in the early twentieth century promoted the idea of the "small family household" (小家庭 *xiaojiating*), consisting of only parents and children (and perhaps a grandparent or two), as opposed to the traditional "large family household" (大家庭 *dajiating*), with multiple generations and various branches living under one roof. The large household was seen as feudal and backward, with conservative family dynamics holding back individual happiness and development. Decisions were made for the sake of the family by the older generations, especially in arranging dutiful but loveless marriages. Small, conjugal households, originating from freely chosen marriages, were now described as the modern ideal. Ba Jin's wildly popular 1933 novel, *Family*, reflected the negative impact of just such a feudal family, in which the three sons find their lives thwarted by the unreasonable demands of their grandfather, the family patriarch. Only the youngest son escapes his fate when he runs away to the bright lights of the city to make his own way in life.

In these same early twentieth-century decades, Chinese women began to seek alternative life options for themselves outside of the family, beyond their traditional roles as wife and mother. A handful of pioneering women blazed trails to become students, writers, newspaper editors, journalists, secretaries, teachers, nurses, principals, doctors, factory workers, civil servants, party loyalists, and even revolutionaries and soldiers. To make a distinction between women working outside of the home and women who still remained at home, taking care of the family, a new Chinese concept was needed. Enter the "housewife" (家庭主婦 *jiating zhufu* or 家庭婦女 *jiating funü*, literally "woman of the house"), the new, modern figure of Chinese female domesticity.

In the modern nuclear family, the entire responsibility for cleaning, cooking, and childcare now fell more or less on the housewife's shoulders. The small family no longer required a staff of servants to cater to its needs and might at most engage the services of a single housemaid. Meanwhile, housework for women gained an association with virtue and diligence. In 1915, Gao Junyin, a female contributor to a Chinese women's periodical, admonished middle-class women to "Do all of the housework yourself." Doing without servants, she reckoned, could demonstrate a woman's industriousness and her frugality. A similar tone was struck in a 1939 article, which warned housewives, "Don't entrust all your housework to servants. They are ignorant and unreliable, and the dishes they cook are not hygienic." The caricature of a middle-class or wealthy woman who relied entirely on her husband's income and the work of servants, while frittering away

her own time in wasteful leisure pursuits, such as shopping or playing mahjong, was frequently criticized in early twentieth-century
Chinese writings.

By the late 1940s, popular audiences easily recognized the figure
of the Chinese housewife and her many household duties. A 1947 cartoon from the prominent *Central Daily News* (*Zhongyang ribao*), for
example, shows all the steps involved in the middle-class housewife's
preparation of dinner each day. Entitled "Lesson for a Housewife," the
six panels depict the housewife as she thinks about what to cook, carries home the shopping, washes all the vegetables, chops all the ingredients, cooks in a wok over a charcoal brazier, and finally serves her
husband and child. Each stage becomes more and more labor intensive,
sweat dripping from her brow as she chops, hands moving frantically
as she cooks, until by the end she is too tired to eat, while her husband
and child happily gobble down their food. The cartoon assumes that
the housewife is already familiar with and skilled in all aspects of
cooking, even as she must perform them alone, with no assistance.

These changing Chinese family structures and domestic arrange-
ments acquired yet another layer of complexity as they were carried
across to Taiwan in 1949. Few mainlander women came to Taiwan
without any family connections and poorer mainlander women could
not afford to come on their own. Without this labor pool to work as
housemaids, mainlander families could for the most part only find
young Taiwanese girls to work as housemaids once they arrived on the
island, if they were able to afford any domestic servants at all. Class,
linguistic, educational, and culinary differences meant a frustrating
experience for both sides. Young Taiwanese girls could not be expected
to know how to cook the kinds of typical regional comfort dishes
mainlanders had known all their lives. All the same, this did not pre-
vent some mainlander families from placing ads in newspapers seeking domestic help from their home provinces, as in this 1950 example:
"*Wanted: Maid.* Seeking a maid from Jiangsu or Zhejiang Province on

behalf of a friend. Age should be around 30 years old. Main qualification is cooking family dishes well. Inquire any afternoon, Kaifeng St., Section 1, Number 114, Yu Building. Ask for Mr. Zheng."

In those early postwar decades in Taiwan, the most common Chinese term used for a housemaid was 下女 (Ch—*xianü*, Jp—*gejo*), borrowed from the Japanese during their colonial occupation of Taiwan, which literally meant "low girl." The housemaid usually lived with her employers and was given a monthly salary, room, and board, in exchange for helping with cooking, cleaning, childcare, shopping, and other household tasks. The challenge of finding and retaining a housemaid in Taiwan was seen as a common problem for postwar housewives. The monthly magazine *Zhongyuan* devoted its entire July 1964 issue to the subject. "Any time you get three housewives together, they won't have spoken ten sentences, and they will have touched upon the topic of housemaid problems," explained the editors. "Once they start talking, it is like the Yellow River has breached its banks, speaking without stopping." High demand for housemaids and growing opportunities for employment in new factories created a fluid labor market, in which a better salary or improved working conditions encouraged young women to jump ship quickly to work elsewhere. Ye Man (pen name of Liu Shilun, 1914–2017), a Hunanese woman and newspaper essayist, had settled in Taipei with her husband in 1967, after several years of following her husband's diplomatic career abroad. She had hired housemaids in Japan and the Philippines, so she was not worried about doing the same in her home country. Yet in the year and a half since their return, wrote Ye Man with a sigh, they had run through a succession of thirteen maids who had been hired, fired, or left.

Ye Man thought the problem was one of cultural difference, between her Taiwanese maids and herself as a mainlander. But hiring mainlanders yielded no better results. Not only did these women demand higher salaries and work less, but they also gave Ye Man a feeling of wordless unease. The unspoken message was that "they had all been happy before, but now had no choice but to come out to work for others. They felt wronged, so they deserved exceptional pity and tolerance. Thus everything in the house got covered in grease and a layer of dust, white clothes were washed into gray, but I still didn't dare say a word, and didn't even dare lift a finger, for fear of hurting their already broken hearts."

Frustrated by maids continually quitting or performing so badly they must be fired, after the tenth maid Ye Man decides to do all the housework herself. But the results are equally dismal. She doesn't mind doing the hard work, it is instead the complete absence of any time to herself that suffocates her. "It wasn't just that I never saw my own relations, but I never once stepped foot out of the house. I busied myself all day long with making three meals and washing the clothes. It got to the point where I didn't even have the time to read the newspaper anymore." Any other intellectual work and interests, such as writing newspaper essays or letters, were piled up high on her desk without ever being touched. "Every day I was worn out like a coolie. I only had the lowest, basic abilities of an animal: eating and sleeping," she writes. She recalls wistfully the short time she lived in the United States with her husband, enjoying modern home appliances and kitchen conveniences. There, "if a housewife wants to be lazy, she doesn't have to start a fire to make a meal, she can just open a can, and that can satisfy her family's stomachs." She could just stuff dirty clothes into the washing machine, and in the time it would take to do a load of laundry, she could sometimes finish writing an essay of one or two thousand characters, and then hang the clothes up to dry. Such luxuries were not available in Taiwan, which meant both doing all the cooking from scratch and washing clothes by hand—or hiring a housemaid to help.

Stories of woe (as well as some heartfelt tales) from mistresses about their maids filled newspapers of the time—and the stories were almost exclusively from the perspective of middle- or upper-class mis-

tresses, who had the education and social capital to access the publishing establishment. But one sympathetic essayist writing in 1964
could at least imagine the plight of the Taiwanese housemaid, who had
to satisfy the competing demands of her employer's different family
members, particularly when it came to food. The large, middle-class
Wu family, for example, relied upon a housemaid to cook all its meals,
since Ms. Wu was in poor health and could no longer do the work
herself. Yet no one in the family had the same tastes: "The same dish
that satisfies the master will not satisfy the mistress. If the older and
younger daughters think it's fine, the older and younger sons are not
content." Going food shopping was its own headache, since the maid
had to inquire after Ms. Wu's daily wishes, and then try to see whether
she could stretch the budget to pay for the desired ingredients. Moreover, each family member did not eat at the same time, and schedules
would shift according to the day of the week: "Number Three brought
a bento lunch to school, Number Four brought a bento supper in the
evening, the master got home late, the oldest had to eat early." It was
enough to drive anyone mad, especially when the family felt free to
complain. At least a maid could take her services elsewhere if they
were underappreciated: a housewife, however, could not quit and find
a new family.

• • •

These dramatic changes in family structure and domestic arrange-
ments in the transition from mainland China to Taiwan are best illustrated through the story of Huang Yuanshan (1920–2017), who was
the pioneer of Chinese cookbook writing in Taiwan in the 1950s and
Fu Pei-mei's most immediate predecessor. Huang was from a well-
to-do family in Hong Kong, whose father was cofounder of a popular film production company in Shanghai. Huang married Qi Ying,
the younger son of the famous scholar of Chinese opera, Qi Rushan,
in 1942, during World War II. As young newlyweds, Huang and Qi

returned briefly to Beijing to live in the Qi family compound for a few months, to give Qi Ying a chance to see his parents and to allow the whole family to get to know Huang. The entire extended family lived together in a large compound, with three main branches: Qi Rushan's family, which had seven children, the family of his older brother, with five children, and the family of his younger brother, who also had five children. The thought of living with the entire Qi clan made Huang "tremble with fear before moving in." All the cousins of the same generation were counted by gender and birth order, in one continuous sequence. Thus, Qi Rushan's own five daughters were denoted as Oldest Big Sister Qi, Seventh Big Sister Qi, Tenth Big Sister Qi, Twelfth Little Sister Qi, and Fourteenth Little Sister Qi.

To her own surprise, Huang Yuanshan remembered her time in Beijing with the Qis with much fondness. "When a household has lots of people," Huang later wrote, "some people say it's easy to stir up trouble and be at odds with one another." But in truth, she added, disagreements had more to do with individual behavior than the size of the family. "If you are an argumentative sort of person, then even a family of just two, husband and wife, can argue all day long." (Huang's rose-colored vision of life in a traditional Chinese multigenerational family might also be attributed to the short time that Huang stayed with her in-laws. It only lasted one year, not her entire lifetime.) The entire clan owned a large grain shop, which was the family's main source of income. Qi Rushan's elder brother took care of the family grain business, while Qi Rushan adjudicated over all family matters within the joint household and stayed home to write. (This left their youngest third brother with nothing to do but happily drink.) Though Qi Rushan handled all major family matters, he always waited to consult with his elder brother before acting on anything truly important. The less important household details were handled by Qi's wife, while the household accounting was handled by the third brother's wife.

The move to Taiwan in 1949 meant a radical shift in the Qi family's living situation: the once-grand clan was greatly reduced and scattered to the winds, living in separate households. At first Huang's father-in-law, Qi Rushan, tried living with his oldest son, who had married a German woman, and their children. But the German daughter-in-law spoke no Chinese and could not communicate with him, so Qi Rushan moved in with his younger son, Qi Ying, and Huang Yuanshan (the couple had no children). Now Huang Yuanshan was entirely responsible for managing their small, three-person household, with minimal help from a housemaid.

Cooking was of particular importance in their small household because her father-in-law, Qi Rushan, had a reputation as a man of great taste. Both her father-in-law and her husband would frequently entertain guests at home, and this meant that Huang Yuanshan, as housewife, was now "personally responsible for going into the kitchen to make all the food." Housemaids at the time, Huang explained, were all young girls, who would work for a few years before quitting to get married. Their own housemaid was a young Taiwanese girl who didn't know how to do anything in the kitchen, so she had to be taught. "I became her teacher," Huang wrote. In those early years in Taiwan, Huang thus gained experience in both cooking and in teaching her housemaid the basics of cooking.

Yet despite her own initiative and skill, whenever she discussed the start of her culinary career, Huang always credited the palate of her father-in-law, Qi Rushan. Huang's relationship with Qi echoed the earlier eighteenth-century dynamic between Yuan Mei and his chef. Since her father-in-law was well-traveled, had eaten all kinds of dishes at famous restaurants in China and had dabbled in Chinese food history himself, Huang always asked him for culinary guidance. "He would tell me in general how to make something, then I would go and experiment. My father-in-law would then taste it, and if he said it was good, then I would make a record of it." Eventually Huang began to teach other housewives how to cook at women's association meetings, and the editor of the women's weekly at the *Central Daily News* (*Zhongyang ribao*), approached her to write a regular cooking column. Huang's first cookbook was published in 1954, followed by four more cookbooks in the next decade.

Fu Pei-mei, by contrast, had no connections to the traditional world of Chinese culinary arts, as it had been described by generations of male literati. She was not born into an important family of great culinary or cultural renown, nor did she demonstrate any special early aptitude for cooking or tasting. Fu's husband was anything but supportive and encouraging in matters culinary. She had no famous father-in-law to help smooth the way for the publication of her cookbooks by lending them the imprimatur of traditional culinary legitimacy, as Qi Rushan had done for Huang Yuanshan by writing prefaces for her cookbooks. Fu's own frustrating experience as a housewife formed the basis for her culinary authority, and she then gained prominence through the new mid-century medium of television. She developed her own palate and sense of taste through repeated trials and experiments, not from the opinions of others. This made her a distinctly modern Chinese culinary figure, as an entrepreneurial woman relying upon her own resources, without the extensive support of a family from the cultural elite. To be sure, her middle-class status gave her important advantages, the most obvious being that Fu could afford to spend both her leisure time and personal funds on cooking lessons and costly ingredients. Yet Fu's ultimate success relied upon her hustle, tenacity, and motivation. It didn't matter whether it was typewriting or stir-frying: Fu could throw herself wholeheartedly into any new endeavor and make things happen.

● ● ●

Fu Pei-mei may never have read Ban Zhao's *Admonitions for Women*, yet the influence of these ingrained gender expectations extended well into the twentieth century. Fu mused that she had been well-trained since childhood to be obedient. At home, her traditional mother frequently espoused the notion that serving a husband should be the principal function of a woman's life—no matter how he behaved. Fu's mother was gentle and devoted, but long-suffering. In Dalian, Fu's father liked to play billiards at the Japanese mama-san's den every night after dinner, so Fu's mother sent Fu tagging along to keep an eye on him. But every night the mama-san would beckon her over, give her candies, and let her fall asleep on the tatami mat. "At the time I didn't understand," Fu wrote, "but now when I think about it, the way women have had to defend against their husband's extramarital affairs has always been the same, then and now." All her adult life, Fu felt tremendous guilt about not taking better care of her mother, whom she did not see for the sixteen years that the two were separated on the mainland and in Taiwan. By the time Fu's mother arrived in Taiwan in 1962, Fu was already thirty-one years old, with three young children, and busy with her new career on television. She simply did not have much time to spend with her own mother.

As it happened, Fu's husband was also a typical northern Chinese "male chauvinist," as Fu described him: "He always regarded himself as the head of the family. His wife and children should always listen to him, no matter what." All the lessons she had been taught, in word and deed, "made me think that everything that I did for him was just as it should be, a matter of course." It was only after forty-eight years of marriage, following her husband's death, that she began to rethink some of these unquestioned attitudes about her role as a dutiful wife.

Fu gave birth to her three children by the time she was twenty-five. She would have liked to have had a larger family, but a dangerous ectopic pregnancy shortly after the birth of her third child led her doctor to recommend tubal ligation. Her husband still hoped to try for more sons, but a neighbor finally convinced him that it was too risky. Fu was saddened but put the abrupt end to her childbearing years in perspective: "It was only because of this that afterwards I was able to throw myself into teaching my cooking classes." She recognized that her life would have been different had she had more children—not better or worse, necessarily, but different—and she chalked it up to fate. Moreover, because Fu had given birth to her children early in her marriage, they were soon in preschool and elementary school, giving her some time and space to teach her cooking classes. Later, Fu's in-laws and a housemaid were also at home to help watch the kids. Starting in middle school, her children went to boarding school during the week and came home only on the weekends. (When Fu's oldest daughter told me this, everything clicked into place: Fu had not been a superwoman after all, but had had help caring for her kids.) Fu's three adult children cherish (and burnish) their memories of their mother as *the* ultimate loving mother. "When we were young," recalls her oldest daughter, An-chi, "mother liked to sit on the floor, spread out her big circle skirt, and let us scramble for a spot. We would sit on it and play or listen to her tell us stories."

By the mid-1950s Fu, her husband and their three children had moved into a three-bedroom apartment in Taipei, with a yard in the back for the children to play in. Since the children were now in school, the mahjong players took over their living room again, and Fu once more faced the daunting task of trying to learn how to cook. (Fu never mentions reading any of Huang Yuanshan's cookbooks in her autobiography, perhaps in order to depict herself as a trailblazing pioneer in her own right.) Fu wanted to make delicious dishes that she could be proud of, and more, that her husband would appreciate. This time she had the idea to write to various restaurants advertising in the phonebook, to ask if any of their chefs were willing to teach her how to cook, for a generous fee. Fu quoted the old Chinese adage: "With money you can get a ghost to push a millstone." She offered half a *liang* of gold for an hour-long lesson. At the time, Fu recalled, one *liang* of gold was worth the equivalent of NT$1600, so she was spending NT$800 to learn to cook three dishes in an hour. (By contrast, in 1956 the Nationalist government set the minimum wage at NT$300 per month, making Fu's expenditures extravagant by any measure.)

With these generous financial terms, all the restaurants soon sent one of their chefs to teach her. Yet to call these demonstrations lessons was something of a stretch. "All of these chefs had the same problem: they didn't want to talk. I'd ask a question, and they'd say a word. I'd bend my head down to take notes, and they'd take the opportunity to throw something else into the wok." Because Fu had asked to learn the most characteristic specialty dishes of each restaurant, the chefs were reluctant to share their house secrets. As soon as they finished, they rushed off so she could never ask questions. Still, she persevered, writing down her observations as best she could, tasting and experimenting, making the dishes herself from her notes the next day. For two years she learned in this way, hiring chefs from six regional restaurants, which specialized in the cuisines of Sichuan, Jiangsu/Zhejiang, Beijing, Guangdong, Fujian, and Hunan, to teach her.

This secrecy was typical of the master–apprentice relationship in the traditional Chinese restaurant kitchen. A master might never reveal his secrets until an apprentice had proven his worth, often after a period of many, many years. Most kitchen apprentices never earned any salary from the master chef, but still had to work from morning until night. Any learning that happened was entirely coincidental and relied on the apprentice's own initiative. "The master would not even teach them properly or say anything about the theories of cooking or any techniques," wrote Fu. "It was entirely dependent on your going to steal a glance and learn in secret. You would learn through intuition, and gradually fumble around for three years until you graduated. I was one hundred percent opposed to this cheap, exploitative model." The fear was always that a more youthful competitor might steal your culinary secrets, profiting from them and putting you out of business. The attitude was not only common among master chefs—housewives could be just as guarded about their specialty dishes. In sharing openly what she had learned about cooking, Fu was again breaking a traditional pattern, this time the typical Chinese system of culinary transmission. She was very proud that she always passed on every trick and tip of what she had learned about cooking to her viewers and readers, to ensure that they could properly duplicate the results of every dish, every time.

Thanks to the informal training she received from restaurant chefs, Fu gradually gleaned enough to tackle some complex and delicate dishes from Jiangsu and Zhejiang—the eastern provincial homes of most of the other mahjong players. With gusto they ate her braised eel with chestnuts, pork with fermented tofu, and braised pork chin, and praised her to the skies—even going so far as to send their own wives over to her to learn how to make these same dishes. By the end of the 1950s, Fu had received so much interest in her cooking advice that she decided to start to teach cooking classes more formally. One night when her husband was out playing mahjong, Fu hired a trishaw to take her around the neighborhood to put up handwritten fliers for her first class. When her husband discovered her plans, he was angry, and refused to allow her to "bring a bunch of random strangers into our house." Fu responded to his objections by erecting a tent in the backyard to conduct her classes, and she only taught in the afternoons while her husband was at work and her children were in school.

The first class had eight students, including Miss Zhang from the national auto company, Mrs. Lin, a surgeon's wife, Miss Liao from the Bolero Western Restaurant, Mrs. Zhao from a construction firm, and two wives of university professors. Several of these students were from wealthy Taiwanese families, which suggests Fu's cross-ethnic appeal, at least among the island's elites. (Miss Liao's father had opened the Bolero Western restaurant, named after Maurice Ravel's hypnotic music, in Taipei in 1934. The restaurant served exotic dishes such as French duck rice and was a favorite for blind dates among well-to-do Taiwanese, who would look at each other shyly while sipping coffee and listening to classical music.)

A large part of Fu's appeal as cooking instructor was precisely her familiarity with China's major regional cuisines. Most housewives at the time, recalled Fu, knew almost nothing about how to cook the dishes of different regional cuisines. But by that point, Fu herself had already taken lessons from six different regional chefs, from Sichuan, Jiangsu/Zhejiang, Beijing, Guangdong, Fujian, and Hunan. "Everyone wanted to learn how to cook, but at the same time they couldn't find any well-known teachers. I had already spent so much money on learning how to cook myself, I wanted to earn some back in order to make up for it," Fu wrote. Having met migrants from different parts of China, housewives in Taiwan grew curious about how others ate and were eager to replicate their neighbor's unfamiliar regional specialties at home. My aunt encountered a similar situation among overseas Chinese in Malaysia in the 1970s. She learned how to make Shanghainese-style *zongzi*, sticky rice dumplings wrapped with bamboo leaves and filled with red bean paste, from older housewives from Shanghai, Fujianese-style *zongzi* with savory meat filling from my uncle's Fujianese relations, and how to roll out proper *jiaozi* dumpling wrappers by watching neighbors who came from Shanxi and Shandong Provinces in northern China.

As Fu got her cooking classes underway, it became an all-encompassing endeavor. "The first two or three years when I started, every table in our house was covered. Under every bed and everywhere else were soy sauce bottles, salt containers, sugar jars, scallions, garlic, and every sort of ingredient for cooking." Despite her enthusiasm and dedication, Fu had not yet accumulated much experience and would occasionally make mistakes. Cooking over a charcoal stove in a tent made it especially difficult to control the heat. "When I just started, I had no experience, and the dishes I made, if they weren't too salty, then they were undercooked. I had to fix the recipes right there in front of the students. It was extremely embarrassing." Still, she was always honest with students and never shied from critiquing her own cooking. "I'd tell the students not to make the same mistakes when they went home to try it."

Housewives appreciated her honest and direct approach. She was one of them, a home cook, not a professionally trained chef (a career path open only to men at the time). "I figured, everyone is human, who has never failed? If you know something, you know it, and if you don't know something, you don't know it. Best not to mislead your students for the sake of saving face." Her reputation as a cooking teacher grew, and eventually, opportunity came knocking. One of her students had recommended her to a Taiwan Television producer who was looking for hosts for a cooking program that would debut at the launch of the new medium in 1962. Curious and encouraged by her students, Fu said yes, never imagining how this single opportunity would catapult her culinary career onto a new level. Out of the frying pan and into the fire—or more accurately, out of the wok and onto the television.

The Housewife

*MY MOTHER'S YOUNGEST SISTER, HUANG MINLIN,
known to us as Siyi, or "Fourth Aunt," has always been the
most storied cook and spirited personality among my mother's sisters. She is known as much for her chili crab as she is
for telling hilarious stories, filling her accounts with exag-
gerated voices and facial expressions. In 1972, she married
an overseas Chinese man from Malaysia and moved with
him from Taipei back to a small, bucolic former mining town
near Penang, in order to join the family building materials business. She started a crash course in learning to be a
competent housewife, in part by reading Fu Pei-mei's cookbooks. For my aunt, cooking is a critical part of bringing a
family together, and all her efforts in the kitchen aim to give
her children "a taste of Mom." In my own family, I have often
reminded my children about the tender loving care someone
puts into a dish when it has been cooked expressly for them.
The message must have sunk in, as my then five-year-old son
finally labeled an empty jar "TLC" and put it in our spice
rack. When he wants to add TLC to a dish, he brings it out
and shakes it on.*

How did you learn to cook?

Your uncle's family in Malaysia is a large, traditional family. Every meal had twenty or thirty people, including all the workers from their shop. The maids cooked; it never fell upon me to cook for everyone. The dishes weren't great, but the quantity was always enough. Your uncle was a favorite of his paternal grandmother. She could see that I didn't like the food and couldn't get used to it, and your uncle kept telling her how great the food was in Taiwan. So, his grandmother would buy a large, expensive piece of meat, either pork or beef, two or three times a week. She would say to me, "Minlin, whatever you want to make, go ahead and make it." So, I had to think of how to prepare that big piece of meat. I pulled out my copy of Fu Pei-mei's cookbook that I had brought with me from Taiwan, one that didn't even have pictures. That's how I got started cooking.

What did you think of Fu Pei-mei's cookbooks?

In our generation, there is no one who doesn't know who she is. Using today's viewpoint to look at them, her cookbooks are written very simply. But using the standards of back then, there was no one else doing this. She was the only one. If you had no idea of cooking whatsoever, then you could read her cookbooks and learn something. A friend who moved to America in 1970 reminded me that I gave her a copy of Fu Pei-mei's cookbook the year she moved. I had totally forgotten! But she still has it, even today. Another friend from Taiwan living in Malaysia told me she brought back a copy of Fu's cookbook two years after she arrived here. I asked her, "Did you read it?" She said, no, she gave it to her servant and asked her to cook from it! That really made me laugh.

How did your own cooking improve?

It was only in 1980 that I really took charge of kitchen matters and cooking. Why? After your uncle's grandfather passed away, the extended family split up, and each brother established his own household. We lived separately, with my mother-in-law, my two younger unmarried brothers-in-law and my unmarried sister-in-law, your uncle, and our three children. That counted as immediate family! I started to cook for all nine of us. My mother-in-law was busy helping as a cashier in the family business, so it fell to me to cook.

Did you learn anything about cooking from your mother-in-law?

My mother-in-law did everything precisely. She didn't know any English, and she only went to school until the fourth grade or so for Chinese. But you really had to respect her. Looking at her recipe books, she wrote down everything diligently, even if there were some wrong characters, especially for the special cookies she baked. In her fruitcake recipe, she wrote, "9 eggs." But above it in brackets, she wrote, "500 ml." I asked her why, and she said, "Because eggs come in large and small, don't you know?" She would write down exactly which brand of butter to buy, to get the right taste. Now I realize that even though she never received any formal education, her mind was very nimble.

Did she invent these recipes on her own, or did she learn them from someone else?

She said if you asked someone, no one would tell you. Everyone would hold something back because these recipes were so dear. Even though she would ask and ask and ask, when she would come back to test and experiment, it would often be a failure, because they had tricked you and told you wrong. My mother-in-law said those were precious recipes she had written down, and they could not be shared with others.

Why not?

I'll tell you a story. Once, I was cleaning out the kitchen. And there was a very large wooden spoon. I wanted to throw out that useless thing, but she wouldn't let me. She said that on the spoon was a mark. I said, "What's that for?" She said that in the past, she made hot sauce and sold it to other people. Her hot sauce was different from Sichuanese hot sauce; it was made with local hot peppers, garlic, sugar, vinegar, very fresh. She said you had to slowly simmer, simmer, simmer, until the liquid reached the mark on the spoon, then you would know it was done. She made a woman who worked for her vow never to reveal the secret after she married out. Why? Because if you told people how to make it, how much of this or that, then people would steal the recipe. She said, "If the day ever comes when we have no more money, we can rely on this to live." I told this story to your grandmother, and she said, "Hnh! Impressive! Ask her to come to Taiwan, so she can make her hot sauce and I'll open a factory!" [*Laughs.*]

What do you think is the most important thing in cooking?

The first thing about cooking you have to consider is your economic ability. There's a Chinese saying: "Even the cleverest housewife cannot cook a meal without rice." If your family really has nothing, you can't do much about it. When I first got to your uncle's house, I would ask my mother-in-law, "Why don't you make things this way or that way?" My mother-in-law would respond, "If we were to do it like you suggest, we would have been bankrupt long ago!" They were from a working-class family and really frugal. If not for all that saving, they wouldn't be here today. So, if you ask, "What did you cook?" I say, it all depends on your economic ability.

So do you cook at home to save money, or to create a family atmosphere?

Well, there's a trend today that I don't really approve of. People have the economic ability, but they think that eating out is better. Every meal they eat out. If you took that same money and cooked something at home, you could make something really nice. Mothers are really important. They make all the plans. I cook for the happiness of the family. Your children will miss it: this is a taste of Mom! If you don't give them this to think about, then they won't have much of a concept of home. In order to sustain a family, three meals a day are an important fact. If you have children, you should cook for them.

3

SQUIRRELED FISH ON
THE SMALL SCREEN

Fu Pei-mei in her debut appearance on Taiwan Television in 1962, demonstrating how to make squirreled fish.

THE SET FOR FU PEI-MEI'S 1962 DEBUT ON TAIWAN Television was little more than a makeshift wooden countertop in the middle of the television studio. The only special touch was a simple background featuring the outline of a cartoon fish made of black fabric, stapled to the wall, with the staples still plainly visible. For the live broadcast, Fu had chosen one of her favorite dishes, sweet and sour "squirreled" fish (*tangcu songshu yu*), an attractive dish from Jiangsu Province that requires careful deboning and scoring of the interior flesh of a whole fish, such that the entire fish puffs up like a squirrel's tail when deep-fried. Squirreled fish was one of Fu's favorite dishes to demonstrate in front of audiences because the end result was visually stunning and demonstrated the two pillars of Chinese cooking, knife skills (*daogong*) and heat-time (*huohou*). Precise knife skills and a properly sharpened cleaver were needed to scale, gut, debone, and score the fish, while keeping the tail intact and attached to both fillets. Precise timing and heat control were needed to deep-fry the fish in a wok without overcooking the delicate flesh.

Yet in order to accomplish all of this on the live television broadcast, Fu not only had to supply all the ingredients for making the dish—a whole fish, flour, egg for deep-frying, plus shrimp, tomato, mushrooms, peas, scallions, ginger, garlic, sugar, soy sauce, vinegar, wine, and starch for the sauce—she also had to bring along all her own cooking equipment, including a cutting board, wok, wok spatula, strainer, chopsticks, bowls, plates, and spoons. Fu's three children and her mother, who had by then arrived in Taiwan from the mainland, were pressed into service to help carry everything to the television studio. With no connections for gas, electricity, or running water, Fu even had to lug along her own brazier, the heating element upon which she would actually cook. The brazier, commonly used at the time by housewives in Taiwan, was a heavy clay bucket with an opening on the side to tend to the lit charcoal while the wok sat on top—only a slight improvement on cooking over a campfire.

At the last moment, as she was carrying her equipment into the studio, Fu realized that she had forgotten to bring her cleaver. Along with a wok, this was the most essential piece of equipment for any Chinese cook. There was no way to demonstrate how to debone or score the fish without it. The assistant director told her to borrow one from the broadcast station's cafeteria, so she ran off to find one. By the time Fu went on the air, the fire in her brazier, which she had lit in the corridor, had nearly burned out and the borrowed knife was too dull to saw off the fish's head. When Fu had just managed to get the fish frying in the wok, she saw the director making circular hand movements signaling her to hurry. Fu ignored her and went on preparing the rest of the dish, which included covering the fried fish with a thickened sauce of stir-fried vegetables and shrimp. As she finished, she didn't even have a chance to say goodbye to the audience before the director cut her off. Still, she had managed to bang out the dish on live television in more or less the allotted twenty minutes, all while sweating profusely.

When she got home, her husband, who had been watching her on the living room television, chided, "You were in such a rush! You really botched that one!" Fu, already upset that she had agreed to appear on television in the first place, was convinced that she had humiliated her-

self in front of the whole world. (This was a dramatic exaggeration—
the broadcast did not reach the central or southern parts of Taiwan,
and even in Taipei not that many families owned television sets yet.)
So, Fu was doubly shocked when the following week she was invited
to return to the cooking program by the producer, who told her that
viewers had responded enthusiastically to her first appearance. Perhaps braised sea cucumber for the second episode?

The introduction of television broadcasting to Taiwan in 1962
marked the beginning of a new media age. Television gave housewives
in Taiwan a whole new way of learning what and how to cook. Little
could Fu have imagined as she was rushing to finish her squirreled fish
that this would be only the first of thousands of appearances on television, launching her eventual forty-year career as a television cooking
instructor. Americans tend to think only of Julia Child when it comes
to television cooking pioneers, but in truth, *The French Chef* debuted a
few months *after* Fu Pei-mei's first television appearance. For millions
of postwar viewers in Taiwan (and around the world), Child, with her
warble of "Bon Appetit!" and her pot of boeuf bourguignon, was not a
household name. Although Fu Pei-mei may have been introduced as
the "Julia Child of Chinese cooking" to American audiences by the
New York Times in 1971, for audiences in Taiwan, it made more sense
to call Child the "Fu Pei-mei of French food." There, it was Fu who
served as the ultimate popular culinary touchstone, the televisual
figure against whom all other cooking authorities were measured, no
matter where they were from. British television host Delia Smith, for
example, was profiled in a Taiwan newspaper as the "Fu Pei-mei of
England," while cookbook author Elinor Schildt was described as the
"Fu Pei-mei of Finland."

Fu's success in television was by no means a foregone conclu-
sion. Television cooking was *modern* cooking, and modern cooking
in Taiwan explicitly meant two things: learning how to cook a variety of regional Chinese dishes *and* how to bake Western desserts. In

the first three years of broadcasting, more than three dozen culinary experts demonstrated how to do both for the cooking segment of the women's program on which Fu also appeared. Yet in the end it was Fu and Fu alone who would become Taiwan's household name for television cooking. On one level, Fu's television success was a testament to her tremendous culinary skill: she could cut anything into a thousand different shapes with a fast and furious flash of her cleaver or wrap dumplings with lightning quick speed and the precision of a military drill sergeant. But, as she herself would have admitted, she was not the only cooking teacher in Taiwan, nor was she the most experienced. How, then, did Fu manage to stand out from a crowded field of other would-be television cooking instructors, eventually becoming *the* face of Chinese cooking on Taiwan Television?

●　●　●

The elegant Madame Chiang Kai-shek, flanked by the reigning and former Miss Chinas, graciously extended her white-gloved hand to press the remote-control button that started the first official broadcast of Taiwan Television, the island's first (and for seven years only) television network. By the second month of broadcasts, TTV had settled into a regular schedule of five hours of programming per evening, from 6 p.m. to 11 p.m., with an extra hour at noon on Sundays. In the first month, broadcasts only reached viewers within a one-hundred-mile radius of Taipei, mostly in the city itself and along the northwest coast of the island. Within three years, the signal was strengthened to reach the central and southern regions of the island. At the start of broadcasting, Taiwan had only three thousand television sets out of a total population of over nine million, but by the end of the decade, almost one-third of households owned a black-and-white television set. By 1975, almost three-quarters of households owned one.

Men, women, and children in Taiwan were enthralled by the magic of the moving picture, beamed right into their living rooms. In

1963, in honor of its founding anniversary, TTV held an essay contest, with the winning essays printed its *TTV Weekly* guide. Song Jiajin, the first-place winner in the children's division, described how she had previously gone with her parents to live in the United States for one year. While she had seen skyscrapers, subways, and "chocolate bars piled high like a little mountain," the thing that she loved the best about America was television, beyond a doubt. Her parents had bought her a small TV set, and all she wanted to do was live in front of it, eat in front of it, and fall asleep there before being carried off to bed. When the family prepared to return to Taiwan, she begged her parents to bring the television, but her mother laughed and said, "We're taking a plane and it's too heavy to bring back. There's no television in Taiwan anyway, so even if you have a TV set there's no point." Jiajin was thrilled when a television station was finally built in Taiwan, and, like so many other mesmerized consumers, at first she watched TV while standing on the street, looking through shop windows. Later a friend's family bought a set, and then finally, to her great delight, her own family did. "Now I have to work exceptionally hard, and my little brother has learned to behave," she lamented. "We are afraid that if mom gets mad, she'll give us the most horrible punishment, telling us: 'Today you aren't allowed to watch television.'"

TTV offered three basic black-and-white television sets to consumers, each produced by a different Japanese electronics company. Model 14T-511, made by Toshiba, stood high on four spindly wooden legs, with a small fourteen-inch screen surrounded by a large plastic console. A few knobs protruded from its face, one to turn it on and off, and another to adjust the volume. (There was little need for a channel changing knob because there was only one network in the country at the time.) The sets were gray and utilitarian at best, but they soon became beloved and cherished members of the family. A fifth grader described his family's television set as his "long-legged older sister," while a second grader asked her mother to make a special dust cover for the family's television set out of red cloth and made sure to wipe it clean every day.

A television set in 1962 cost more than 5,000 yuan, yet time and again, families scraped together whatever it took to bring one into their home. (To appreciate how expensive a television set was, consider that my mother earned 800 yuan per month working as a teaching assistant in 1963, while minimum wage was 450 yuan per month in 1964.) One young father impulsively spent three years' worth of his family's entire savings in one afternoon on the 14T-511, with one jiao left over. A Taipei housewife described how she borrowed 400 yuan from each of twelve friends in order to circumvent her husband's opposition to buying a television, arranging to pay the loans back a year later. She reckoned that with five hours of broadcasting per day—every hour of which her family planned to watch—in one year her family would have watched more than eighteen hundred hours of programming, which meant that each hour of entertainment cost less than two yuan fifty, surely making it the cheapest way to entertain an entire family.

As a half state-owned, half privately-owned partnership, TTV programming was intended by its producers to straddle the line "between education and entertainment," with something for "every class and every generation." It broadly promoted an acceptable set of aspirational, middle-class (and government-approved) values for Taiwan's nascent television viewers, through a variety of genres. One zealous viewer, whose workmates now called him "Mr. TTV," made up his own mimeographed program guide for the communal television in his work dormitory: there were cartoons and *The Children's Quiz Show* for kids; movies, music, sports, and dance for teenagers; homemaking and cooking programs for the women; current affairs, news, weather, dramas, art and literature, and chess for the men. There were traditional Peking operas for older viewers, but also many imported programs from America, such as *I Love Lucy* or *Leave It to Beaver*, for the younger ones. Viewers of both genders and every age described how they loved to watch the entire five-hour broadcast at night, as a new form of total entertainment. Lonely single men, in particular, wrote about how they eagerly anticipated settling down in front of the television with a cup of hot tea or a cigarette, such that an older man no longer had to wander aimlessly around the streets and a young sailor no longer wasted money chasing after women and drink. "I can miss a meal, but I can't miss watching television in the evening," "It has become my best friend," they chorused.

The original "women's program," in which Fu Pei-mei took part, was a twenty-minute-long live broadcast show, which featured one different homemaking skill for women in each program, in a regular rotation. During Christmas week in December 1962, for example, viewers could tune in to tips on how to select and use cosmetics on Monday (beauty), how to celebrate Christmas on Tuesday (family), how to bake a coconut tart on Wednesday (cooking), how to wash clothes on Thursday (fashion), and how to put into practice household management ideas from experts on Friday (home economics). Other regular segments featured home decorating, flower arranging, child-rearing, and health advice. TTV producers saw their efforts to engage women as both aspirational and broadly appealing, designed for women from every walk of life, from "elite women and intellectual classes, down to illiterate old women in rural villages." In truth, however, it was not easy for a short, twenty-minute program to appeal to such a broad audience of women and the programming instead presented a fairly narrow vision of the interests of urban, middle-class women, who were most likely to purchase a television.

Cooking, a major segment of the women's program, was featured on Wednesday evenings from 6:50 p.m. to 7:10 p.m. No doubt the timing of the TTV cooking program was at least partly intentional. The editors of the *TTV Weekly* reminded viewers, "If there are any housewives who happen to be making dinner during the scheduled program, please don't forget about whatever you are cooking in the kitchen while you watch, so it doesn't burn." Another housewife shared how her husband would tease her whenever she was engrossed in watching television: "When I have just fallen under the spell of the television, my old man says to me jokingly, 'Ai! Wife! The rice is burning! The water has boiled off!' I just ignore him." Audiences in Taiwan were certainly getting a very different version of a "TV dinner" from those in the United States settling down to their Swanson's trays. After her squirreled fish debut, Fu made braised sea cucumber for her second television appearance, then shrimp with kidneys and cashews for her third. (This last dish looked so mouth-watering that TTV executives elsewhere in the building, who happened to be watching the live broadcast, asked for it to be sent over from the studio so they could try it for themselves.) This was no Betty Crocker boxed cake mix, nor was it a simple French omelet as debuted by Julia Child on American television in 1962. This was serious Chinese home cooking, and Fu made it all seem possible to Taiwan's housewives, armed only with a cleaver, a wok, and a charcoal brazier.

● ● ●

In its first few years on the air, the TTV cooking program featured dozens of different individual cooking instructors and several regular program hosts. Pan Peizhi, a self-taught grandmotherly woman from Jiangxi Province who had established her own cooking school in Taipei in 1962, appeared on TTV most often in the first year of cooking broadcasts. She demonstrated thirteen Chinese main dishes from different regions, some familiar and others a bit more unusual and elaborate. Jiang-Zhe dragon-phoenix legs for Chinese New Year celebrations featured a mixture of chicken and pork meat shaped like legs, mounted on top of a chicken claw, wrapped in caul fat, and then deep-fried. The Hangzhou specialty, Milky Way fish lips soup, was a seafood soup with shrimp, scallops, and fish or shark skin. She demonstrated Sichuanese spicy carp and Cantonese roast pork, as well as dishes designed to fill lunch boxes for hungry children and husbands, such as braised quail eggs. In addition to teaching her own cooking classes, Pan wrote cooking columns for two newspapers, hosted a weekly cooking broadcast on the radio, and later authored two cookbooks of her own.

Hu Peiqiang, who was known as a Western dessert specialist, demonstrated lemon pie, raisin pudding, and something called country soup (with ham and vegetables) in her first appearances on TTV. Hu wrote recipes for newspapers and later published her own cookbook. She had opened her own cooking school in Taipei in 1961, where she taught dishes from her original recipes, such as a banquet dish called Smooth Sailing, for those traveling to distant places, made from stuffed sea cucumber with triangular pieces of bamboo stuck into their tops to represent a flotilla of sailboats. (To my delight, I discover that my own grandmother took a cooking class from Hu Peiqiang, since she learned this very dish and made it for my mother and her siblings.)

But certainly the best-known of all cooking instructors in Taiwan at the time had to be Huang Yuanshan (discussed in Chapter 2). By 1962, Huang was a professor of home economics at National Taiwan Normal University and had already published two volumes (1954 and 1957) of her popular cookbook series, plus one cookbook on desserts and snacks (1956) and another on Western foods (1960). She had traveled to the United States in 1961 in order to promote soy sauces and other Chinese food products manufactured by the Wei-Chuan Food Company, and she had appeared on American television programs in Seattle and Chicago to demonstrate Chinese cooking. She published her recipes in the *Central Daily News* (*Zhongyang ribao*), and the *Women's Weekly* (*Funü zhoukan*). Yet the tragedies of Huang's personal life prevented her from taking a bigger role on television. First her father-in-law, Qi Rushan, and then her husband, Qi Ying, passed away within six months of each other in 1962. With no children, Huang was suddenly left completely alone in the house. "The thing that made me feel the worst was that there was no one to eat with and taste food with me," she wrote. Though she appeared on TTV a handful of times in 1963 and 1964, soon after she emigrated permanently to the United States, where she got remarried and made a fresh start in life.

Fu may have had less actual cooking experience than some of these other women, but she had other, even more valuable skills that made her an excellent fit for the new medium of television. In her first year on TTV, Fu demonstrated eight dishes on Taiwan Television—fewer than Pan Peizhi, but more than Hu Peiqiang. Yet before the second year of the cooking program broadcasts had begun, Fu's role on Taiwan Television had expanded. Fu was promoted to serve as producer and host of the newly named program *The Weekly Dish* (*Xingqi candian*) by August 1963, and she also was appointed host of a new regular cooking program, *The Weekend Dish* (*Zhoumo candian*). Chinese main dishes were the focus of *The Weekly Dish*, while *The Weekend Dish* featured Western main dishes, Western desserts, Chinese snack foods, and Chinese wheat flour recipes, such as buns, noodles, and pancakes.

The original producer and host of the women's program, Sun Bufei, was not yet thirty years old, but she had worked as both a schoolteacher and a home economics correspondence course teacher. Normally in America and Europe, Sun explained to *TTV Weekly* readers, television producers spent forty to one hundred hours to prepare for a single hour of programming, but in Taiwan, various limitations gave hosts very little time to come up with an idea, draft the program contents, prepare for the performance, and then go on the air. It was so stressful and difficult, she said, that she had lost six pounds in the previous month of serving as producer and host. In her new role as producer and host, Fu did not necessarily demonstrate how to cook every dish herself, but she invited different chefs on to the programs to showcase their own specialty dishes and was responsible for arranging for their appearances. Later, Fu would also take on the role of editing *The Television Cookbook* (1965), which included all the recipes from previously broadcast cooking programs.

TTV editors summed up the promotion of Fu Pei-mei to program producer in the summer of 1963 by explaining, "Every time after she comes on the air, we get heaps of letters praising her." Viewers were impressed by her "extreme conscientiousness, one-hundred percent detailed explanations, well-practiced and proficient technique" in teaching both "the famous dishes of each province of our country" as well as Western desserts. Others praised her "accurate recipes and ingredients... [and] kind and genial demeanor." The editors were effusive about their decision: "When considering the selection of a program host, in the end we felt that Miss Fu was qualified and competent in every regard."

A great part of Fu's appeal and television persona was the visual impression she made on the screen. She looked like the consummate modern housewife and maintained this look throughout her entire career. From the start, her standard formal on-air uniform was a *qipao*, or Chinese fitted dress with mandarin collar, covered by a trusty apron, of which she owned hundreds. Her hair was always neatly coiffed, either blow-dried into a bouffant, or wound up into an elegant bun. As one fan later recalled, "Teacher Fu Pei-mei... completely fit the fashion trends of that era.... She was certainly quite distinct from the figure of my own mother in the kitchen, with her messy hair and grubby face, battling against the oil and smoke." Media scholars Ti Wei and Fran Martin suggest that Fu managed to simultaneously represent "a symbol of traditional, orthodox mainland Chinese culture," while she "also conjured an imaginary of modern life for her audience." The impression Fu made extended beyond her clothing; she always exuded an air of calm competence, despite the nonstop movements of her hands. No doubt it also helped matters that at thirty-one, Fu was young and attractive, especially compared to several of the other more mature (and experienced) cooking instructors, such as the grandmotherly Pan Peizhi.

Yet Fu's most valuable attribute for television cooking success was neither her face or figure, nor was it the skill of her hands: it was instead what came out of her mouth. On the air, Fu could easily and simultaneously cook and talk, talk and cook, explaining in clear, methodical fashion how to achieve success step-by-step with complex Chinese dishes. *TTV Weekly* repeatedly shared viewer praise for Fu for her ability to "point out all of the secrets and where to pay special attention in making a dish." The distinction is most apparent when watching episodes of Fu's cooking show from later decades, when she often invited different guests onto her program to demonstrate their specialties. More than a few guest chefs remain totally silent or utter a few monosyllables while their hands move dexterously to perform a tricky technique. Only Fu's persistent questions and commentary fill the air, prompting the pros to explain what they are doing. Unfortunately, when she would ask her guests to explain something, they would often stop moving their hands, making it difficult to complete an entire dish without rushing at the end. "When they lost track of time, I could see the panic in their eyes, and I would have to scramble to think of ways to smooth things over, so they did not lose face or appear awkward in the moment," Fu recalled.

Essayist Ai-ya had a front row seat to Fu's live cooking program in the 1960s. Ai-ya worked as a voiceover actor on a TTV puppet show, which followed Fu's cooking show in the evening lineup. As Ai-ya and the other voiceover actors gathered in the studio, they frequently watched the live broadcast of Fu's program. There was another benefit to watching in person too: after the broadcast, Fu always doled out the dishes she had cooked on air to the in-studio crew. This became so popular that Fu would purposely cook two sets of dishes ahead of time, so that the entire crew could have a taste of everything. Fu's unflappable professionalism made a lasting impression on Ai-ya: "When [Fu] was cooking live, she would at one and the same time chop and explain, cook and explain, all the while paying attention to the oil in the pot, the movement of her knife, the actions of her assistants, the location of the camera, the allocation of time, as well as the instructions of the director." Yet every time she watched Fu, Ai-ya could not help but be nervous for her:

> What if the spatula fell on the ground, or the lid of the pot clanked, or the match didn't light the gas stove, or her knife cut her hand? What then? Without warning the in-studio director might use his index finger to draw circles in the air, which meant that she was to speed it up, and immediately after, the director upstairs might issue another set of instructions through the headphones, so that the in-studio director would use both hands and slowly pull them apart, right and left, in order to indicate that she was to slow down, slow down.

Occasionally Fu might notice the change and stumble over her words, but mostly, Ai-ya reports, Fu was "steady as a rock." Fu did indeed embody a "show-must-go-on" mentality, but she had little alternative in an era of live television broadcasts. There were never any rehearsals, only a single set of ingredients, and one chance to get the dish completed and broadcast in the allotted time. Occasional cooking mishaps such as cuts or burns had to be bravely endured, at least when humanly possible. During one episode, a nail protruding from the set gouged a three-inch gash in her arm, which hurt so badly she immediately started to cry. Crew members rushed to stanch the wound.

In the context of postwar Taiwan, Fu's television cooking demonstrations did more than teach women how to cook. Her comprehensive televisual survey of Chinese regional cuisines united an otherwise fractious and fragile nation, brought together by the universal Chinese

appreciation for good food. It was crucial that Fu, born in the northern province of Shandong, could speak in clear, unaccented, standard
Mandarin. Mandarin had been spoken as a common language for centuries by court officials in Beijing, in northern China, and had been
designated as the official language of the ruling Nationalist Party in
Taiwan. Fu was praised by the *TTV Weekly* not only for her "excellent
enunciation," but also for her ability to speak "standard Mandarin,
Japanese, Taiwanese, and other dialects." With so many mainlander
migrants from different provinces in Taiwan speaking a vast range of
mutually unintelligible Chinese dialects, a Mandarin-speaking television host like Fu projected the image of linguistic unity so desired
by the Nationalist Party and underscored the importance of Mandarin as the officially imposed *lingua sinica* of the day.

Fu herself saw it as a pity that so many talented local or regional
cooks were sidelined for their lack of linguistic, rather than culinary
skills. In her introduction to *The Television Cookbook* (1965), Fu
explained that she frequently sought out regional cooking instructors, famous chefs, and housewives alike, to demonstrate their specialty dishes for the program. Unfortunately, she admitted, "Among
them are some who are not so good at speaking standard Mandarin
due to their advanced age, or who have stronger local accents and can't
quite grasp the right expression when trying to explain something."
This, she felt, was only a "small blemish" and insisted upon continu-
ing their in-person demonstrations "in order to preserve the unique
flavor and true essence" of these famous regional dishes. The diversity
of Fu's guests underscored the depth and breadth of Chinese regional
cuisines, and clearly demonstrated that no single individual, including Fu herself, could claim to be an expert on *every* type of regional
Chinese cuisine, let alone every dish.

Once she became the producer of the cooking show, Fu attempted
to introduce the dishes from a different province every month. From
Guangdong Province, she made scallion oil chicken, sweet and sour

pork, beef with oyster sauce, spareribs with black bean sauce. From Sichuan, she cooked *bangbang* chicken, fish fragrant pork shreds, fish with chili bean sauce, and *mapo* tofu. Later, she introduced dishes by main ingredient, showcasing a different ingredient every month. Beef would be stir-fried, braised, made into meatballs; fish would be dry-fried, deep-fried, braised, steamed, smoked, paper-wrapped, and stir-fried. During holiday seasons, she would demonstrate special dishes, such as *yuebing* (mooncakes) for the Mid-Autumn Festival, *zongzi* (sticky rice dumplings) for the Dragon Boat Festival, *tangyuan* (sticky rice balls) for the Lantern Festival, and different regional specialties for the Lunar New Year. And afterward, she would invent new ways to use up holiday leftovers. The cooking program remained on the air under the name of *Family Recipes* for another twenty-one years, with Fu churning out dish after dish. All the while, Fu continued to juggle teaching a full roster of classes in person at her popular cooking school.

● ● ●

Chinese regional dishes were only part of the modern housewife's necessary kitchen arsenal. Women in Taiwan were also eager to expand their culinary horizons with new Western dessert recipes. Chinese gourmet Qi Rushan had already conceded decades earlier that Western baking was the only area in which Western cuisine clearly surpassed Chinese cuisine: "Their ovens are many times more complete and convenient than in China, and their baked goods outnumber ours by many types." By adding Western desserts to the cooking program slate, Taiwan Television producers were actively responding to viewer demand. One early article explained that while "many famous dishes"—meaning Chinese ones—had already been shown, "with regard to Western desserts, there have been few demonstrations in the women's homemaking program. In the future we will certainly accord with viewer wishes and arrange for a rotation of Chinese dishes and Western desserts to be demonstrated."

Fu never claimed more than a basic knowledge of Western cuisine, desserts or otherwise, but she was more than happy to invite guests onto her program who could instruct women in Taiwan on the Western art of baking. The first volume of *The Television Cookbook* (1965) included recipes for Western desserts and snacks such as egg pudding, birthday cake, pineapple pie, banana bread, coconut tart, steamed chocolate pudding, orange sponge cake, egg tart, plum jam, raisin pudding, butter pound cake, lemon pie, marble cake, butter sponge cake, and curry triangles, a meat stuffed pastry popular in Hong Kong bakeries. Guest instructors demonstrated most of these dishes, but Fu showed viewers how to make chilled fruit milk, by combining corn starch, egg whites, canned milk, sugar, and diced fruit.

Numerous real-life American Betty Crockers were ready and available to pick up the whisk and share their baking experience with television viewers in Taiwan. Mrs. "Ai-bo-te" (probably Abbott), an American woman, was the first foreigner to appear on Taiwan Television in December 1962, when she came on the cooking program, with Fu Pei-mei as host, to demonstrate how to make banana bread. The ingredients and recipe would have been familiar to American housewives of the time: "1) Mix ½ c. lard, 1 c. sugar, and two eggs together well, then add three mashed bananas. 2) Stir together 1¾ c. flour, a dash of salt, 1 tsp. baking soda, ½ tsp baking powder. 3) Mix the dry ingredients into the wet in two batches, and slowly stir. Add ½ c. of chopped walnuts. 4) Get a rectangular baking pan, place a piece of wax paper inside, then pour the batter in. Put it in the oven at 300 degrees for one hour. After taking it out, let it cool and then cut into thin slices." After the episode aired, Fu claimed that it led to a huge surge in the number of Western bakeries in Taipei.

However, everything about the recipe (with the exception, perhaps of the bananas, which grew splendidly in Taiwan's tropical heat) would have seemed exotic to an ordinary housewife in Taiwan at the

time. Most Chinese kitchens did not even have ovens, let alone baking pans, whisks, or measuring spoons and cups. (In order to meet this
need, the last page of *The Television Cookbook* (1965) featured an ad for
a Taipei store that specialized in baking equipment, including pans,
molds, whisks, measuring tools, along with small countertop ovens.)
The ingredients, too, were expensive and difficult to find. Wheat flour
was not a domestic crop in Taiwan; in the postwar period, subsidized
American food aid was the source of most wheat imports. (Even today,
Taiwan imports more than ninety-nine percent of its wheat, of which
about seventy-five percent is purchased from the United States.)
Canned or powdered milk and butter, other common ingredients in
Western baking, were also pricey, as Chinese diets did not generally
incorporate anything in the way of dairy products.

Yet despite these challenges, curiosity and demand for learning
about *both* Chinese dishes *and* Western desserts remained high. How
else to demonstrate one's newly found, modern, cosmopolitan tastes?
The first edition of *The Television Cookbook* (1965) included more than
one hundred sixty Chinese recipes for main dishes and desserts, but it
also included more than forty recipes for Western main dishes (*xicai*)
and Western desserts (*xidian*). Western dishes included American
favorites such as grilled steak and lobster salad, but also Hungarian
goulash, Spanish omelets, and French fish rolls. Western dishes and
dessert recipes represented anywhere from a fifth to a third of all the
recipes in each of the first three volumes of *The Television Cookbook*.

To be clear, interest in Western dishes in Taiwan did not origi-
nate with TTV broadcasts—the station was merely responding to a
larger social trend. Huang Yuanshan, for one, had already published
a cookbook entirely devoted to Western cuisine (which included her
own recipe for banana bread) in 1960. Huang's book also featured
descriptions of place settings, modern kitchen appliances, and eti-
quette guidelines. ("Cut your food up into small pieces before put-

ting it in your mouth. Chew and swallow quickly, so that if someone speaks to you, you can answer without having an unattractive mouthful of food.")

What was so different about the TTV broadcasts was the impact of television as a *visual* medium. It made all the difference to *see* the very blonde Mrs. Abbott mix the banana bread batter herself, while standing next to Fu Pei-mei in her *qipao*, rather than merely reading the measurements and directions in a printed recipe. Likewise, it was a totally different experience to *see* Fu Pei-mei demonstrate how to score the fish in a delicate pattern for the squirreled effect, or how to hold onto the tail while frying the body in the wok to achieve its signature rounded shape, before letting the entire fish slip into the oil. "It may seem difficult to make the dish absolutely perfectly using these ingredients and instructions," read the editors' notes to one printed recipe in the *TTV Weekly*, "but after you have seen a famous cooking instructor's demonstration, we believe the results will be quite good."

● ● ●

Within a few years of her start on the TTV's cooking programs, Fu Pei-mei had already helped to change what women cooked and how families ate at dinner tables across the country in Taiwan. Taipei housewife Meng Lei, the winner of the housewives' division of TTV's fifth anniversary essay contest in 1967, described how she and the other women in her neighborhood gathered each week to watch the cooking program. The TTV cooking show served as aspirational culinary instruction, motivating these women to make new dishes for their families. For busy housewives like them, Fu Pei-mei was a welcome friend, joining for an evening chat. "The words 'Yesterday, Fu Pei-mei said . . .' are often stuck into our conversations, as if she were living among us," Meng Lei wrote.

The ritual is the same every week. "On Wednesday nights," Meng Lei writes, "I always cook dinner early. After eating, I leave the front and back doors unlocked, to avoid guests ringing the doorbell when they arrive." The women gather at Meng Lei's house to watch, most likely because her family is the only one in the neighborhood to own a television set. The rest of Meng Lei's family make themselves scarce, so that there will be enough seats for the women. One of the visitors invariably brings along a special treat, such as cold beverages, seasonal fruits, a carefully made practice dish, or a special snack sent from southern Taiwan by relatives.

During the broadcast itself, Mrs. Li, the "speediest notetaker" is designated as the "recording secretary, carefully writing down every word and gesture of the presenter, to be shared and copied by everyone later." Once, during a demonstration for birthday cake, Mrs. Ye laments that she can never make her buttercream frosting into pretty flowers. The other women rush to reassure her, telling her that her desserts are already great, and she never needs to learn how to make frosting flowers, because people don't eat them for fear of getting fat. More of the usual chatter erupts, when suddenly Mrs. Li has a brainstorm: "We should have a dinner party!" Meng Lei adds wryly, "Because we are embarrassed that we have eaten so many of Mrs. Ye's Western desserts, everyone immediately approves." Mrs. Li will make a main dish, Mrs. Ye will make a Western dessert, and they will serve as instructors for everyone else, who can pay for ingredients. Quickly their plans expand: Mrs. Wu must bring her dumplings; Mrs. Zhang makes a great eight treasure rice. "Mrs. Cheng, who has four kids, stubbornly insists that each child needs to pay one *fen*, so that everyone participating can have a clear conscience, and also so the wives who have fewer children won't mutter and complain." The women agree to allow their husbands to join for free. The neighborhood potluck is set in motion as "the people in front of the television set have become members of a planning committee."

After a week of frenzied preparation, the neighborhood get-together finally takes place. The table is laden with Chinese dishes—

cold platters, hot stir-fried dishes, deep-fried dishes, gravy fried dishes, sweet soup, desserts—along with a second table filled with large platters of Western desserts. "It was truly a great *Television Cookbook* display," Meng Lei writes. The neighborhood potluck is so successful, it becomes a monthly ritual. Thanks to the cooking show, all the women now have experience with drawing up a menu, deciding on the sequence of dishes, choosing accompaniments for vegetables, determining how to balance colors, and knowing what various cooking terms mean. And now, whenever one of the women in the neighborhood has guests over for dinner, she first prepares the ingredients and then asks one or two of her neighbors to oversee the kitchen, so that she can change her clothes and entertain guests properly as hostess alongside her husband. "It has increased the nutrition of our families and improved relations in the neighborhood. Thanks to television, *Family Recipes* has truly been a blessing!"

It was no wonder that Meng Lei's essay won the first prize in the housewives' division that year. TTV executives could not have wished for a more ideal summary of what they hoped television programming would bring: an immediate, explicit, and dramatic improvement in the daily lives of viewers at home. For Meng Lei and her middle-class neighbors, their families were now eating a variety of economical, healthy, novel dishes, both Chinese and Western, and often more ambitious than the women would have attempted on their own. Watching the cooking program together even helped reunite feuding neighbors, as another essay writer describes: "It used to be that Mrs. Zhao and Mrs. Wang argued and did not speak to one another. But now in front of my family's television, they shake hands and chat amicably, having made up their differences." Such was the unifying power of television, married with the nurturing possibilities of food: when combined in the form of a cooking program such as Fu Pei-mei's, it brought everyone to the table.

When Fu made her debut on television in 1962, she was the right person at the right time. Fu's tidy, youthful appearance, proficient standard Mandarin, and her deft ability to cook and talk simultaneously on camera made her an ideal choice for the new medium. Eventually, in the 1970s and 1980s, both the picture-perfect image of domestic middle-class femininity and Taiwan Television's emphasis on Mandarin language would be challenged as women overturned traditional gender roles and non-Mandarin-speaking linguistic groups asserted their cultural identities. Yet in terms of conveying complex culinary ideas over the small screen, Fu translated techniques and specialty dishes from different Chinese regions into a common idiom that could be shared with a broad public audience, demonstrating a modern, national sensibility in cooking across regional lines. With a dish of squirreled fish, a new television star was born.

4

FOR THE SAKE OF
FOREIGN READERS

Fu Pei-mei teaching a group of eager American women at her Chinese cooking school in Taipei (undated).

W HEN FU PEI-MEI RECEIVED HER FIRST BOUND copy of *Pei Mei's Chinese Cook Book*《培梅食譜》(*Pei-mei shipu*), she could not bear to put it down. It had that new book smell. It had rows and rows of words arranged neatly in their proper sequence. Her name featured prominently in yellow Chinese characters down the left-hand side of the front cover, while it stood out in bright blue English capital letters across the top. The vibrant front cover photographs had been carefully staged, with a rich, red fabric backdrop (her sofa cushion) draped behind a blue and white ceramic table setting. The back cover featured a cold appetizer platter artfully arranged in the shape of a phoenix. She pored over every detail: it was a thrill to see it all finally in print. "I had no way to describe the joy and excitement I felt inside," she recalled. The book had been the result of intensive research and recipe testing, time and effort measured out by every catty, ounce, cup, and spoon. Many dishes required painstaking tinkering to perfect each measurement and direction. How much stock, sugar, wine, or soy sauce did a dish need? How could every dish achieve the proper color, fragrance, and taste? Fu was determined to include only those recipes that she could guarantee readers could replicate on their own.

When *Pei Mei's Chinese Cook Book* made its debut in 1969, there was nothing else like it in Chinese publishing. In an age when cheap, small format, softcover paperbacks were the standard, Fu's expensive, large format, hardcover book made an immediate visual impact. Fu proudly boasted that her self-published Chinese cookbook was the first to include full-color photographs. At the time, color photography was still a new technology in Taiwan, and Fu spent an entire day to prepare and style each dish for the photographer, using costly ingredients. Yet because of his incompetence—he either forgot to take off the camera's lens cap or pressed the wrong button—none of the first batch of photos turned out, so Fu had to cook another round of the same dishes again the next day. "That day I nearly fainted," she wrote. Later editions would expand to include full-page, full-color photos of every dish in the book. There were photos of formal place settings for the traditional, round Chinese banqueting table; later editions named each ceramic dish and added color photographs of frequently used vegetables and other special ingredients. Fu also included a series of black-and-white photos of her multiple professional engagements, as she appeared on television, judged cooking contests, and taught different groups of students.

The results may seem modest to our eyes today, but at NT$80 (roughly equivalent to today's US$20), Fu's cookbook was a definite extravagance. One woman in the southern city of Tainan recalled that as a girl, she would buy a copy of *TV Weekly* every week, so that she could cut out the featured recipe and picture, and paste it into a special album. She watched Fu's television program for several years before she finally saved enough of her pocket money to buy a color edition of *Pei Mei's Chinese Cook Book*, "reading it until I could recite each dish by heart. When I finally had the chance to try things out in the kitchen for myself, I really did treat this cookbook as a kind of 'sacred text,' practicing everything in it." Her comments underscore a major distinction between Fu's domestic fans and her international ones.

The front covers of Fu Pei-mei's most iconic, eponymous three-volume cookbook series, *Pei Mei's Chinese Cook Book*, (L to R) Vol. I (1969), Vol. II (1974), and Vol. III (1979). The covers are distinguished by the dominant background color, red (I), blue (II), and green (III).

While Fu's domestic fans had a chance to get to know her personality through their television screens, most of Fu's international fans would only ever know her in print, through her cookbooks.

Beyond the splashy, full-color layout with photographs, by far the best marketing decision Fu made was to publish her cookbook in a bilingual, Chinese–English format. It was a brilliant move, crucial to launching her global career. The book itself is printed in Western style, bound on the left, with the text read horizontally from left to right. By contrast, Chinese-only books printed in Taiwan at the time, including Huang Yuanshan's cookbooks, Pan Peizhi's cookbooks, Hu Peiqiang's cookbook and *The Television Cookbooks*, were bound in traditional Chinese style on the right, with the text running vertically, read from top to bottom and right to left. Each recipe in Fu's cookbook appears in Chinese on the left-hand page, with the corresponding English version of the recipe on the facing page on the right. All other textual elements of the book, including the introduction, photo captions, and list of foodstuffs in the back, also appear in both Chinese and English. The cookbook's bilingualism allowed Fu's name and vision of Chinese cuisine to spread beyond the borders of Taiwan and the Sinophone world, circulating among international, English-

Photographs of dishes from the first edition of *Pei Mei's Chinese Cook Book* Vol. I (1969), which includes (L top) "Spiced Pork," (L bottom) the infelicitous "Mould Pork in Brown Sauce," and Fu's favorite demonstration dish (R), "Sweet and Sour Fish." Note the raisins sprinkled on the fish, which are included only in the Chinese version of the recipe.

Bilingual recipe layout for Fu's Sweet and Sour Boneless Fish/松鼠黃魚 *songshu huangyu* (which I have translated more literally as "squirreled fish" throughout this book), from the first edition of Fu's eponymous cookbook (1969). Several differences mark the Chinese and English versions of the recipe, beyond the actual dish name. The Chinese version specifies using either a whole yellow croaker or black carp and calls for two optional tablespoons of raisins for the sauce, details omitted in the English version. Meanwhile, the English version notes that "our foreign friends prefer" this preparation, while the Chinese version notes that this preparation suits "the average person's taste" (*yibanren kouwei*).

speaking audiences. Indeed, it is the cookbook's accessible bilingualism that continues to give it a robust afterlife in the used book market in the United States today, with pristine original copies often priced online for several hundred dollars.

The bilingualism of Fu's cookbook allowed her access to an entirely new, global audience, but few of her readers, whether Chinese or English-speaking, have probably ever given this essential fact much thought. We often imagine the act of translation to be like a clear soup, 清湯 *qingtang*, which allows you to see through to the bottom of the bowl. The meaning reflects back to you directly, in an instant. Instead, it is much more like a bowl of rice gruel, 粥 *zhou*, where the meaning is cloudy and veiled, and you can never see the bottom of the bowl. (Even here, for example, I wonder which English word best evokes the concept of *zhou*. I've seen it translated as everything from "rice gruel" to "rice porridge" to "congee," a derivation from a Tamil word, and transliterated from the Cantonese pronunciation as *jook*. To make things even more complicated, it is also known in Mandarin as *xifan*, which literally means "diluted rice.") In the case of Fu's cookbook, despite tidy appearances to the contrary, English readers are *not* always getting a precise translation of the original material in Chinese. Although the recipes themselves are by and large accurate, some of the rest of the English copy bears only a passing resemblance to the Chinese original. It is as if every assiduous non-Chinese restaurant-goer's worst nightmare has come true: Chinese readers *do* get a separate menu, and English readers don't even realize it.

Take, for example, the very title of the book. Although in English it is called *Pei Mei's Chinese Cook Book*, in Chinese it is simply "Pei Mei's Cook Book" (*Peimei shipu* 培梅食譜), without any elaboration on the type of cuisine. For Chinese audiences, there was no need to spell this out because the default cuisine of *all* cookbooks published in Taiwan at the time was Chinese cuisine. Only cookbooks featuring *non-Chinese* cuisine, such as Huang Yuanshan's *Yuanshan's West-*

ern Cuisine Cookbook (*Yuanshan xicanpu*) (1960), necessitated an explanatory adjective. On the one hand, these linguistic differences may appear to be minor because they make no material difference to someone just trying to learn how to make eggrolls. On the other hand, such differences in translation are precisely the point: Fu Pei-mei was speaking very deliberately and consciously in two different ways to two different audiences at once.

Sometimes the English translations of Fu's recipes read like coded riddles. One example is Fu's recipe for Mold San-Sze Soup. Does it actually contain mold, or is that a way of naming an unfamiliar fungus? Only after learning the Chinese name of the dish, 扣三絲 *kou san si,* do its everyday qualities come into focus (at least for Chinese readers). "San-Sze" (three shreds) refers to three main ingredients shredded evenly into strips: in this version, Fu uses chicken breast, ham, and eggs fried in an even layer. The shreds are arranged artfully in sections in the bottom of a medium-sized bowl, steamed, and then, just before sending it to the table, the steamed bowl is inverted into a larger bowl and removed. Soup stock is carefully added such that the ingredients retain their original form and arrangement for an attractive tableside display. Mystery solved: the "mold" is not fungus after all, but rather the culinary technique (扣 *kou*) of arranging ingredients neatly into a bowl, steaming, and inverting so that the dish retains its shape—plausibly a "mold" in English. (Fu's Mold Pork in Brown Sauce, 走油扣肉 *zouyou kourou,* uses the same cooking technique and suffers from the same infelicitous translation.)

Oddly translated Chinese dish names (whether in Fu's cookbook or your average Chinese takeout menu) might seem funny at first glance to English speakers, but they hint at a much more fundamental dilemma of cross-cultural culinary translation. For anyone fluent in Chinese, it can seem like an impossible mission to convey even the most basic notions about Chinese cuisine to English speakers who have no reference points to Chinese geography, history, language, or culture. Direct equivalencies often do not exist in English for Chinese cooking techniques or ingredients, to say nothing of dish names incorporating historical, geographical, or poetic allusions, which might require elaborate footnotes to explain fully. Capturing the multiple embedded meanings of a Chinese dish name in a few evocative English words requires almost as much skill and creativity as cooking the dish in the first place.

•   •   •

The bilingualism of Fu's cookbooks bears the strong imprint of their immediate Cold War context. From 1951 to 1978, the United States sent American servicemen and CIA operatives as part of the Military Assistance Advisory Group (MAAG) to Taiwan, dubbed "Free China," as opposed to Communist "Red China" on the mainland. These American service members worked as advisers to their counterparts in the Republic of China's military. As one ROC government magazine explained in 1966, "Of all U.S. activities around the world, military advisement probably brings Americans into the closest contact with the nationals of other countries. The working level is direct—man-to-man. MAAG in the Republic of China is no exception. Americans and Chinese have come to know and understand one another—and many have formed close friendships that continue through the years." Yet it was not only "man-to-man" contact that MAAG initiated—woman-to-woman contact thrived too. "MAAG wives" figured prominently in the American presence in Taiwan, with six hundred out of eight hundred MAAG servicemen stationed in Taiwan living there with their families, for a total community of more than twenty-seven hundred in 1966.

While their husbands were stationed in Taiwan, American military wives enjoyed taking advantage of one of the many cultural opportunities available to them: Chinese cooking classes taught by none other than Fu Pei-mei. This intimate link to the American presence in the country was illustrated in Fu's cookbook by the inclusion of a foreword from Dorothy D. McConaughy, wife of Walter P. McConaughy, the American ambassador to the Republic of China from 1966–74, when the two countries still had diplomatic relations. No doubt Dorothy McConaughy had American audiences in mind when she explained in the foreword that Fu had "skillfully compiled and up-dated recipes for more than one hundred traditional dishes which will appeal to both western and eastern tastes." McConaughy hoped that Fu's cookbooks would build diplomatic bridges, to "increase interest in Oriental cuisine" and to "further advance the friendship and interest between the Chinese and American people."

Fu herself explained in the Chinese version of her introduction that her original motivation in writing the cookbook was to have a convenient way to share recipes directly with her students: all the recipes included in the cookbook were for dishes taught at her cooking school. "For many years now," Fu wrote, "many Chinese and foreign ladies have hoped to buy my lectures notes or recipes in order to be able to refer to them when making a dish. This need has felt especially urgent for those going abroad or those with friends or relations overseas. Also, many overseas Chinese have encouraged me, hoping to have Chinese food recipes written in English that are both correct and authentic." Fu spoke some English herself, but never felt entirely at home in the language. Still, it was the only way for Fu to communicate with her American students, as well as with overseas Chinese who did not speak Chinese.

Yvonne Zeck accompanied her husband Frank from Illinois to Taiwan from 1966 to 1968, during his posting there as a colonel in the US Air Force. In Taipei, the Zecks enjoyed the typical life of American expats. Their photo albums from the time show pictures of their black dog Ching-mi, their attractively appointed home with Chinese motif furniture, and their amah (housemaid), Miss Lee. For fun, Frank and Yvonne rode in a three-wheeled pedicab, golfed at Tamsui, shot skeet, and gathered for cocktail parties with fellow military officers, both American and Chinese. There are pictures of their travels in and around Taipei, to the National Palace Museum, which had only just opened in 1965, and around the island of Taiwan, to the tourist attractions of Taroko Gorge and Sun-Moon Lake. Zeck was fascinated by the bustling cityscape that surrounded her, often involving food, with ducks and fish hanging on a line to air dry outside, a pedicab delivering pork, narrow back alleys lined with street food vendors, or two boys grinning impishly as they stand at a roadside food cart. The Zecks also visited Hong Kong, and in the New Territories caught of hazy glimpse of Red China in the distance. Their photos evince a moment in Taiwan's modern history when it stood on the brink of massive urbanization and industrial development. A few pictures showcase the rural beauty of terraced rice paddies, and traffic occasionally included water buffalo, but change was already on the way. Zeck saved a clipping of a news article with the headline, "Taipei's Pedicabs on Last Legs," which captured how these old-school, human-powered, three-wheeled vehicles were now being phased out in favor of automobiles.

In January 1968, Zeck, along with a dozen or so other American military wives, took part in a series of cooking classes taught by Fu Pei-mei, organized by the Foreign Affairs Office of the ROC Joint Logistics Headquarters. Zeck's black-and-white photos depict a simple classroom, with a blackboard listing ingredients and plastic checkered tablecloths. In that particular session, Fu had a male assistant, who is "making covers for spring rolls," according to Zeck's photo album notes. Fu stands next to him, holding up an example wrapper, clearly in the middle of an explanation. Another photograph shows Fu using a cleaver to chop the ingredients for the filling. The American women, decked out in pearls and beehive hairdos, look on attentively, waiting expectantly for something delicious to happen.

At the time she was teaching Zeck's class, Fu had been working on translating her cookbook, but felt that she needed a native

English speaker to help. "I had not studied English much myself," she explained, "but even a foreign language major in college might not have been able to translate all the specialized cooking actions and nouns. In English there was simply no exact equivalent for these terms." Fu was not the only Chinese culinary expert to feel that English terminology was wanting. Qi Rushan, playwright, scholar, and gourmand (whose views on Chinese cuisine have been discussed in Chapter 1), considered these distinctions not simply as differences, but as deficiencies on the part of Western cuisine. In 1954, Qi claimed that "Chinese cooking techniques have long surpassed Western cooking techniques" because there were twice as many distinct words for them. Although both Chinese and Western cooking techniques encompassed a range of slow-cooking methods, such as 煨 *wei,* 滷 *lu,* 燒 *shao,* 燴 *hui,* and 燜 *men*—all variations of simmer, stew, roast, or braise—Western cuisine made no such distinctions with quick-cooking methods. There were no precise English equivalents for techniques such as 爆 *bao,* 溜 *liu,* 烹 *peng,* or 爆炒 *baochao*—frying methods which might be rendered as quick-fry, sauté with sauce, quick-fry followed by sauce, and quick stir-fry at high heat. Only the Chinese cooking term "stir-fry" (炒 *chao*), first coined by Buwei Yang Chao in her cookbook for American wartime audiences, *How to Cook and Eat in Chinese* (1945), had made much headway in English. Unfortunately, the popularity of the term had the unintended consequence of giving foreigners the mistaken impression that stir-frying is the only essential technique of Chinese cooking. As Fu later explained, there are dozens of Chinese words for distinct cooking techniques (she once named more than thirty in a 1993 article), which are often difficult to translate concisely into English equivalents.

This was why Fu was keen to approach Zeck for help. Every time Fu translated ten pages of her cookbook, she would bring them to Zeck's house in Tianmu and ask her to make corrections. Zeck spoke no Chinese herself, though she occasionally taught English classes to

ROC military personnel. When the cooking techniques were particularly tricky to explain, such as how to fold a dumpling, how to squeeze out meatballs by hand, or how to score in a crisscross pattern, Fu would even bring the ingredients over to Zeck's house to demonstrate for her in person. "To write the recipes in English that first time was tremendously difficult," Fu recalled, "but for the sake of future students, it would be a million times more convenient. So all of the hard work seemed worth it."

After the cookbook was finally published, Fu sent a copy to Zeck, who by that point had already returned to the United States, accompanied by note handwritten neatly in English:

Dear Mrs. Zeck,

How are you and your family? I miss you very much. My cook book just come out. I got many trouble from Printing Co. . . . . Please let me know as soon as possble when you received this book, so I will be send more books to you later.

Please give my kindest regards to your family.

Sincere

Pei Mei

30. May. 1969.

The note is charming in its intimacy and reminds me of my own grandmother's careful looped, English handwriting, written with fountain pen, which I read on the thin blue airmail letters she regularly sent to my mother. Yet in the slightly uneven English conjugations of Fu's note, I also hear the echoes of every Chinese auntie and uncle I've ever known who has stumbled over the illogical grammatical constructions of English and its tricky and infuriating pronunciations. This is how I imagine I sound when I speak in my second-generation

Chinese or what it looks like to others when I write in my schoolchild's Chinese scrawl. I know what it is like to sweat as you think about pronunciation, word choice, grammar, diction—and still get it wrong. In Chinese, it is enough of an effort for me to get my meaning across in whatever way I can, but in English, I have no worries: I make puns, tell jokes, make up silly rhyming songs with my kids, and write anything at will. No wonder Fu wanted a native English speaker to read through and smooth out her translations; in her place I would have done the same.

The second volume of Fu's bilingual cookbook, published in 1974, had a different translator, with better but still imperfect results. Monica "Nicki" Croghan was in Taiwan at the time as a graduate student from the University of Pennsylvania, studying Chinese. Croghan communicated with Fu entirely in Chinese, and never spoke English with her. She met Fu after taking one of Fu's cooking classes (in which Croghan was the only foreign student); Fu asked for her help in translating the second volume of her series. As Croghan recalls, Fu was eager to complete the project quickly because she was aware that a competing bilingual cookbook from another author (likely the revised edition of Huang Su-huei's *Chinese Cuisine* cookbook, published by the Wei-Chuan Food Company) would soon appear on the market. "She didn't think there was room for two cookbooks to come out at approximately the same time. So she wanted hers to be out first," says Croghan. Croghan translated the Chinese manuscript into English, which then got typed up by young women "who didn't really have much education in English, so their typing skills weren't exactly up to par." However, because Fu was in such a rush to get it out, she "was more interested in the time frame than correct English. Some of the typing mistakes were corrected, but a lot of them were not corrected," Croghan adds. The rush job paid off, however, when Fu's second volume did ultimately come out before Huang's, to Fu's great pleasure and relief.

● ● ●

Fu made one more radical decision in the presentation of her first bilingual cookbook. She offered a four-part regional framework to organize the vast expanse of Chinese cuisine. "In this book," Fu explains in the Chinese introduction to the first volume, "Chinese cuisine is divided into large sections by East-South-West-North." (Here, Fu uses the traditional Chinese sequence of cardinal directions, as opposed to the typical North-South-East-West sequence of English speakers.) "The East has Shanghai as its center and contains Jiangsu and Zhejiang cuisines; the South includes Fujian and Guangdong; the West indicates Hunan and Sichuan cuisines; the North primarily indicates Beijing cuisine." Fu seems to have been the first Chinese cookbook author ever to use this organization of culinary regions by cardinal direction; later Chinese cookbook authors writing in English, such as Florence Lin (1975) and Deh-Ta Hsiung (1979), would follow. Fu's immediate predecessors in Taiwan had instead arranged their cookbooks by cooking method, main ingredient, dish type, and even season.

Fu anticipated that Chinese readers might object to her four-part organization of Chinese regional foods as overly simplistic, yet as she explained in her Chinese introduction, such a general schema was necessary "for the sake of foreign readers." China had more than thirty provinces and dozens of cities large and small, each with its own famous local dishes. How could a foreigner, who was already not familiar with Chinese language or geography, keep all their names straight? The organization by cardinal direction was elegant and concise, and attended to the most obvious distinctions of Chinese regional cuisines.

At the same time, most dishes Fu selected for her cookbook also took into account "the difficulty of buying ingredients or the lack of various ingredients in foreign countries," and featured common cuts of chicken, beef, pork, and readily available fish, shrimp, vegetables, and eggs. Only a handful of recipes called for what a foreign reader might deem as exotic (though typically Chinese) ingredients, such as shark's fin, abalone, winter melon, or sea cucumber. (The Chinese master chefs who prepared the welcome banquet for President Nixon's historic visit to China in 1972 strictly avoided serving sea cucumber, a worm-like marine invertebrate with a highly prized gelatinous texture. A Chinese protocol officer remarked to an American reporter, "we found that our European guests hardly ever touched the seaslugs, so we dropped them.")

Finally, Fu chose to include recipes for dishes that would be most familiar to foreign restaurant-goers. Theresa Lin, Fu's daughter-in-law, confirmed that the cookbook was conceived of as much as a potential guide for Americans to order dishes in a Chinese restaurant as it was meant to be followed as an actual cookbook. Color photographs were included in the hopes that foreign students, in particular, would be enticed to purchase the cookbook to give to friends as gifts. This is why you can find a recipe for Peking Duck in her cookbook, even though it's too elaborate for most amateur cooks to replicate successfully at home, and a recipe for Chop Suey, the signature dish of mid-century Chinese American restaurants. (Though chop suey (*zasui*), a Cantonese dish, originally featured stir-fried animal entrails, its American incarnation included any mishmash of stir-fried meat and vegetables served with a sauce over rice or noodles. Fu's version features a stir-fried and sauced mix of pork, pork kidney, smoked squid, shrimp, ham, bamboo shoots, carrots, green peppers, bean sprouts, and spring onions.)

None of this logic or rationale, however, for the cookbook's organization or selection of recipes, is made apparent to English readers of Fu's cookbook. The English version of Fu's introduction says nothing about how or why Fu came to write the book, why she organizes in it four regional sections, or why certain well-known dishes appear but not others. Instead, English readers get a simple, direct lesson on regional distinctions in Chinese cooking: "Looking at a map of mainland China one understands why each area soon developed its own style of cuisine. Easy transportation was unknown and the provinces made best use of its own products. Several main types evolved which include the famous Peking roast duck from the North, the Szechuan food also known as Honan [Hunan Province] or western style featuring highly peppered food and camphor-smoked duck. The Foochow [Fuzhou, a city in Fujian Province] and Cantonese style specializes in light tasting dishes often stir-fried to preserve texture and flavor. The eastern area around Shanghai is noted for its oily food and wonderful special sauces." Foreign readers unfamiliar with Chinese geography might not realize that Fu had collapsed Sichuanese and Hunanese cuisines—distinct regional culinary identities—into one category of dishes from western China, or that she has done the same with Fujianese and Cantonese cuisine, collapsing the two into a single category of dishes from southern China. Nor is any mention made of accommodations for foreigners who have difficulty accessing specific ingredients. Instead, "American cooks" were instead merely reassured by Fu that the selected dishes were "typical of my country."

Given her own limited English skills and the complex collaborative process of translation that required the help of Zeck, who knew no Chinese, there were many pragmatic reasons why Fu's presentation might have been simplified for foreign audiences. There may have been limitations of page space and layout to consider—the condensed grammatical structures of the Chinese language can make texts pithy, and translating them fully into English often requires more space. Or perhaps, after years of teaching American students, Fu had taken the measure of her typical foreign audience and decided that a handful of Chinese place names was enough. English readers didn't necessarily need more geographical or historical details than they could handle anyway, if the big picture was more or less accurate. If you aren't already familiar with Chinese history and geography, will the storied culinary city names of Yangzhou, Hangzhou, or Ningbo (or for that matter, Jiangsu and Zhejiang Provinces) and the distinctions of their cuisines even mean anything to you? Or will your eyes glaze over at yet another list of unpronounceable Chinese place names that you cannot locate on a map? At the end of the day, the most important feature of the cookbook—the bilingual recipes themselves—correspond in their lists and measurements of ingredients, and largely overlap in their instructions. If you tend to head straight to the recipes in a cookbook and skip everything else, or if you are already very familiar with Chinese regional cuisines, then these linguistic differences may not matter much to you.

The plethora of Chinese *or* English-language Chinese cookbooks today underscores the singular importance of Fu Pei-mei's bilingual Chinese *and* English-language cookbooks. In that particular postwar moment, when both Chinese-speaking and English-speaking audiences were hungry for guidance on how to cook Chinese food, Fu was the first one to claim, audaciously, that she could and would speak to both audiences at the same time, within the covers of the same book. (Later cookbook authors from Taiwan, such as Huang Su-huei, who wrote for the Wei-Chuan Foods Corporation cooking school, would follow very closely in Fu's bilingual footsteps.) Bilingualism made Fu's work truly transnational, appealing to domestic and overseas Chinese and to foreign audiences all over the world. Although some of the cookbook's English translations may have been a little vague, in practice they worked well enough to impart Fu's general ideas about Chinese cuisine. Most importantly, Fu's cookbook gave audiences useful versions of reliable recipes for a range of typical, regional, home-style Chinese dishes. This was a huge step forward over most other English-language Chinese cookbooks available at the time, which gave foreign readers little sense of that vast regional variation.

• • •

Other American military wives stationed with their husbands in Taiwan were just as eager as Yvonne Zeck to learn how to cook Chinese food, and they did so by taking classes with Fu Pei-mei at her school. Some were so excited to share the fruits of their study that they taught their own Chinese cooking classes upon their return to the United States, where they found audiences hungry for more than chop suey and chow mein. Curiosity about Chinese food, particularly its distinct regional cuisines, increased steadily through the 1960s as Americans became more aware of a broader range of Chinese food, thanks in part to new restaurants established by postwar Chinese migrants to the United States who were not Cantonese, such as Cecilia Chiang (owner of The Mandarin in San Francisco), who was from Jiangsu Province, and Joyce Chen (owner of the Joyce Chen Restaurant in Cambridge), who was from Beijing.

Judy Getz, of Camden, New Jersey, was featured in her local newspaper in 1973, under the headline, "She Studied Chinese Cooking With Taiwan's 'Julia Child.'" Getz had lived in Taiwan from 1968 to 1970, while her husband, a surgeon, was stationed at the US Naval Hospital in Taipei. "If you think television cooking shows are a strictly American venture," the article begins, "you haven't been to Taiwan, Republic of China." Getz proudly describes what she learned under Fu. "It wasn't the 'chop suey' type of Chinese cooking," Getz explains. "I was taught the dishes enjoyed by the wealthy Chinese." (Ironically, of course, Fu had indeed included a recipe for Chop Suey in the first volume of her cookbook.)

The article specifically mentions that Getz learned "the gourmet foods of many regions," including Canton, Shanghai, Hunan, Peking, Yunnan, and Sichuan. Getz shared Fu's recipes for Chicken and Cucumber Salad, Paper-Wrapped Fried Fish, Egg Roll Soup made with homemade pork stock, and Eight Treasure Rice Pudding. "After the first few sessions," the article enthuses, "Mrs. Getz' students were using chopsticks like pros when they sat down to enjoy the food prepared in the lesson." Other American military wives, such as Ruth Aston in Bangor, Maine, Val Sterzik in Petoskey, Michigan, or Midge Jackson in Tyler, Texas, had similar stories written about them in the pages of their local newspapers throughout the 1960s, 1970s, and 1980s. All of them were profiled for introducing their families, neighbors, and home communities to the flavors of Chinese dishes they had learned from Fu Pei-mei.

But American military wives were not the only foreigners inspired by Fu Pei-mei. American men were equally excited to share what they had learned about Chinese cooking from Fu. Ed Faist, a sanitation worker from Passaic, New Jersey, was such a fan of Chinese cooking that, after years of taking classes whenever he could in New York's Chinatown, he traveled to Taiwan in 1976 for the sole purpose of studying for a week with Fu. "To the Chinese, the way Americans cook their food is a joke," Faist explained to a local reporter. Faist too taught adult education classes in Chinese cooking, complete with tours of New York's Chinatown. Bruce Borthwick, a political science professor at Albion College in Michigan, took a six-week cooking course with Fu Pei-mei in the summer of 1974. The following year, he taught his own ten-week class on Chinese cooking to a group of college students and community members. The students learned how to make soy sauce chicken, fried wontons, fried rice, egg rolls, various noodle dishes, egg foo young and sweet-and-sour pork. In Borthwick's opinion, learning how to cook was the best way for Americans to get over their fears and get to know a foreign culture.

As a graduate student in Asian history at Indiana University, Michael Drompp traveled to Taiwan for the first time in the early 1980s. His homeward journey each day in Taipei happened to pass right through Fu's neighborhood, so one of his colleagues suggested that they take cooking classes there in the evenings, both to learn how to cook and to improve their Chinese. They would scan the teaching schedule ahead of time to see which dishes would be taught that week and sign up for the specific classes that interested them. All the dishes Michael learned were taken from the first volume of *Pei Mei's Chinese Cook Book*, a copy of which he purchased and in which he took copious notes, including his own hand-drawn illustrations. "What helped me most as a foreigner, sitting in on the class, was having the [cook]book with me," says Michael. "I'd have it open to the right page, and there it was bilingually. Now, sometimes the English isn't perfect in the book, but that's where my Chinese was good enough that I could look over and see what it should be. I could understand what was written."

The cooking school's one and only classroom occupied the floor directly below Fu's own family apartment, making the daily commute an easy one. Students sat on tiers of risers, in the manner of a small lecture hall, with the focal point on the teaching kitchen in the front. The classes were taught entirely by lecture and demonstration, with no active student participation, but this didn't bother Michael. Fu was an excellent teacher, earnest and conscientious. The tone was not formal, but neither was it "giggly or funny or laughing. It wasn't that kind of entertainment. It was serious, in the sense of 'I'm here to help you. You can do this. And here's how you do it. Just watch. And if you have questions, ask.'" He adds, "To me it struck a perfect note, and that's why I enjoyed it." Michael would go home to his tiny, shared apartment in Taipei and practice what he had learned, though not every dish was a smashing success. On one occasion for a dinner party, he had planned to make Crispy Chicken 脆皮肥雞 (*cuipi feiji*), which requires dipping a whole chicken into hot oil and then cutting it into pieces. "It was a hot chicken, I had my cleaver, and I was nervous anyway because I had company." Michael slipped and cut his finger badly, bleeding all over the kitchen. The dinner party ended with a trip to the hospital. "I never made that dish ever again," he laughs.

Besides learning directly from Fu, the experience of strolling through Taipei's back alleys was itself a first-rate culinary education, one that Michael had not anticipated before he arrived in Taiwan. Growing up in a small town in northern Indiana, he mostly ate "standard Midwestern fare," such as hamburgers, spaghetti, and fried chicken, dishes he had learned from his mother and grandmother. There were no Chinese restaurants nearby. Moreover, the Chinese restaurants that did exist in larger towns did not serve high-quality food. As his horizons expanded in his first year of college, Michael distinctly remembers trying to make "what I thought was Chinese food," using packages and cans of La Choy processed food, then available in the local grocery store. "It was awful," he admits. "So I never had good Chinese food until I went to Taiwan, and suddenly I'm faced with this smorgasbord of incredible food. Taipei is an eater's paradise."

Michael describes how in Taipei, "there was food around me all the time. Not just food, but people making food right in front of me." In every back alley of the city, people cooked and sold foods of all kinds, all day long, from breakfasts of *doujiang* (soymilk) and *youtiao* (fried dough sticks) when he walked to work in the morning, to vats of tofu prepared for sale the next day when he went home at night. Many food stalls were open at midnight, when he could grab a late-night snack with coworkers or friends. "Taiwan opened my eyes to the quality of everyday food and the incredible diversity" of regional Chinese foods, he says. "I think most Americans, if they went to China and got a chance to eat in restaurants where Chinese people eat, would be surprised at the variety and the quality. It doesn't really taste like a lot of what they get here; it's not all sweet and sour," he says.

This culinary experience has made Michael dissatisfied with what he can find eating out in Chinese restaurants in the United States, especially outside of urban centers with large Chinese populations. Instead, he prefers to cook with his battered copies of Fu's cookbooks at home. Michael purchased all three volumes of Fu's cookbook series while in Taiwan but finds that he uses them in "descending order." He turns to Volume I, with its familiar regional homestyle dishes "a lot," Volume II with an expanded list of dishes "some," and Volume III "very rarely," because the last volume focuses mainly on fancy banquet foods. Drompp likens the comprehensive approach and universal impact of Fu's cookbooks to the two volumes of Julia Child's *Mastering the Art of French Cooking* (published in 1961 and 1970, respectively), except that he uses Child's cookbooks "far less than my trusty Fu Pei-mei books!"

•   •   •

What did all these Americans ultimately gain from their study of Chinese cooking with Fu Pei-mei? Did they learn more than simply how to make fried rice, egg rolls, and sweet and sour pork? Did they begin to think about Chinese people and culture differently, after learning about Chinese cuisine? Dorothy McConaughy, the American ambassador's wife, certainly hoped that learning how to cook Chinese food would "advance the friendship and interest between the Chinese and American people," and Fu Pei-mei agreed. When asked to give the keynote address at the fiftieth anniversary meeting of the Chefs de Cuisine Association of America in Los Angeles in 1976, Fu emphasized the role of cuisine in promoting cross-cultural friendship and understanding: "I think that cooking is a vital part of a country's culture. . . . By sharing our various cuisines, we can increase mutual understanding and friendship around the world."

On good days, I want to believe in Fu's dream, that "mutual understanding and friendship" might blossom from a bowl of noodles. Why not? Cooking classes with Fu Pei-mei and daily strolls through the back alleys of Taipei certainly changed the eating habits and palate of Michael Drompp, opening his eyes to the amazing variety and deliciousness of regional Chinese cuisines. For a young man starting out from small-town Indiana, it is no small personal journey to undertake, to go from La Choy to 拉麵 *la mian* (hand-pulled noodles) in a lifetime. The same might be said about Fu's influence on other American women and men, including Yvonne Zeck from Illinois, Judy Getz from New Jersey, Bruce Borthwick from Michigan, Midge Jackson from Texas, or any number of others profiled in their local newspapers.

But on not-so-good days, I wonder: does loving the food of a place necessarily translate into a deeper, more compassionate, and more humane understanding of its people and culture? I think about this question repeatedly during the recent coronavirus pandemic. At one 2021 event in New York City protesting the sharp rise in anti-Asian violence, a young woman, Jessica Ng, holds up a sign that poses the idea not as a question, but as an imperative: "Love our people like U love our food." The slogan quickly goes viral, copied not only onto other protest signs, but also onto T-shirts, sweatshirts, stickers, magnets, egg tarts, and frosted cakes alike. The slogan's popularity among Asian Americans demonstrates that it has struck a deep nerve, situated right at the confluence of food and identity, demanding that we be seen not just as a source of tasty food, but as human beings deserving dignity and respect. But perhaps the very existence of the slogan instead implies that the opposite sentiment largely prevails: although Asian food is readily loved and accepted in the United States, it is not such an easy path of acceptance for Asian people.

Fu Pei-mei's bilingual cookbooks were the product of her historical circumstances and context as much as her own hard work. They are also utopian statements of hope: that it is indeed possible to bridge cultural and linguistic divides in the world through the language of food. Maybe it is easy to be so confident when you live in a world where Chinese cuisine is the default, so obvious as to be unnecessary to include in the title of your cookbook. Fu spoke from a position of respected culinary authority, in a world where foreign students clamored to learn how to cook Chinese cuisine. From everything she had experienced, of course Fu could believe that teaching and learning about Chinese cuisine would lead to "mutual understanding and friendship." Yet the ultimate work of translation, it seems to me, lies not in what Fu was able to accomplish on the page, rendering her Chinese into English with the assistance of Zeck and other translators. The real act of translation lies instead in the hands of her foreign readers. By choosing a cookbook over takeout, will they no longer see these dishes as a delicious end unto themselves, ready to order and devour? Getting results in cooking requires time, effort, and patience: these are small, hopeful steps in a lifelong journey of understanding, making real the possibility of connecting distinct peoples and cultures through food.

5

MUST A HOUSEWIFE
FORGET HERSELF?

Fu Pei-mei at the public exhibition of her collection of more than
three hundred aprons in Taipei, 1977.

FU PEI-MEI'S FAVORITE APRON WAS A SIMPLE DESIGN made of navy-blue cotton, with a light blue appliqué scroll pattern on the top bib and bottom corners. It had two generous pockets trimmed and decorated in the same light blue fabric, handy for catching kitchen odds and ends. To Fu, aprons were pragmatic and attractive "symbols of industriousness and competence" for housewives. They not only protected clothes from oil stains and kitchen spills; they could also serve as fashion statements, demonstrating a housewife's "abilities and graceful bearing" should an unexpected guest drop by for a cup of tea. Fu never appeared on television without an apron over her clothes, anything from a frilly pink number to a tidy blue floral print trimmed with buttons to one made of elegant hand-painted silk. She had purchased some of the aprons on her travels; others were gifts from grateful cooking school students. Television viewers often wrote to her to ask how they could copy a specific apron that they had seen her wear on air. (*Families Magazine* obliged by printing the measurements and sewing instructions for two different examples of Fu's aprons.) Over the course of her long career, Fu amassed a collection of more than three hundred aprons, which she proudly displayed in a public exhibition at her cooking school in 1977.

But by 1977, other women in Taiwan were ready to cut their apron strings and leave the kitchen entirely—or at least question whether they wanted to fulfill social expectations of caring for their families and households in this manner. The modern Chinese social ideal of the small family household and the central role of the housewife in managing it had always been shaped by the desires of men. Now women in Taiwan were vocally challenging these gender norms. The pioneering postwar feminist of Taiwan, Lu Hsiu-lien, published her manifesto, *New Feminism* (*Xin nuxing zhuyi*) in 1974, critiquing the unequal standards for men and women that had developed from centuries of Confucian gender ideology. "The tradition of 'men manage the outer, women manage the inner' has meant that men take on all the responsibility for everything public-facing that happens outside of the home, while women are confined to the kitchen, among diapers and baby bottles, sweeping, cooking, giving birth and raising children." She added, "Men get to live on all of heaven and earth, 'like a fish swimming in water, like a bird soaring in the air,' while women have only one path in life, that of the 'dutiful wife and loving mother'—an incredibly narrow and cramped path."

Presented in this way, the choice seems stark: either women are in the kitchen obediently donning aprons to cook for their families, or they are throwing them off to reject domestic duties entirely. Is it possible to square any kind of feminism with cooking for one's family, or is the daily act of cooking dinner itself, given the long history of women's invisible domestic labor, an unfair, gendered expectation that ought to be rejected? A new generation of feminist scholars has pushed back against the wholesale rejection of women's work in the kitchen, attempting to recuperate the space of the kitchen and the act of cooking as significant realms of female experience and identity. As sociologists Kate Cairns and Josée Johnston argue, "We support struggles toward gender equality and do not believe that this requires women to reject the significance of food in their lives—to throw in the apron, so to speak. We certainly do not want to diminish the history of women's food labor, knowledge, and love in the kitchen." Other scholars have focused on examining the caring work of feeding the family, including planning, shopping, cooking, and cleaning— duties that have often fallen to women, whether or not they work outside the home.

There is, in other words, more than one way to think about aprons, which do more than just keep a woman tethered to her place in the kitchen. Fu's favorite blue apron was her most treasured possession because her mother had hand-sewn it for her initial television appearances, after her mother had finally been allowed to emigrate from mainland China in the early 1960s. At her apron exhibit, Fu had included a poem she had written about her mother's handiwork:

慈母巧構思　My loving mother skillfully laid out the design

親手縫又紉　Sewing and stitching by hand

殷殷勤指導　Earnestly guiding with diligence,

望女擅烹飪　Hoping that her daughter would be an expert at cooking.

Fu's mother was barely literate, and only learned how to write Chinese characters phonetically. Yet sewn into the fabric of that apron was her loving care and every best wish for her daughter. As Fu explained in her autobiography, her mother never taught her any kind of academic or intellectual form of knowledge, "but in her everyday life, through the way she behaved toward her husband, her children, her friends, her neighbors, and even the servants, she made a deep impression on me, both directly and indirectly. It was a kind of 'embodied knowledge,' or teaching by example." Fu's poem recalled the famous lines of the Tang dynasty poet Meng Jiao (751–814), who had written centuries earlier of another loving mother, sewing clothes for her traveling son: "Loving mother, thread in hand, / Stitching the garment tight / That her son will soon wear on his journey." It turns out those particular blue apron strings tie Fu not to the kitchen, but to her own mother. There is much more an apron can tell us about Chinese women, their domestic labor, and their professional aspirations, if we attend closely to the many potential messages stitched into its very fabric.

• • •

Although her roles as wife, mother, and daughter-in-law within an extended Chinese family were central to Fu Pei-mei's experience, self-identity, and public persona, as she neared the end of her life, she questioned the submissive role she had taken on in her marriage. For the entirety of her forty-eight-year marriage (which only ended with the death of her husband in 1999), she kept family harmony by deferring to her husband in all things, taking care to never challenge his sense of control. She asked for her husband's permission before going on any overseas trips and would strategically wait until shortly before she intended to depart to speak with him. Near the end of her life, she wrote, "I never thought about it back then, but times are different now, and a lot of things were really just unreasonable models of behavior." Cheng never seriously obstructed Fu's career, but he also did not appear to do much to actively support or encourage it. She does not mention, for example, Cheng's help in any activities related to her career, such as delivering cookbooks by car or carrying supplies into the television studio, assistance that her children and mother provided. Fu's oldest daughter An-chi even recalls her father saying to her mother, "It's not like I can't take care of you, so why do you still need to show your face on television?" For her part, Fu simply responded that it was work she enjoyed doing; later, she felt that she had a mission to help the world learn about Chinese cuisine.

The point that most galled Fu in looking back on her marriage was that she never controlled any of her own earnings. When she first started teaching cooking classes in her backyard, she agreed to turn over all the tuition money to Cheng, since he had studied accountancy, his job was in finance, and he was much better with numbers. This established a pattern of financial control in the family, such that her children believed that it was natural that their father "had the authority and the money," while she herself had never so much as opened a bank account in her own name. She never even had her own pocket money to spend and always had to ask her husband for even trifling amounts—which he always gave to her magnanimously.

Early in their marriage, at the urging of some of her more liberated friends, she tried to keep back some of her own earnings. "This is money that you earned yourself!" "How could you be so dumb?" "By what rule should you turn it all over to him?" Yet there wasn't really any place to hide money in their small apartment. The only place she could think of was the wardrobe in their bedroom. She wadded up 20,000 yuan in bills, which she divided in two, stuffing each half into the pockets of one of her husband's suits. Later, she forgot all about it, and when her husband went on a business trip to Kaohsiung, she helped him pick out a suit to wear. She was even happy for him when he excitedly called to tell her he had found a large wad of cash in his pocket—until she remembered that had been her own savings stash.

All this talk about financial control makes us reconsider Fu's culinary origin story, in which she paid a series of chefs to teach her how to cook their regional specialties. In multiple interviews, Fu repeated that she had used her own dowry, in the form of both gold and jewelry, in order to pay for those cooking lessons. In 1999, she told a foreign journalist, "It was *mianzi*. Face. I was ashamed that I didn't know how to cook. I hired a chef to teach me, at half an ounce of gold per lesson. I used all my gold, sold my diamond ring, changed chefs every three months for two years." The journalist adds that Fu "grimaced recalling her dogged determination." In another interview, Fu said that she learned some three hundred dishes the first year, and one hundred dishes the next. "By the end of the second year," the reporter writes, "she had exhausted her dowry, but had also become an exceptional cook." Each hour-long lesson consisted of three dishes, and cost half a liang of gold, which at the time, Fu recalled, was worth the equivalent of NT$800. Using Fu's own figures and estimates, she spent over NT$100,000 of her own money on cooking lessons over two years, making Fu's expenditures extravagant for the time by any measure.

Whether or not these figures are entirely accurate, what is significant is the idea behind the story: Fu always claimed to have exhausted the only money she would ever call her own, her dowry, on the expense of private cooking lessons. Initially, she only intended to placate her picky husband's tastes, yet when one considers the impact of these lessons on her later career, they turn out to have been a wise investment. An enthusiastic commentator from mainland China, writing an essay about Fu in 2011, observed that another person might have gotten angry or given up, after her husband had repeatedly criticized her cooking. But Fu Pei-mei was determined to "study to make up for any deficiencies, and even launched a new business opportunity." No doubt after she started paying chefs exorbitant sums to teach her how to cook, "she may have heard a lot of gossip or had others secretly laughing at her, believing that she was truly wasting her money!" However, it was Fu who would have the last laugh. "Her choice to 'invest in herself' was the right one, which paid off beyond measure!"

Both things can hold true at the same time: Fu *was* subject to patriarchal control, in a household ruled almost absolutely by her husband. But she also made the smartest financial investment of her life *in herself*, with her own funds, which eventually bought her professional freedom, the chance to travel worldwide, and public accolades. Though no aspect of her career had been planned in advance, Fu created a one-of-a-kind path for herself in the world of culinary arts that would span decades and influence generations of Chinese home cooks.

After her husband passed away, Fu was sad, but serene. "I had not one ounce of regret or remorse when it came to my husband. I did everything for him that a wife should do, and even did for him many things most wives could not—or would not be willing to—do."

* * *

Even as Fu was privately struggling to assert control over her own earnings, other women in Taiwan were ready to take their fight for women's rights public. Lu Hsiu-lien made a name for herself as the leader of Taiwan's nascent feminist movement in the 1970s. Lu was born in Taoyuan just before the end of World War II, to a Taiwanese family with both Hokkien and Hakka ancestry. She excelled in her studies and graduated with a law degree from National Taiwan University in 1969; she then spent two years on a graduate fellowship at the University of Illinois Urbana-Champaign for her masters of law degree. During those pivotal developmental years, she rejected a woman's traditional path when she said no to her only serious marriage proposal. (Ultimately, Lu never married or had children.) She returned to Taiwan in the summer of 1971 and, at her mother's urging, did not go back to the United States for further graduate studies as she had planned, but instead accepted a civil service job at the Executive Yuan Law and Regulations Commission.

Lu's path to feminism had been inspired in part by Western feminists such as Betty Friedan, whose work Lu had encountered while studying in the United States. In her landmark book, *The Feminine Mystique* (1963), Friedan critiqued the constricted role of the housewife and the home as the site of uncompensated labor. Friedan believed that a liberated woman could find fulfillment only in a wage-earning career, taking her rightful place in both public and political spheres. (Friedan had little to say about the domestic help these liberated women would often need from lower-income women to keep their families and households running.) American artist Martha Rosler's early video, *Semiotics of the Kitchen* (1975), follows this critical vein of Friedan, capturing a sense of rage against the confines of middle-class American women's postwar domestic roles in the kitchen. Spoofing television cooking programs of the time, such as Julia Child's, Rosler, wearing all black, stands in a small kitchen behind a table piled high with various utensils. She proceeds to recite a kitchen alphabet, miming the action of each implement as she solemnly says its name. She very deliberately dons an "apron," then holds up a "bowl" while motioning the mixing gesture with her other hand, and then uses a "chopper" to hack into the bowl. As she continues through the alphabet, Rosler moves with increased force and violence, clanging, banging, slashing, stabbing, until she slices a Z through the air with a knife.

To American feminists like Friedan and Rosler, Fu Pei-mei's notions about home, family, and women's roles within them must have seemed positively retrograde. In Fu's first edited cookbook, *The Television Cookbook* (1965), Fu had written that cooking was a paramount life skill for women, with the implication that feeding their families was solely their responsibility: "The importance of cooking to women surpasses any other kind of life skill. All three meals a day have a direct impact on the health of the family's minds and bodies and an indirect impact on a family's mood and spirits." Elsewhere she expressed the opinion that women in her cooking classes were primarily motivated to learn in order to take care of their families and loved ones, never just for themselves or their own pleasure.

Yet how much did Friedan and her American feminist contemporaries really have to say to postwar women in Taiwan, especially with regard to their work in the kitchen and cooking responsibilities? Friedan had little opportunity in real life to interact formally with feminists from Taiwan. Although Friedan said she was eager to sit next to a Chinese delegate to speak "woman-to-woman" at the first UN conference on the status of women, held in Mexico City in 1975, the members of the Chinese delegation all came from the People's Republic of

China (PRC) on the mainland, not the Republic of China (ROC) on Taiwan. Conference organizers had invited Lu Hsiu-lien to attend, but she was refused a Mexican visa after the PRC delegates objected to the presence of a representative from "the renegade province of Taiwan."

An ordinary housewife in Taiwan in the 1970s might well have felt a sense of curiosity and wonder, not a sense of sympathetic rage in the unlikely event that she even encountered Rosler's video: why on earth did this American woman need so many gadgets in her kitchen anyway? What was the purpose of this mysterious "egg beater," "hamburger press," or "juicer," and what kind of elaborate dishes necessitated this amount of kitchen gear? What kind of self-respecting home cook needed anything beyond a cleaver, a cutting board, a wok, and her own two clever hands to make a complete and satisfying meal?

● ● ●

After her return to Taiwan, Lu began to write and speak about social issues from a feminist perspective. "I was the first one to ask why women should accept the stereotype, perpetuated by male patriarchal society, of *nan wai, nu nei*, or men outside the home and women inside. No one had ever questioned in public the idea that it is the duty of men to work while women handle the tasks of child rearing and cooking." Eventually she became a regular columnist for the *China Times*, writing about women's issues. She tried to open a feminist coffee shop so that activists would have a place to gather, but it became a magnet for government snoops and had to be closed. In 1974, Lu published her landmark manifesto on the feminist movement, *New Feminism* (*Xin nuxing zhuyi*). Two years later, Lu and several other feminists started a publishing company, Pioneer Press (*Tuohuangzhe chubanshe*), which aimed to introduce translations of Western feminist texts to Taiwanese readers. Lu soon realized that these translated texts were not enough. "I soon found that Taiwanese women have different cultural reference points from those of Western women.... I decided to com-

mission the writing of books specific to the Taiwanese experience."
Many of the original books published by Pioneer Press were banned
by government censors because they focused on the so-called "dark
side of society to promote social disorder," such as prostitution, rape,
or the profile of a successful madam. Yet the blanket censorship also
suppressed stories about Taiwanese rural women and working-class
women, which were included in these same volumes.

In 1976, Lu Hsiu-lien and the Pioneer Press, along with the Taipei branch of Junior Chamber International, organized two special
events in Taipei to commemorate International Women's Day and
to raise funds for Taipei's first women's hotline and resource center.
The first event was a men's cooking competition. The purpose of the
competition was "to encourage cooperation and division of labor" at
home in the kitchen "in order to achieve the harmony of the two sexes
in society." The organizers invited amateur men of all ages to apply for
one of the sixty spots and explicitly encouraged mixed gender teams:
"We welcome husbands and wives, fathers and daughters, brothers
and sisters, and sweethearts to join together to take part." Each team
had one hour to cook two Chinese dishes, either an entrée or dessert
for twelve people, "proving that the kitchen can no longer be the sole
territory of women." On the day of the competition, almost a thousand
spectators came to watch the teams in their frenzied preparation.

The wide range of dishes cooked by the winners more than sub-
stantiated the claim that men also belonged in the kitchen. The overall winner was seventy-one-year-old Zhou Qifan, who made fish-head
stew in a clay pot (a Jiangsu dish). Second place went to Li Fan's specialty quick-fried pork kidneys (a Fujianese dish), which required
skilled knife work to score the kidneys so that they would transform
into an attractive flower shape when quick-fried. Zhao Shuijun's sweet
and sour spareribs won third place. One husband and wife team, Li
Jigong and Ye Yingxiu, were both in their sixties and had been cooking together for forty years. At the other end of the age bracket was

Liu Zhiyang, who at eighteen was the youngest participant. He came with his older sister; their mother had taught both siblings how to cook. Another participant, Zhang Youcheng, a mechanical engineer, had cooked for himself while studying abroad in America, and after he got married, his wife asked him to teach her how to cook. Liu Mao-tong cooked the two fastest dishes, bringing his cold mixed shredded dry tofu, and scrambled eggs with shrimp to the judges' table within ten minutes.

Before the cooking competition got underway, spectators were treated to a song and dance number about men's talents in the kitchen, performed by a group of ten elementary school students. The original tune, composed in Taiwan in 1952 by Bai Jingshan, included lyrics that cheered on older brothers and fathers fighting against Communist bandits on the mainland. Lu Hsiu-lien cleverly upended the martial spirit and masculinist intent of the original, rewriting the lyrics to encourage male domesticity. In the original song, one of the lines read, "Older Brother and Father, don't worry about household matters!" ("*Gege Baba, jiashi buyong nin qiangua!*"), but Lu transformed it into a strong claim about men's domestic qualifications: "Who says a gentleman stays away from the kitchen? / They are as good as Mother!" ("*Shei shuo junzi yuan paochu? / He mama yiyang hao.*"). Lu was referring to the classic quotation from the philosopher Mencius on benevolence, who wrote in the third century BCE that in the case of ritual sacrifices, a gentleman should "stay far from the kitchen" because he cannot bear to see animals suffer once he has seen them alive. The phrase had since, however, been commandeered by modern Chinese male chauvinists to justify their refusal to even step foot in a kitchen, let alone cook. Instead of catching Communist bandits, the older brother and father in Lu's lyrics were enjoined to boil, fry, and braise.

One of the five judges at this gender-role reversal cooking competition was none other than Fu Pei-mei. What did Fu make of all these men cooking? She had plenty of male students in her cooking school, most of whom were doing so in order to open restaurants, either in Taiwan or abroad. Yet the men in the cooking competition were amateur home cooks, who did so for the pleasure of it and to feed their families. Fu had praised the artist Zhang Jie's beef with oyster sauce, saying that its color, fragrance, and taste were all superior. Did Fu ever wish, even the tiniest bit, that her husband Cheng Shao-ching might learn from these men, who were happy to take up cleaver and wok at home? In her autobiography, Fu talks quite a lot about her husband's food likes and dislikes, but she never once mentions him lifting a finger to wash a dish, let alone cook one. At the same time, Fu took pride in her own cooking skills, and her ability to care for her family in this way—would she even have welcomed her husband's participation in the kitchen? As the artist Zhang Jie suggested, "Some wives think that a man who goes into the kitchen loses his male dignity. Others are just annoyed that their husbands get underfoot and make a mess in the kitchen."

The second commemorative event that year was a "Tea Talk on Women Outside the Kitchen," which was billed as a direct counterpart to the men's cooking competition. However, the audience for the tea talk was far smaller than it was for the cooking competition, with only seventy or eighty younger women participating. The idea was to bring together exemplary women who had built careers outside the home and to have them speak in an informal setting about their experiences and the reasons for their success. Yet the tea talk manifested everything that was challenging about pushing forward a women's movement in Taiwan. Compared to the men's cooking competition—a fun event for all ages—the signature event for women was serious talk about *everything* else. To make matters more confusing, the messaging was mixed. Two female psychologists, for example, urged the women not to think of sex as "dirty"—but also cautioned that premarital sex was "unwise." A female journalist encouraged young women studying journalism "not to be afraid" of forging their careers—but they were also cautioned to put marriage and family first. There were so many knotty issues to grapple with—double standards for sexual behavior, equal opportunities in work and education, marriage and family issues—where even to begin?

After the cooking competition and tea talk, the well-known advice columnist, Madam Weiwei (pen name of Yue Chaijun), wrote a short opinion piece to explain the larger meaning of both events to dispel any misperceptions. She explained to readers that the aim of both events was neither to push men into the kitchen, to get them to do all the cooking going forward, nor was it to push women out of the kitchen, insisting that they "must leave the kitchen far behind" to "count as a modern, new woman." It was much more a matter of every-day practicality in figuring out who should tackle any given household task. "If the wife is a working woman whose work is very arduous," wrote Yue, "the husband does not need to stubbornly stick to his traditional roles and 'responsibilities,' sitting in the living room reading the newspaper while waiting for his wife to get off work to come home and cook, when she is so exhausted her head is steaming." (It was a pity that Yue could not speak directly to Lin Yutang, who twenty years earlier had described listening to his wife and daughter debate recipes in the kitchen while he sat comfortably in the living room.) The issue was to "flexibly" assign household tasks to preserve the "feelings of a modern couple." At the same time, Madam Weiwei wrote of the women who participated in the tea talk that "none of them have refused to go into the kitchen because of their work outside of the kitchen." Again, the answer was not in absolutes, but in flexible accommodation.

In 1977, the following year, a new research project, sponsored by the publishers at *Family Magazine* (*Jiating yuekan*) and the Pioneer Press, aimed to shed light on the daily lives and desires of Taiwan's housewives. Social science researchers from local universities, along with their students, fanned out to survey almost one thousand Taipei housewives, ranging in age from nineteen to fifty-four, with

educational levels from illiteracy to college graduates. The results of
the survey were shared at a symposium on life after marriage, sponsored by *Family Magazine*. The symposium was promoted as a way for
housewives to learn how to improve their life situations: "Do you wish
that your own married life was more satisfactory? Do you wish to be
a happy housewife? Do you understand the real facts of marriage?"
Expert panelists, many of whom were male academics, shared their
views on various topics, including the idea of self-sacrifice, time management and efficiency, managing the family budget, women's general status in society and within the family, sex and marriage, and the
future of housewives.

The most riveting part of the symposium proceedings were the
question-and-answer sessions that followed each expert presentation. These unscripted, free-wheeling discussions, reprinted in the
magazine, shed some light on the wide variety of attitudes that ordinary housewives in Taipei had about their own lives and roles, in their
own voices. Most people in the audience were housewives, but a few
husbands also attended. Mr. Liu Zhaoqing, who had been married for
more than fifty years, offered his opinion on divorce, discouraging
women from going through with it. Regarding extramarital affairs, he
said, "I'm not making excuses for men, but I hope that women can bear
it, and not take the most serious step of getting a divorce, or else definitely both sides will lose." Mr. Hu Qingheng stood up with his mother
and his wife at his side—and then proceeded to speak on their behalf,
in admiration of their self-sacrifice.

One lively audience debate began with the question, "Must a
housewife forget herself?" That is, should a housewife sacrifice her
own desires for the sake of the family? At one end of the spectrum
was Ms. Xiao Yanyao, who felt that a housewife's self-sacrifice for her
children was "not necessarily a bad thing for a woman." The success of
raising children well, she argued, "is certainly not any less than that

of a career woman working outside the home." At the other end of the spectrum was Ms. Qiu Qiqi, who introduced herself as a housewife with twenty years' experience. (Qiu was also an essayist and editor of the women's weekly of the *Taiwan Daily*, with numerous books to her credit.) Qiu felt that all too often, women sacrificed themselves for their families and at the end were forgotten for it. She gave the example of feeding her family a plate of chicken. While her husband and children would eat the tastiest parts—legs, wings, and breasts—she would always end up eating the neck and rump. "If you ask the kids, 'What does your mother like to eat?' they will answer, 'Mother likes to eat chicken rump.' Does mother really like to eat chicken rump? No, she doesn't. But because she has given all the good things to eat to her husband and children, a false impression is created." Qiu urged the women in attendance to hold themselves in higher regard. "If you don't value yourselves," she cautioned, "then your husbands will gradually forget you. And your children will also overlook you."

The real housewives of Taipei were not out of touch with the rising feminist consciousness of the day. They *were*, in fact, questioning different aspects of their lives and had a wealth of experience upon which to draw. In this regard they already brought much to the table, such as the homespun philosophy of Qiu Qiqi, which cut through the pontificating of the academic experts (often male), who offered numerous suggestions on ways to "improve" the lives of housewives. But like any random group of women that might gather today, not all the women at the symposium agreed on what they wanted or needed. The provisioning of food and its careful preparation represented *both* a desire and opportunity to demonstrate care for the family, *and* a potentially onerous domestic burden. The struggle to define a fair and appropriate division of labor in the home was not a matter of making a firm distinction between the struggles of career women and the struggles of housewives, or even just a simple matter of dragging reluctant gentlemen into the kitchen. Instead, all these consciousness-raising events illuminated the frustrating problem of how to manage domestic labor, an issue that almost all women with families still face today.

• • •

The question of whether a woman should don or remove her apron, and thereby accept or reject the responsibility for family cooking, was only half the story. What about a woman who might take off the family apron, only to put on another apron in a professional kitchen outside the home? The act of cooking did not simply demonstrate a house-wife's physical and emotional care for her family; it could also give rise to an entirely new professional identity. Fu Pei-mei herself, after all, had trodden the path from familial domesticity to professional culi-nary authority, without any plan or formal training.

Of all Fu's cooking school graduates with professional culinary careers, Susanna Foo (no relation to Fu Pei-mei) achieved the high-est level of public acclaim. Susanna is the retired chef-owner of her namesake restaurant, Susanna Foo Chinese Cuisine, which opened its doors in Philadelphia in 1987 and closed in 2009. Over the course of her culinary career, she was named one of America's Ten Best New Chefs by *Food and Wine* magazine, won the James Beard Foundation Best New Chef Award for the Mid-Atlantic Region, was awarded the Robert Mondavi Culinary Award of Excellence, and published two acclaimed cookbooks. In every newspaper interview published about her, Susanna never fails to mention that she took cooking classes with Fu Pei-mei while still a housewife in Taiwan, a foundational part of her early culinary education. Working as a chef and owning a successful modern Chinese restaurant, however, was never part of Susanna's plan.

As a young woman, Susanna tells me, she never had any intention of becoming a chef: "When I was in college, my generation was very different from your generation. We wanted to be good housewives. I was just thinking I should learn how to cook food well so when I marry a good person, I could take care of the children, cook, and entertain guests. I didn't really like to study. I just wanted to be a housewife." Susanna went to her first cooking class at Fu Pei-mei's school in the company of her future mother-in-law, who was already an accomplished housewife and home cook from Hunan Province. Susanna took more classes with Fu after she got married, and thoroughly enjoyed cooking for her own house guests.

The transformation from passionate home cook to professional chef was a painful one. Family obligation prompted Susanna to enter the restaurant business. In the early 1970s, her parents-in-law emigrated to the United States and opened a Chinese restaurant near Philadelphia's Main Line. The restaurant soon became a neighborhood institution. A few years later, in 1979, her in-laws informed Susanna and her husband, who by then had also moved to the United States, that they had purchased a second restaurant property in Philadelphia's Center City—and they wanted the two of them to come and help run it. To Susanna's dismay, her husband agreed. "I was so upset," she recalls. Susanna and her husband helped in the front of the house, while her mother-in-law took charge of the kitchen in the back. Business was bad. "Everything was frozen, everything was canned, all the sauces were ready-made," recalls Susanna. "I was shocked at how much MSG they were using. I never saw so much MSG in my entire life."

Susanna's fate took an unexpected turn when she crossed paths with Jacob Rosenthal, the former president of the Culinary Institute of America, who had retired to a condo two blocks from their restaurant. Every time he came in, Susanna cooked for him personally— and Rosenthal loved her cooking. He took the couple under his wing, introducing them to the best restaurants in New York City. He also encouraged Susanna to take an eight-week course on French cooking techniques at the Culinary Institute. She loved her time there, comparing herself to "Alice in Wonderland" before the rows and rows of cookbooks in the library and the gleaming equipment in the professional kitchen. But a demanding schedule of weekly commutes to New York City, classes from 6 a.m. to noon, and afternoon apprenticeships were not the only challenges. Susanna's fellow classmates—all white, male, professional chefs—didn't respect her and didn't understand why she was even taking the course. Once, when Susanna attempted to lift a heavy stock pot, another student purposely bumped into her, causing her to drop the pot and burn her arm.

Back in Philadelphia, Susanna returned to the everyday grind of working in the family restaurant. Business was still bad, and she resented that her in-laws forced her to work there: "I was crying all the time because it was so hard in the kitchen." (Neither was the irony lost on Susanna that she was often so busy at the restaurant cooking for customers that she was never at home to cook for her own children. Instead, she gave them money to buy cheeseburgers at McDonald's.) Still, Susanna was determined to take small steps to apply what she had learned at the Culinary Institute to their existing menu. She insisted on making her own sauces, such as *kung-pao* sauce using French techniques, and standardized prep procedures for marinating chicken. She bought fresh fish instead of frozen and stopped using MSG. Over time, she would gradually merge her Chinese tastes and French technical training, creating new fusion dishes such as wild mushroom dumplings in chanterelle sauce, filled with mushrooms, parmesan cheese, and cellophane noodles.

Owning her own namesake restaurant was another unplanned career development for Susanna. As property prices rose in the 1980s, her husband's family abruptly decided that they wanted to sell the building that housed their restaurant. Susanna and her husband were forced to lease another building (a former steakhouse) less than a mile away, which they would rebuild, reopen—and rename. "We were trying to find a name—Imperial Kitchen, Forbidden City, even Mongolian Shanxi cooking. But friends said you should use your own name, because the food is what you are making now." Susanna was reluctant to include her husband's family name on the restaurant, since they had made things so difficult over the years, but in 1987, Susanna Foo Chinese Cuisine opened its doors. For the first few months, they had no customers and were in constant fear of failure. Then the *Philadelphia Inquirer* published a review calling it "the best Chinese restaurant in Center City," and suddenly (after only eight long years) a new star chef was born. No doubt Fu Pei-mei would have recognized all the blood, sweat, tears—and pride—behind the restaurant's singular name.

● ● ●

Beyond serving as a symbol of domestic competence or professional success, an apron could carry other, more deliberate messages. Back in Taiwan in the 1970s, Lu Hsiu-lien had demonstrated her willingness to embrace creative, sometimes zany, ideas to gain attention and publicity for her feminist cause. She brought that same creative spirit to her first run for public office in 1978, for a spot in the National Assembly, the body whose primary purpose was to elect the president. Lu stood for election in her home county of Taoyuan, just southwest of Taipei. Yet despite her feminist newspaper writings and the establishment of the Pioneer Press, compared to the other candidates, Lu was a relative unknown.

Lu thought of a way to get her name in front of urban voters by meeting them where they could easily be found: shopping for food at traditional vegetable markets. "To increase my appeal," Lu explained, "I designed an apron displaying the island of Taiwan, 'Hello, compatriot,' and 'I love Taiwan,' and my name. The idea was a little wacky but eye-catching. I arranged to make 6,000 large shopping bags with a similar logo design, which my campaign volunteers distributed in local vegetable markets." Most people had no idea who she was, but gladly accepted the freebies. "Soon the vendors were wearing my aprons in their stalls and people were walking around with shopping bags that bore my name," Lu recalls. "It was a somewhat comical sight." Who else but an entirely unapologetic feminist politician would think of using two ubiquitous symbols of women's domestic drudgery, aprons and shopping bags, as a way to announce her candidacy? On this point, at least, Fu Pei-mei and Lu Hsiu-lien could agree: aprons were indeed symbols of "industriousness and competence"—for Taiwan's aspiring female politicians as much as for its housewives.

In the end, Lu never got to stand in those elections. In December 1978, President Jimmy Carter announced that the United States would now formally recognize the People's Republic of China—which meant that it would be forced by the PRC to break off diplomatic relations with the Republic of China on Taiwan. The resulting uncertainty and instability prompted Taiwan's President, Chiang Ching-kuo, to announce that all elections would be suspended indefinitely starting in 1979. Later that year, Lu took part in organizing a human rights demonstration in the southern city of Kaohsiung to promote democracy on the island. The Nationalist government used the demonstration as an excuse to crack down on opposition leaders, and Lu was sentenced to twelve years in prison for making a speech at the event. She would eventually be released in 1985, after five and a half years as a political prisoner. After her release, she would join the newly established Democratic Progressive Party and successfully wage campaigns for the Legislative Yuan (Taiwan's legislative body) and then for Taoyuan County magistrate. She worked her way through the party ranks, and, at the apex of her political career, Lu served as Taiwan's first female vice president from 2000 to 2008. Yet the story of women's participation in Taiwan politics does not end there. In 2016, forty years after the initial Pioneer Press tea talk, Tsai Ing-wen, a law professor and trade negotiator, soundly beat her male opponent to make history as Taiwan's first female president. Tsai, like Lu, a member of the Democratic Progressive Party, handily won a second term in 2020, with an even greater share of the popular vote.

Is it possible to think that the road to women's personal liberation, professional success, and even political power is at least partially paved with aprons? Although Fu never explicitly called herself a feminist, she recognized the societal demands on both housewives and working women, and took their needs, concerns, and desires seriously. Her pragmatic purpose was to help any woman who might find herself floundering in the kitchen, wondering each night what to make for dinner. Like Susanna Foo, Fu Pei-mei occupied both domestic and highly public culinary roles, having carved out her own path as a successful cooking instructor and television personality through her experience as a housewife and mother.

An apron can indeed tie a woman to the kitchen and gendered norms of domestic behavior. But it can also remind a woman of the sacrifices of her mother, and the strength of women passed down from generation to generation. In the form of chef's whites, it can turn a reluctant restaurant chef into a local celebrity, capitalizing on gendered expectations of women's labor in the kitchen. Who knows? An apron might even pave the way from the kitchen to the highest public office in the land, as housewives and professional women alike band together to change the world around them.

KITCHEN CONVERSATION

The Working Mom

AT OUR ANNUAL CHINESE NEW YEAR CELEBRATION gathering in Midland, Michigan, when other mothers would bring their specialty Chinese dishes, Catherine Chen would always bring the solid Midwestern standby and perennial kid favorite, pigs-in-a-blanket (hotdogs wrapped and baked in ready-made Pillsbury crescent rolls). Her main interest in cooking is how to save time doing it. Yet before our interview, Catherine still prepared five dishes for our lunch from scratch—beef with peppers and onions, egg with wooden ear fungus and carrots, peppered shrimp, fishball soup, and a green vegetable—all of this even though she insists that she is "not a food person." I have known Catherine Chen all my life—she and her husband have been friends with my parents since they were all in graduate school at the University of Minnesota in the early 1960s. I wanted to interview her precisely because she focused her primary energies on her career and never cared much about cooking. She started out as a part-time reference librarian at a local college, then climbed the ranks to become head librarian, academic dean, and eventually, provost, the second-highest ranking administrative position at the university. All the same, she still undertook the basic task of making daily meals through the many decades of raising her family.

How would you describe yourself as a cook?

I make do, survival cooking! Your mom is a good cook—she makes fancy things, like seven-layer salad. One layer is enough for me! Uncle [*what I call her husband*] is a much better cook. He's more patient and will take whatever time it takes to cook something; he'd put on music and be singing and cooking. But his cooking is very time consuming and very messy! [*Laughs.*] I'm impatient. I just want to stir-fry everything, that's it. So over the years I took over, to simplify everything and make it in a time saving mode. I can do everything in one pot, but his food definitely tastes better. I'd give him that.

How did you learn how to cook?

I never stepped foot in the kitchen when I was growing up. My grandfather was very progressive at the time. He had a rule that his daughters would never learn how to cook. He didn't want them to serve food to others. That was to our detriment because my mom never learned how to cook! His daughters all went to college, and that was very rare for that age. When I got to the United States, I stayed in a sorority house at USC with ten other girls. We divided up the meals and everybody cooked for the whole group. That was a problem! I thought, "What am I going to do?" I didn't even know how to cook rice; I burned it. Good thing we had a garbage disposal! But there was another girl from Hong Kong, who taught me how to cook rice. Sometimes I just bought frozen vegetables and frozen hamburger meat, cooked them together, and put some soy sauce on it. That's how I ate. My parents did send me Huang Yuanshan's cookbook, *The Television Cookbook*, and then Fu Pei-mei's cookbooks, but only the simplest ones.

What did you cook for your kids?

When the kids were younger, I'd let them have a choice, American or Chinese. I'd say, "What do you want?" and they'd say, "Spaghetti," so I'd make spaghetti or lasagna. I learned to make Chinese dishes too, like *shizitou* [lion's head meatballs] or *niuroumian* [beef noodles].

How did you get your start working?

In 1970, we had just bought a house in Midland when the University of Michigan needed an instructor for Chinese, so they reached out to me. I went to Ann Arbor with Jim [*her oldest son*], while Uncle stayed by himself to work. I would go to the library to work on my dissertation in the mornings, and Jim would go to the babysitter.

So for one year, you were basically on your own doing your degree, working, pregnant, and taking care of Jimmy. That sounds like a lot!

Yeah, it was a lot. But at the time, you don't feel it because you're in the middle of it, you know? During the winter there was a lot of snow, and we had to walk all the way from the bus stop to our apartment. It was a long way. I was pregnant with John [*her second son*] and really big! And every car would stop and offer me a ride. [*Laughs.*] That was embarrassing. I never took a ride. I'd say, "We're OK. We live just right over there." I got a lot of exercise since we were walking all the time.

Did you ever feel like it was difficult for you as a woman, working in position of authority?

I didn't even notice it. I think going to an all-girls' high school helped. Growing up you are very self-possessed. Our university [*in Midland, Michigan*] had a lot of connections with the big three auto companies, and I would often have to go to meetings with those executives to improve our business curriculum, get resources, donations for scholarships, or whatever. Once I went to a meeting—it was always all big, tall, white men in those meetings—and everyone was standing by the conference table. So I went to stand there too. After a while, I asked my neighbor, "How come everybody's standing for so long?" And he said, "They're waiting for you to sit down." [*Laughs.*]

How do you think it is for working women today?

Nowadays it's a lot harder for young people. It's more competitive, and technology makes it easier but also more complicated. You always have to upgrade yourself. I think my nieces are doing a great job; it takes a lot of organization, strength, and determination to do it. They have to train their children to fit into a schedule, because otherwise how could they function? I think it's great to see these two-career families strive. Think about the wasted potential of women all these years—we could have been on Mars a long time ago if we had developed the potential of all minorities, all women! It's a selfish thing, male domination, and it's lasted so long.

6

CULINARY AMBASSADOR
TO THE WORLD

Fu Pei-mei meeting Chiang Ching-kuo, Premier of the Republic of China and Chiang Kai-shek's eldest son, in 1974. Chiang Ching-kuo would eventually serve as president of the ROC for two terms, from 1978–88.

THE WALNUT CREAM SOUP BROUGHT A SWEET FINISH to the week that changed the world. It was served at the end of the closing banquet at the Great Hall of the People in Beijing, after a historic week of negotiations that began the normalization of diplomatic relations between the United States and the People's Republic of China, in February 1972. At the closing banquet, US President Richard Nixon and China's Premier Zhou Enlai toasted each other's delegations while they feasted on pea sprouts and quail egg soup, three delicacies (sea cucumber, velvet chicken, and shrimp balls) with egg white, duck cubes in spiced sauce, a vegetarian medley (mushrooms, bamboo shoots, water chestnuts, and broad beans), and the ever-present squirreled sweet and sour fish, in addition to the walnut soup and assorted side dishes not even listed on the menu, such as steamed dumplings, sesame balls, and rice flour cakes. Although diplomatic relations between the two countries were not formalized until 1979, Nixon's week in China was a political—and culinary—triumph. The image of Nixon gingerly using chopsticks to pick up delicate morsels of Chinese food at the Great Hall would forever be seared in the minds of American audiences, who had watched the dinner banquet unfold live on their television sets over breakfast, thirteen-and-a-half hours and a world away.

The so-called walnut cream soup had no cream in it at all. It was a simple mixture of crushed, deep-fried walnuts, sugar, salt, and water, thickened with a cornstarch paste. The *New York Times* printed the recipe for it, "for those interested in approximating the dishes served" at the closing banquet. The recipe had been copied from the first volume of *Pei Mei's Chinese Cook Book*, which had been published just three years earlier. American readers could purchase the cookbook by sending $2.50 to Fu's mailbox in Taipei.

By the time of the dining détente, Fu had already put a dent in the consciousness of Americans seeking authentic Chinese food, thanks to the publication of her bilingual Chinese–English cookbook. Unfortunately, only lucky cognoscenti could get their hands on a copy, as the books were only published in Taiwan. The food critic Raymond Sokolov had dubbed Fu "the Julia Child of Chinese cooking" in a 1971 *New York Times* article explaining the basic differences in Chinese culinary regions. "The four main regions of China are as different, one from the other, as France is from Italy," wrote Sokolov. Yet Americans could gain little sense of these regional distinctions from typical Chinese restaurant fare in America. "Part of the problem is that no truly authoritative cookbook exists in English. Except on Taiwan, that is. *Pei Mei's Chinese Cook Book* was published there, and unhappily only there, a few years ago," Sokolov wrote.

The publication of Fu's recipe in the *New York Times*, and the reference to her cookbook as *the* "authoritative cookbook" on Chinese cuisine, should have been unmitigated triumphs for Fu, a reflection of her growing reputation among international audiences. It *was* an achievement that her recipe was printed in the *New York Times*, but that it should appear as part of the newspaper's coverage of the banquets celebrating Nixon's historic trip to China—a trip that marked the beginning of the end of the existing diplomatic relationship between the United States and Taiwan, and the subsequent decline of Taiwan's status on the international stage—demonstrated the pitfalls of Fu's promotion of modern Chinese cuisine in a global context.

During her entire professional career, Fu consciously took up the mantle of "culinary ambassador" (*meishi dashi*) on behalf of the *Republic of China* on Taiwan, promoting the island as the last bastion of authentic Chinese cuisine. This was in marked contrast to the *People's Republic of China* on the mainland, where decades of Maoist political revolution had nearly destroyed traditional Chinese culture, including its culinary culture. It was often said that Chiang Kai-shek had not only transported the funds of China's central bank and the most prized items of the imperial art collection to Taiwan in 1949— he had also brought along a coterie of China's best chefs, who were national treasures in their own right. Yet foreign reporters seemed oblivious to these significant political differences and made little of them when it came to Fu and food. For most foreigners, Chinese food was Chinese food, not ROC food and PRC food.

Even now, American food writers tend to look back fondly on the Nixon–Zhou banquets and celebrate them as the moment of awakening for American palates, at least with regard to Chinese cuisine. Television viewers were spellbound by the parade of unfamiliar Chinese delicacies they saw President Nixon eating in Beijing and clamored for such dishes stateside. Before the banquets, it was chop suey and chow mein. After the banquets, it was Peking duck and Sichuanese *kung pao* chicken. But the aftermath of the banquets looks very different from the perspective of Taiwan. In the decades since the 1970s, Taiwan has endured the loss of its place at the international table in favor of a much heftier dinner guest, one that has grown ever more confident in demanding a rearrangement of the seating chart and even changes to the menu itself.

● ● ●

There have always been Chinese connections made between food and matters of state, in both the practical and metaphorical senses. The classic *Book of Han*, written in the first century CE, includes the line, "To the emperor, the people are heaven. To the people, food is heaven." In other words, if basic sustenance is of utmost importance to ordinary people, then the well-being of the people should be of utmost importance to the emperor. He should always ensure that the people had enough to eat—particularly if he did not want them to rise up and rebel. This classical Chinese formulation was updated in the twentieth century when Sun Yat-sen (1866–1925), the founding father of the Republic of China, replaced the figure of the emperor with the nation itself. In his signature political manifesto, the *Three People's Principles* (1924), Sun wrote, "The nation considers the people as its root, while the people take food as heaven."

In his foreword to Fu Pei-mei's 2000 memoir, James Soong, a mainlander and career politician in Taiwan, quotes this classic Chinese text. Soong explains the broader political implications of Fu's culinary career, both foreign and domestic. "At a time when the Republic of China has met with difficulties and distress in its foreign relations," Soong writes, "Fu Pei-mei has used her consummate culinary skills to open a new page for foreign relations between citizens. She not only has pupils everywhere; she has also spread the fame of Chinese cuisine far and wide." He adds, with a touch of regret, "If only today's politicians could manage the affairs of the state as Fu Pei-mei has done for the culinary arts, the country would have a much brighter and broader path into the future." Were it only so easy as Soong imagines, changing foreign hearts and minds through their stomachs.

Soong also reminds readers of a long-held Confucian perspective, that families are the fundamental units of social order and serve as a crucial foundation for the state. Confucius explained this in *The Great Learning*, a collection of his teachings possibly compiled in the fifth century BCE: "Wishing to order well their states, they first regulated their families.... Their families being regulated, their states were rightly governed. Their states being rightly governed, the whole kingdom was made tranquil and happy." By improving the lives of families everywhere through her culinary contributions, Soong argues, Fu had done her part for good governance of the nation as a whole.

Fu herself gladly took up the mantle of culinary ambassador, a role that fulfilled her father's early ambitions for her. Her father had admired the Japanese actress Yoshiko Yamaguchi (known in Chinese as Li Hsiang-lan and in English as Shirley Yamaguchi), who had been born to Japanese parents in Japanese-occupied Manchuria and could speak Chinese, Japanese, and English. He sent Fu to a Japanese elementary school, hoping that she might someday become an interpreter and have an international career. Fu's father was right about her potential. ROC government agencies, such as the foreign affairs ministry, the overseas Chinese office, news agencies, and the tourism bureau, realized what a great asset they had in Fu, and they frequently invited her to join in cultural demonstrations abroad "to propagandize for Chinese culture." Likewise, whenever foreign journalists came to Taiwan, these same government agencies would send them to Fu for an interview, to teach them more about Chinese culinary culture.

Like other loyal mainlanders of her generation, Fu promoted the idea that Taiwan alone had preserved authentic Chinese culinary traditions. This perspective was part and parcel of the Nationalist Party's broader claim that traditional Chinese culture flourished only on Taiwan, while it had been destroyed on the Chinese mainland after the Communist takeover. When asked to give the keynote address at the fiftieth anniversary meeting of the Chefs de Cuisine Association of America in Los Angeles in 1976, for example, Fu "did not forget to conduct a little person-to-person diplomacy" on behalf of her country, extending an explicit invitation to the "beautiful island": "You're welcome to visit our country, Taiwan, the Republic of China, where you can experience the joy of eating authentic Chinese food."

Fu also emphasized in her speech the role of cuisine in both pre-serving national identity and promoting cross-cultural friendship and understanding.

At the time, there was some merit in these grand Nationalist claims: in the same decades that Fu's career took off, mainland Chinese were preoccupied with getting enough to eat and surviving political upheaval. They could not afford, financially or politically, to pay attention to the bourgeois pleasures of cuisine. "A revolution is not a dinner party," Mao Zedong had famously declared in 1927. Food in the PRC was framed as a "problem" (*wenti*) to be solved for the masses, not a matter of gourmet judgment and taste. Mao had insisted in 1934 that Communist Party cadres "pay close attention to the well-being of the masses, from the problems of land and labor to those of fuel, rice, cooking oil, and salt," in order to mobilize the peasantry and spread revolution. After the Communists came to power in 1949, Mao began his program of widespread land reform in earnest. Tragically, over-zealous and misguided attempts at reform ushered in the disastrous economic, industrial, and agricultural policies of the Great Leap Forward (1958–61), which resulted in a famine that killed tens of millions.

One of the many "improvements" of the PRC's Great Leap Forward was the collectivization of all aspects of domestic life. Everyone was a member of either an agricultural commune or urban work unit and ate all their meals at communal canteens. Meals were free, and families were discouraged from cooking and eating at home. Likewise, young children were cared for in communal crèches. The collectives would thereby take over two major tasks of the housewife, cooking and caring for children, so that women would be able to join the revolution and work outside the home. At first, workers were encouraged to eat their fill—which ironically led to waste and meant that collectives consumed their food stores more quickly than usual, worsening the later famine. In some cases, communes ate through a six-month food supply in twenty days. A cookbook for communal canteens published at the height of the campaign in 1959 described canteens as "solving" the "issue of eating" for the masses by "changing people's habits of living that have held for thousands of years." To encourage people to eat collectively, it was "necessary to make people feel that eating in a public cafeteria is truly better than preparing food and eating it at home." A propaganda poster of the time simplified this message into a rhyming ditty to trumpet the cause:

公社食堂強   People's canteens are great!

飯菜做得香   The dishes there all taste first-rate!

吃着心如意   Stuff yourself and fill up your plate,

生產志氣揚   So the drive for production won't abate!

Though the policies of the Great Leap Forward were eventually rolled back, the political upheaval in China only continued with the subsequent chaos of the Cultural Revolution (1966–76). In its early phase, groups of young students loyal to Mao, known as Red Guards, fomented revolution on their own terms, rising up against those in positions of authority. Later, after the violence grew out of control, Red Guards were sent to the countryside, to give them an education in labor and help the peasants with production. During this time, food was rationed, and could only be procured with coupons issued through one's work unit. Cookbook author Sasha Gong, who grew up in Guangdong in the 1960s, recalls the time as "an era in which the traditional food culture of China . . . went into near-total eclipse. Shortages were the order of the day, and one was lucky to consume as many calories as one burned on any given day. . . . People ate whatever they could get their hands on, and there was almost never enough to go around."

In this context, the ROC's claims of upholding traditional Chinese culinary culture in the Cold War decades were not unjustified, and *Pei Mei's Chinese Cook Book* helped significantly in substantiating these claims. Her books served as an unparalleled vehicle for the ROC to export a greater understanding of Chinese cuisine to the rest of the world. Fu boasted that the first volume of her cookbook had been officially commended by the government as "substantive" and "useful to Chinese culture," and frequently selected as exhibition material for international book fairs. Indeed, in these decades, most new Chinese cookbooks were printed in Taiwan or Hong Kong, with only a small handful printed in Beijing, Shanghai, and other PRC cities. Maoist-era cookbooks from the mainland followed the political orthodoxy of the day, bearing titles such as *Cookbook for the Masses* (*Dazhong caipu*) (1973). These PRC cookbooks targeted restaurants or cafeterias cooking for huge groups of twenty or thirty, not individual housewives cooking for their families. During these postwar decades, it was cookbook authors from outside of mainland China who definitively shaped the world's understanding of Chinese food—and Fu Pei-mei led the way.

●   ●   ●

Fu's comprehensive vision of Chinese food can be seen through her best-known three-volume series, *Pei Mei's Chinese Cook Books* (1969–79). These cookbooks are particularly compelling because their publication coincided precisely with the international shift of diplomatic recognition away from the government of the ROC on Taiwan, in favor of the government of the PRC on the Chinese mainland. Thus the confident tone and celebratory claims about Chinese cookery in her first volume, published in 1969, mirrored the status of the ROC at the height of its international influence. At that moment, Fu had no difficulty laying claim to a common Chinese historical and political lineage stressing the importance of food, stretching back from Sun Yat-sen, modern father of the Republic of China, all the way to the philosophers of the Spring and Autumn Period (ca. 771–476 BCE). "Our country has five thousand years of glorious history, and every aspect of its culture surpasses that of other countries," Fu wrote. Even in ancient times, "there was already detailed knowledge of how to apply knife skills and heating techniques in order to bring out the greatest potential for the most satisfying tastes of all kinds of foods."

Two short years later, in October 1971, ROC representatives were ousted from the United Nations in favor of PRC representatives, beginning a rapid shift of allegiance within the international community. The United States tried to advocate for the ROC's continued presence in the United Nations while allowing a seat for the PRC, but the PRC and its allies would not consent to a two-China system. A few months before the vote, in June 1971, Nixon had privately asked Walter P. McConaughy, ambassador to the ROC (whose wife had written the foreword to Fu's cookbook), to perform two delicate tasks. The first was to reassure their allies in Taiwan of American support, while the second was to warn them of impending changes in status. "Our China position will not support any propositions that have the Republic of China put out of the UN.... We will be strong, steadfast on that point," said Nixon. "But," he added, "they must be prepared for the fact, that there will continue to be a step-by-step, a more normal relationship with the other—the Chinese mainland. Because our interests require it. Not because we love them, but because they're there." As it turned out, only the second part of the message came true, when Nixon made his groundbreaking trip to Beijing in February of the following year and began the normalization of diplomatic relations between the United States and China. As for the United States remaining strong and steadfast about not ousting the ROC from the United Nations, it did not matter: the rest of the body voted to replace ROC representatives with PRC representatives, by a final vote of 76 to 35, with 17 abstentions.

In the second volume of her cookbook series, published in 1974, after the US–PRC détente, Fu now referred to the Republic of China's political and material success more explicitly—in unspoken contrast to the poverty and chaos of the People's Republic of China on the mainland. In the Chinese introduction, she wrote, "Today, citizens in Taiwan, the Republic of China's model province . . . are living in a peaceful, affluent and happy environment as a result of the rapid development of the economy and the progress of society toward prosperity. . . . The most prominent expression of this is within the realm of food. Having already had their basic needs of 'sufficient food' fulfilled, our compatriots can now pay attention to the highest levels of enjoyment of 'fine food' and 'cuisine.'" With regard to Taiwan's rapid economic development, ROC citizens at the time were indeed far better off than those in the PRC. As McConaughy had reminded Nixon, Taiwan's total foreign trade in 1970 was "just over $3 billion, which slightly exceeded the total import and export trade of the Chinese Communists." At that moment, no one could have predicted how drastically and dramatically that relative economic picture would pivot between the ROC and PRC in a matter of just a few decades.

By the time of the publication of the third and final volume of Fu's cookbook series in 1979, Taiwan's political stature was greatly diminished: this was the same year in which the United States switched its diplomatic recognition to the PRC. Mao had finally died in 1976, and Deng Xiaoping soon consolidated his hold on power, instituting the major economic reforms that would allow the Chinese to realize the new maxim of the times, "to get rich is glorious." Deng and Jimmy Carter formalized diplomatic relations between the two countries during Deng's state visit to the United States in 1979, the first for a Chinese leader since Madame Chiang Kai-shek's wartime visit in 1943. Deng donned a cowboy hat, ate veal, and visited the headquarters of Coca-Cola. The introduction to the third volume of Fu's cookbook series reflected the ROC's newly subdued political position. Fu retreated from referencing Taiwan's contested political claims and instead described her country in cultural terms alone, as a paradise of Chinese cuisine in miniature, at least to her English-language readers: "At present, it is only in Taiwan that the pleasure of eating authentic Chinese food from all parts of China can be experienced. . . . In Taiwan, there are people from every part of China, and thus there are restaurants representing each province."

As described in Chapter 4, Fu had mapped the four essential culinary regions of China in her first volume based on the four cardinal directions and arranged the recipes in four corresponding sections. Each section was prefaced with a map highlighting the provinces included under that cardinal direction. For example, the map for eastern China highlighted Jiangsu, Anhui, and Zhejiang Provinces; southern China highlighted Fujian and Guangdong Provinces; western China highlighted Sichuan, Guizhou and Hunan Provinces; and northern China highlighted Shanxi, Hebei, Shandong, and Henan Provinces.

Map of eastern China from *Pei Mei's Chinese Cook Book, Vol. I* (1969). Fu's map is based on the extent of the Republic of China before 1949, not the more familiar contours of today's People's Republic of China.

Yet for today's readers, these regional designations are not the most interesting feature of Fu's culinary maps. If you look carefully, the contours of Fu's national maps are not an exact match for the borders of the PRC as we know them today. (Compare it with the map at the start of this book.) Rather, the maps included in Fu's 1969 cookbook are maps of the pre-1949 Republic of China, preserving intact all thirty-five of its provincial boundaries (including some that no longer existed, such as Rehe Province) and territories claimed (such as outer Mongolia, which had become an independent country) before the Nationalist retreat to Taiwan.

These culinary maps uniquely illustrate the disjuncture between the geographically bound reality of the Republic of China on the island Taiwan and its loftier political aspirations. For decades after its loss to the Communists in 1949, the Nationalist Party claimed itself as the true, legitimate government of China, even as it exercised no actual political authority over any of the mainland territories. The fiction was maintained by the continued existence of the National Assembly, a body of provincial representatives elected on the mainland in 1947. The National Assembly moved to Taiwan along with the rest of the ROC government in 1949, but its representatives could never be replaced because new elections could not be held on the mainland. As a result, these provincial representatives continued to sit on the National Assembly decade after decade, acting as if they still governed China, although they were entirely disconnected from the populations they purported to represent. Moreover, representation in the national governing body did not accurately reflect the population actually governed on Taiwan. It was not until political reforms in 1990s that the last mainlander members of the First National Assembly were forced to retire, before the entire body was suspended and replaced in 2000.

Although the Nationalists could no longer exercise actual *political* authority over any of these mainland areas, they could and did still claim an inherited *cultural* authority over quintessential Chinese qualities and values. In large part, this was the reason that cultural matters were so important in the ROC, to a degree that may have seemed unusual outside the country. Fu Pei-mei's cookbooks could never be value-neutral presentations of Chinese cuisine: with the political gulf separating the ROC and PRC, any discussion of "Chinese" cuisine begged the ultimate question of what this cultural and political identity should now consist of. That Fu or any of her mainlander contemporaries in Taiwan assumed the mantle of culinary traditions from their home provinces was certainly in line with the political orthodoxy of the day. But for contemporary readers, Fu's 1969 maps manifest a kind of magical thinking, or at least a wishful denial regarding the territorial realities ROC Nationalists had to contend with in exile. Interestingly, there were no maps of China in Volume III (1979) of Fu's series, even though it too was also organized by culinary region. Perhaps by 1979 it was too much of a glaring stretch to cover the disparity between the geographical reality of the ROC and its rapidly receding political aspirations.

More than a decade later, in 1993, Fu was asked by the ROC army to teach its kitchen staff about Chinese cuisine, for its new Food Logistics Training Center. Anyone involved in army meal preparation was required to attend, in order to improve the quality of meals served to servicemen. After several decades of rapid economic development, enlisted men, like Taiwan's civilians, were no longer satisfied with having enough to eat, but now wanted good things to eat. Courses covered logistics for kitchen supplies, menus, nutrition, and hygiene. Fu was responsible for teaching about cooking, with six lectures per day.

For her army students as for the housewives who had preceded them, Fu's teaching methods centered on a geographical approach to introducing Chinese cuisine, detailing special regional characteristics, techniques, and flavors. On the first day of class, she would ask one of the army students to come up to the front of the room to draw a map of China on the blackboard. "That person would always draw a hodgepodge picture, a bit like a duck and a bit like a melon, and make everybody laugh." Fu would then go on to use this mixed-up map to discuss China's geography, provinces, and the special regional characteristics of Chinese food. But by 1993, more than forty years after the traumatic retreat of the Nationalists from the mainland to Taiwan, one had to wonder: What if the reason the map was mixed-up was not a result of poor draftsmanship, but rather a different, hazier vision of "China"? No doubt the map of China that Fu held in her head, heart, and memory was not the same as the mental map that these young recruits possessed, who had never set foot on mainland soil.

* * *

Fu's international travels throughout the 1970s, 1980s, and 1990s were part of a culinary charm offensive, using Chinese cuisine to woo the stomachs—and hearts and minds—of potential foreign allies. As her reputation grew, Fu traveled to the Philippines, Japan, Singapore, Hong Kong, South Korea, Malaysia, Australia, South Africa, the United States, and the Netherlands to teach foreign audiences how to cook Chinese food. Yet Fu's hard work to ensure that the ROC made a good culinary impression on foreign travelers began even before she stepped foot on a plane. In 1973 she was approached by China Airlines, the Republic of China's flagship airline, to help improve their international in-flight meals, her first of many outside consulting projects. She developed several set menus that could withstand the rigors and restrictions of air travel, with a hot main meat dish (prone to overdrying when heated in tiny airplane ovens), a cold marinated dish or salad, and either rice or noodles as a starch, all served on a tiny 9 × 15 cm tray. The main dishes included cashew chicken, oil-dripped chicken, or red-braised beef. Unfortunately, the third-party airport kitchen staffs in San Francisco, Honolulu, and Tokyo "didn't understand Chinese food and couldn't even make fried rice," so Fu traveled to each city to teach them in person. The chefs in San Francisco, who were from Switzerland, were very large men who towered over Fu. She tried to teach them how to make meat rolls, but their fingers were too beefy and not deft enough to make three dainty rolls, so they had make do with two chunky ones.

Fu was always very conscious of her responsibility to do her part on behalf of the ROC during her world travels. Once on a personal trip to Florida in 1985 to visit her youngest daughter, who had moved to the United States, she got a phone call from the Taipei Economic and Cultural Representative Office (TECO, the ROC's de facto government organ in the United States) in New York City, begging her to come there and talk about Chinese food on television. The TECO representative urged her, "Do something for your country! Enlist your special skills to promote Taiwan!" Fu was happy to engage in "a little person-to-person diplomatic work for the government" by making appearances on morning television programs in various American cities and was proud that her efforts to demonstrate Chinese culinary arts could help to "achieve the ultimate goals" of the Government Information Office, the ROC's media and propaganda bureau.

Although Fu never occupied any formal position in the ROC diplomatic corps, the Taiwan press, at least, seemed to believe that her overseas appearances not only promoted the unique cultural and culinary heritage of Taiwan, but also promoted the country's diplomatic agenda to foreign audiences. During her first demonstration trip to the Philippines in 1972, for example, an article in the *China Times* extolled Fu's influence abroad, drawing positive attention to Taiwan in a way that other news items had not:

> English newspapers in the Philippines have never much
> emphasized news from our country. But during the time of
> Fu Pei-mei's visit to the Philippines, the four major English-
> language newspapers, the *Daily Mirror, Manila Daily Bulletin,*

Daily Express, Manila Evening News and *Weekend Magazine,*
all had large pictures and lengthy reports on the enthusiasm of Filipino-Chinese women in taking classes and learning [from Fu]. This is successful person-to-person diplomacy
through "eating."

Fu would sometimes advocate for the ROC's diplomatic agenda in a
more concrete and explicit fashion. For example, on Fu's original Chinese cooking program for Fuji Television in Japan, which was broadcast in Japanese from 1978 to 1983, Fu referred to the superiority of
Taiwan's produce and industrial food products at every opportunity:

The color of the bean paste available in Japan is not as attractive as that available in Taiwan. Fu Pei-mei can only tell Japanese viewers, "Making this mapo tofu in Taiwan, it would be a
lot more attractive."

When she has to use rape greens in lieu of green cabbage, she says, "In Taiwan, it's a lot tastier because we use
green cabbage, which is both fat and tender."

When making dry-fried green beans, she says, "At this time
of year in Taiwan, green beans cost only one-tenth of what
they cost here."

She is imperceptibly and continuously propagandizing on
behalf of our treasured island.

At the same time that she was propagandizing on the wonders of
Taiwan's produce, Fu also set out to correct erroneous foreign views
on Chinese food. When it came to strictly maintaining the standards
of Chinese culinary excellence worldwide, Fu minced no words. On
her 1972 trip to the Philippines, Fu suggested that, "Although the
overseas Chinese living in the Philippines still maintain the traditional home cooking of Chinese food, what they understand is still

uniformly a mix of Guangdong dishes and Fujianese dishes. These dishes are sweet, sour, and salty, and not actually all that tasty." She was convinced that if "an expert can guide them on how to take advantage of available native ingredients as substitutes for preparations, then they can also cook up authentic tasting Chinese dishes, thus improving the food and drink of these overseas compatriots." For this particular trip, Fu brought along in her suitcase one hundred rolling pins and fifty colanders to give away to her students, having heard that these two utensils could not be purchased in Manila.

On another occasion, during a visit to Australia in 1984, sponsored by the Australian Meat and Livestock Association, Fu schooled a group of Australian cooking experts, some of whom had had the temerity to teach Chinese cooking to other foreigners. (She didn't think much of Australian food either, which she said had "no special characteristics. They like to eat meat in large pieces. No matter what kind of meat, it's all barbecued, after which they put on all kinds of condiments and seasonings.") The worst of these self-styled foreign experts was Margaret Fulton (1924–2019), whom the press in Taiwan called the "Australian Fu Pei-mei." Fulton had edited a weekly cooking column in *Women's Day* magazine for many years and authored thirteen cookbooks, including a comprehensive encyclopedia of cooking and her own Chinese cookbook. Widely known for having internationalized Australian dining tables beyond strictly meat-and-potatoes fare, Fulton had based her expertise in Chinese cooking on a handful of visits to Hong Kong, Taiwan, and mainland China.

The greatest result of Fu's trip, crowed one Taiwanese magazine, was that she had taught a lesson to these Australians, particularly Fulton, Fu's "Australian shadow," who had only half-baked understandings of Chinese food. Although these women were curious about Chinese food, their questions for Fu were "very amateur." They seemed to have little to no idea about the regional distinctions of Chinese food, and a limited understanding of Chinese cooking techniques, featuring only examples of deep-fried or stir-fried dishes in their so-called "Chinese" cookbooks. Moreover, from their cookbook photographs Fu could tell that their "basic knife skills could not be said to be of particularly high quality." After their session with Fu Pei-mei, even the grand and conceited Fulton had to admit that she had much yet to learn about Chinese cuisine.

Yet these glowing descriptions of Fu's international travels in the Taiwan press seem naïve in their understanding of how foreigners might interpret Fu's overseas cooking demonstrations. Just mention-ing Taiwan or Taiwanese products did not necessarily mean that for-eigners took Fu for anything other than a representative of "Chinese" cooking. For example, Filipino coverage of Fu's 1972 visit appeared in English-language newspapers, complete with large, attractive photos—but only on the Society pages of the *Manila Daily Bulletin* and the *Philippines Daily Express*. In the text caption of the latter, Fu is called a "Chinese cook" and no mention is made of Taiwan, while in the former there is only a single mention of Fu's cooking school in Taiwan. The impact of Fu's visits was always limited to the women's pages, food pages, or society pages, not splashed on the front pages. Without exception, foreign journalists focused solely on Fu and food, not the complex, entangled, and distinct histories or political agendas of the PRC and ROC.

• • •

In many ways, Fu's position as a media celebrity promoting an appeal-ing and appetizing image of Chinese culture abroad prefigures the explicit emphasis in recent decades on bolstering Taiwan's soft power, or global influence in arenas outside of politics, the military, or the economy. Since Thailand first introduced its Global Thai program in 2002, with the aim of increasing the number of Thai restaurants around the world and driving foreign tourism, other countries, such as Taiwan, South Korea, Malaysia, and Peru—all middle state powers with rich food traditions—have followed suit with their own versions of culinary campaigns designed to strengthen recognition of their national brands and extend soft power. Even the United States has joined these countries in the kitchen, with the State Department introducing its Diplomatic Culinary Partnership program in 2012. American celebrity chefs have been invited to assist in state dinners, gone abroad to participate in food tours and cooking demonstrations in foreign countries, and served as hosts to foreign chefs on food visits to the United States. These gastrodiplomatic programs are built on the same premise: that an excellent way to win friends and influence people is to appeal to their stomachs.

The Cold War example of Fu Pei-mei's cookbooks and gastrodiplomatic mission underscores the particular difficulty of Taiwan's use of food as a tool of diplomacy, even today. What is the best way to represent the country's culinary heritage for foreign audiences, who may have little to no idea about the complex, divided political histories of the PRC and ROC, or the internal divisions within Taiwan? One example that comes readily to mind is the immense popularity of bubble tea (*zhenzhu naicha*, also known in English as pearl milk tea or boba tea). The drink was originally invented in Taiwan in the 1980s, but has quickly spread around the world, thanks to dedicated Taiwanese entrepreneurs and the popularity of the drink in overseas Asian communities. In its most basic form, it is a sweetened black milk tea with soft, chewy balls of tapioca in it, but shops now offer dozens of delicious varieties, with fruit flavorings, cheese foams, and all manner of additions.

For Taiwan's partisan boosters, bubble tea's Taiwanese origins matter very much. The drink is now often promoted as a national symbol, found on all manner of tourist tchotchkes representing Taiwan. One of Taiwan's newly established political parties, the New Power Party, which advocates for Taiwanese nationalism and independence and grew out of the 2014 Sunflower Student Movement, sponsored a passport cover redesign contest in 2020 to remove the words "Republic of China" from passports in favor of the single word "Taiwan." Among these graphic visualizations of Taiwanese identity, bubble tea featured in six of the 127 designs. In one entry, bubble tea stands as an enlarged base for a cityscape of other iconic Taiwanese symbols— the Taipei 101 building (one of the tallest skyscrapers in the world), a Pingxi lantern, the Chiang Kai-shek Memorial. In another, Taiwan's national bird, the Taiwan blue magpie, wears a jaunty bubble tea hat. Another envisions bubble tea as a kind of traditional-style watercolor, in a distinctive closeup of beige milk tea with tell-tale black rounded balls at the bottom.

But does the average American or other foreign consumer know or care about the specific origins of bubble tea? Chapel Hill, North Carolina, the college town in which I live, now boasts five dedicated bubble tea shops, all of which have opened within the last few years. Three of them are within walking distance of the campus. Undergraduates seem quite happy to get their boba fix from any or all these shops, but few seem aware of their different backstories. The owners of Cha House, the first bubble tea shop to open in Chapel Hill in 2016, are from Taiwan, and they proudly declare their heritage by calling Cha House an "Asian-inspired tea house, influenced by the tastes and traditions of Taiwan." The shop serves popular Taiwanese street foods, such as popcorn chicken and tea-stewed pork rice, in addition to bubble tea. The second store is Yaya Tea, part of a chain that began in New York City in 2008. No mention of bubble tea's Taiwanese origins can be found on their website, and their food offerings are Japanese snack foods such as *onigiri* rice balls. The latest arrival on the local bubble shop scene in 2021 is Möge TEE. The shop is part of a massive chain, established in the PRC in 2014, with more than three hundred stores in the PRC alone, and dozens more around the world. The website of Möge TEE boasts that it is "inspired by thousands of years of Chinese traditional tea culture"—even though bubble tea is a very recent invention of Taiwanese street food entrepreneurs in the 1980s.

What *should* matter most to a consumer making a choice about which bubble tea shop to patronize? The bounciness of the boba or the background of the store's owners? To judge from Yelp reviews of all three bubble tea shops, most customers don't know or seem to care about bubble tea's origins or the backstories of each shop. Not surprisingly, customers are more concerned with the quality of the drinks or the perceived level of service.

When Fu Pei-mei got her start promoting the diplomatic interests of the ROC through Chinese cooking demonstrations around the world, bubble tea was not yet even a milky gleam in the eyes of Taiwan's entrepreneurial street food vendors. But today the drink is seen as a popular national symbol of Taiwan, exported around the world. The image of Fu sipping on the big straw of a bouncy boba tea, however fanciful, brings together Taiwan's culinary past and present, and underscores the same tensions that plague both. (Fu never drank bubble tea during her lifetime, but her daughter says she would have enjoyed trying it, as she approached any popular new food or drink with characteristic curiosity.) Regardless of whether one is trying to promote the interests of the Republic of China or the interests of Taiwan, it may not matter if your intended audience doesn't get the message. It should have been a triumph for Fu to have her recipe printed in the *New York Times*, just as it should be a triumph that your average American college student now sees bubble tea as their go-to afternoon pick-me-up drink. Yet American audiences in Fu's day made no distinction between the ROC and PRC (seeing them both as interchangeably "Chinese"), just as they now make no distinctions between bubble tea shops (seeing them all as interchangeably "Asian"). In gastrodiplomacy, sometimes the deliciousness of the dish trumps the meaning of the message.

7

DINNER IN SEVENTEEN MINUTES

Fu Pei-mei working in the lab of an industrial food research facility
(ca. 1980s).

EVERY TIME FU PEI-MEI PASSED THROUGH THE WIN-
dowed corridor overlooking the factory floor, she slowed her
step, stealing secret glances at the precise movements of the
gleaming machinery on the assembly line. It was 1979 and Fu had been
invited by the Japanese food company Yamamori to serve as a consultant to improve their line of Chinese dishes in retort pouches that had
been brought to market with disappointing results. Yamamori, whose
late nineteenth-century founder, Sentaro Mitsubayashi, had built his
business on soy sauce brewing, opened the first retort pouch sterilization facility in Japan in 1969, which packaged precooked foods into
soft, flexible, metal laminate pouches. After being placed directly in
boiling water to reheat, the food was ready to eat. Fu was mesmerized
by the efficiency of the entire line, which was arranged in six linked
rows, "like long dragons." The food was first cooked in a huge cauldron, then sucked directly into a pipe, then squirted in exact amounts
into pouches, and finally sealed and sterilized, all without ever being
handled by human hands. "It took your breath away, to see the perfection of all of those specially designed, advanced machines," Fu
recalled. "That was the first time I had seen anything like it."

If the factory floor assembly line was the epitome of tidy, hygienic, automated efficiency, then the small research lab where Fu actually worked developing food products was anything but. Two researchers sat squeezed together at each worktable, while an old sterilization cauldron stood in the middle of the room, emitting steam and the occasional ear-splitting whistle. There was no air-conditioning and the heat was suffocating. Fu's job was to cook Chinese dishes in traditional fashion, determining the exact amount required of each ingredient, seasoning, and chemical component in precisely measured quantities. "When I wrote the recipes for my cookbooks, measuring spoons were used to calculate the amount of each seasoning, but in the lab, grams were the standard unit." The main problem facing the researchers was the negative effect of the sterilization process on the appearance, texture, and taste of the food itself. "Colors would fade, elasticity would be lost, and viscosity would diminish. The chlorophyll in any green vegetable would break down and turn yellow or black." Many powdered starches would return to liquid form after processing, yielding a soupy mess. Moreover, because the food was stored at room temperature, over a long period of time its smell and taste would also change. The research team's ongoing experiments to address these issues within the specific limitations of the sterilization process not only taxed their brains, Fu wrote, it also meant that "our tongues had long ago been numbed by repeated tastings."

In Fu's own eyes, it was not a contradiction for her to work on developing ready-to-eat, industrial food products, even though she had built her reputation as Taiwan Television's home cooking guru. She liked keeping up with the latest developments in food technologies, driven by an insatiable curiosity to learn about anything new. She enjoyed the challenges posed by the problems that arose in the laboratory and did not fear the meticulous labor involved in repeated attempts at perfecting a recipe. It also did not hurt to have an additional income stream through food product consultancies. Fu considered frozen foods and retort pouches as merely the latest stage in long-standing Chinese efforts to preserve food, which had taken different forms over many centuries. "Starting in ancient times there were preservation methods such as air drying, smoking, curing, salting, soaking in oil, and pickling.... In modern times, high-temperature sterilization of metal cans or glass jars has been used to extend the shelf life of food products. In the latter part of the twentieth century, we have started to replace cans with retort pouches." Other, even newer preservation methods, such as vacuum packaging or using an inert gas like nitrogen to flush out oxygen, could be used for foodstuffs that did not require reheating.

Fu's many collaborations with industrial food companies, fast-food restaurant chains, food industry agencies, and a commercial airline in the later stages of her career exemplified her forward-thinking attitude toward Chinese cuisine. Fu did not necessarily want to replace home cooking entirely with ready-to-eat packages of processed foods or restaurant foods—but she was also a realist when it came to modern women's lives and Chinese cooking. Retort pouches, for example, were both simple and convenient. When she first heard about retort pouches on her trips to Japan in the 1970s, Fu thought, "If you could package tasty but time-consuming Chinese dishes in this fashion, it could save many housewives the trouble of preparing meals."

Two decades later, as processed foods thrived and possibilities for eating out had multiplied, the need to cook at home from scratch had diminished dramatically. In an interview from 1992, Fu described how difficult it had been to sustain her cooking classes, with fewer and fewer women interested in enrolling. By the end, Fu had started to teach dishes that could be partially prepared ahead of time, for quick reheating after work. "That's what society needs now," she sighed. "Being housewives and career women simultaneously, modern women are too busy to cultivate much interest in time-consuming

Chinese cuisine. Besides, the smoke from the kitchen deteriorates the home living environment. Lots of young people even refuse to cook at home," she said.

Processed foods and new kitchen technologies revolutionized the way women shopped and cooked in Taiwan in the postwar decades, just as they had in the United States. An ever-growing stream of canned foods, frozen foods, jarred sauces, and retort pouches, all purchased at newly built supermarkets, meant that home cooking could be a simple matter of opening a jar or heating a pan. Refrigerators with freezers meant that busy housewives no longer had to make a daily trip to the market for groceries but could instead buy meat and vegetables to keep for several days, or even weeks or months. Gas burners offered a much safer, cleaner, easier way to cook, replacing messy and inefficient clay braziers fueled by burning firewood, wood charcoal, or coal briquettes. When microwaves came along in the late 1970s, they were even faster and cleaner than burners, without the usual smoke of stir-frying. Each of these products, developed and marketed by Taiwan's burgeoning food processing and appliance industries, was touted as a time-saving improvement, purportedly designed to lessen the burden on housewives in the kitchen. But did Fu's numerous food consultancies help to hasten the demise of home cooking, or did she merely take part in an inexorable social trend toward the industrialization of food? Did the latest version of Fu Pei-mei, in her hairnet and lab coat, push her old self, armed with cleaver and wok, out of a job?

• • •

Even in the early decades of her career, Fu recognized the need for speed and simplicity in the kitchen. She consciously created recipes suitable for busy, modern lives. Volume I of *Pei Mei's Chinese Cook Book* had focused on what Fu had deemed the "traditional" presentation of representative specialty dishes from different regions of China, but her later cookbooks paid more attention to the needs of younger housewives: dishes that were novel, easy-to-make, in smaller quantities, and arranged by main ingredient or basic cooking technique. In the introduction to the third volume of *The Television Cookbook* (1970), Fu explained that the dishes she included relied upon quick-cooking techniques of frying, stir-frying, boiling, and deep-frying, rather than "more delicate and refined" slow-cooking techniques, such as braising or gentle simmering. "Unlike the previous generation," Fu wrote, "we no longer have the mood or leisure to keep watch over a pot of silver ear fungus soup, simmering all day long." Silver ear fungus (*Tremella fuciformis*, also known as snow fungus) soup, cooked with lotus seeds, jujubes, and goji berries, and sweetened with rock candy, had reputedly been a favorite of China's most notorious imperial concubine, Yang Guifei (719–756), to ensure her flawless complexion. Yet the hours required to make it were an idle luxury for modern women.

Fu was aware of the added time constraints facing working women in particular, who juggled their careers and household management. She could sympathize with their plight. Although she spent her days teaching other women how to cook delicious Chinese dishes in person and on television, feeding her own family was another matter. As one reporter explained in a profile of Fu from 1971, "All of her energies are put into her cooking, so she has no time to take care of her family and children. No one would guess that only the simplest and most casual of family dishes land on the dinner table at her house." The article quoted Fu as saying, "It's good that my mother-in-law and father-in-law don't really pay that much attention to the art of eating." The article was headlined "Fu Pei-mei and Speedy Chinese Food," and Fu admitted that although eating well-prepared Chinese food was a distinct pleasure, Chinese cooking could be "overly particular and time-consuming," making it "outdated in the present moment, which demands speed." Fu imagined a day when a family going out on a picnic might bring along a "specially processed, quick-to-prepare meal packaged in a plastic box." When their stomachs are growling and they are ready to eat, the mother simply whips out the box, heats it in a simple fashion (exactly how is not specified), and voila! "The family can sit together and enjoy a delicious, happy time."

One could say that Fu's vision of simple and speedy Chinese food did come to pass only a decade later, as a direct result of Fu's most successful industrial food collaboration: the Manchu-Han Imperial Feast (*Manhan dacan*) line of instant ramen noodles from Uni-President Enterprises, a huge food conglomerate headquartered in the southern city of Tainan. The name was meant to evoke the imperial banquets of the Qing dynasty (1644–1911), when the ruling minority ethnic group, the Manchus, would feast with their subordinate Han officials. The association with imperial opulence hinted at the marketing of the product as a kind of luxury version of instant noodles, with an actual packet of processed meat included, along with a packet of dry seasoning soup powder, a packet of flavored oil, and the dried noodles themselves. Instant ramen noodles had been invented in Japan in 1958 by Momofuku Ando (originally named Go Peh-hok) (1910–2007), who had been born in Taiwan to a Taiwanese family during the colonial period. Later as a young man, he emigrated to Japan, where he eventually established the Nissin Foods company. In Taiwan, Uni-President Enterprises, established in 1967, was the first domestic company to offer its own version of instant ramen noodles in 1970.

Uni-President executives had approached Fu in 1982 to work for them as a consultant, helping to develop new Chinese food products. Based on her prior experience working with Yamamori and her understanding of the processes of high-temperature sterilization and packaging, she was well-suited to the task. Each month she went to Tainan to Uni-President's small research lab facilities, equipped with the by now familiar tools of the trade: a large oven, a fermentation cabinet, a stove, large and small refrigerators, large and small mixers, a packaging machine, and shelves of seasonings and measuring tools. She never knew until she arrived what the assignment for that day might be, so it was a bit like going into battle. "I would have to tackle issues or topics I wasn't always familiar with, and had none of my usual reference materials at hand. I always had to rack my brains to think of creative solutions."

For the first six months, she collaborated on developing twenty different retort pouch flavoring packets for instant noodles. As with Yamamori's product, the biggest challenge was maintaining a suitable viscosity and texture in the prepared food, which tended to get mushy or soupy after high-temperature sterilization. The team experimented with using different cuts of beef and found that parts with more tendon could better withstand boiling, offered a chewier mouthfeel, and could help to hold the lean meat together, to keep it from disintegrating. The accompanying ingredients went through the same rigorous testing, to determine the proper cutting size, the ideal amount of seasoning, and the best sequence for cooking it all together. Of the original twenty flavors they developed, the research team presented six for evaluation by all the section heads of the company, who gathered for a blind taste testing. Their assessment was both qualitative and quantitative. The judges described in words what they saw, smelled, and tasted, as well as assigning each characteristic a specific numerical value. They ate in a dark room so that they could focus on taste alone; after that, the products were examined in the light, for appearance, color, and overall satisfaction. The flavors then underwent another round of testing and improvement, until every element was deemed satisfactory.

When the Manchu-Han Imperial Feast instant noodle line was first introduced in Taiwan in 1983, it was a massive success, with US$3 million in sales in its first year. There were six different varieties, including the best-selling beef noodles, *Dongpo* pork noodles, and winter bamboo slivered pork noodles. The whole line was advertised as a luxurious indulgence, and with the inclusion of a packet of real meat, it was seen as a second-generation improvement over the other instant noodles, which only added a powdered seasoning packet. According to Fu, the "rare delicacy flavor beef noodles" (*zhenwei niuroumian*) were so unexpectedly popular that Uni-President had to order an entire automated assembly line from Japan to meet the demand. (Prior to that upgrade, the flavoring packets had been cooked and packaged entirely by hand at the company's facilities.) The original product packaging featured a picture of Fu Pei-mei, boasting of her "personal oversight" in the product development, alongside a picture of a steaming bowl of noodles. (Less fortunately, the company went with an English rendering of the product name as "President Imperial Big Meal," which sounds more like a cause for indigestion.)

Luke Tsai, a Bay Area food writer, vividly recalls going to visit Taiwan as a child in the 1990s, when his entire family would look forward to eating what they called "Fu Pei-mei's beef noodles." "That was the only brand we ever bought," he says. It was the inclusion of meat packet that made it fancier than other brands, while the dried noodles themselves "weren't anything special." Moreover, the flavors were strong. "It also had a packet of orange grease [chili oil]. That was what made it taste good when you mixed it together," he says. When returning to the United States, Tsai remembers, "We would always smuggle it back on the plane, because it had the actual packets of meat inside of it." Today, the Man-Han noodle packaging no longer bears Fu's image, but with its packets of real meat, the line continues to boost Uni-President's dominance in Taiwan's domestic instant ramen market.

Fu's failures in industrial food development were just as telling as her successes. She worked as a consultant for various frozen food companies and continually tried to convince consumers in Taiwan that frozen foods were convenient and did not lose nutrition or flavor when compared to the fresh variety. Frozen delights such as orange juice concentrate, fish sticks, and turkey TV dinners had been popular with American consumers since the 1950s, but housewives in Taiwan were not so readily swayed when frozen foods arrived there in the

1970s. In a food column she wrote for *Families* monthly magazine in 1978, Fu extolled the virtues of frozen foods. "When you bring up frozen vegetables, a lot of people might turn up their noses. They think that they are not only bad tasting, but they also have no nutritional value. Actually, if they don't taste good, it is due to the defrosting and cooking methods that they don't achieve the best results." Fu shared recipes for stir-fried (frozen) fish slices, an assorted (frozen) vegetable salad, dry-fried (frozen) green beans, jade rice with (frozen) spinach, and stir-fried beef with (frozen) cauliflower.

Despite Fu's endorsement, frozen foods did not gain acceptance in the domestic market in Taiwan for many years. A 1992 article in *Taiwan Review* explained that annual per capita consumption of frozen foods in Taiwan, at 6 kilograms, was still far less than frozen food consumption in United States (51 kg) or Japan (11 kg). "Many people feel that however tasty these frozen foods may be, they still lack that home-cooked touch," concluded the reporter. This view may have explained the failure of a line of frozen Chinese dishes by the Japanese food company Ajinomoto, which Fu worked on in the 1990s. She first cooked fifteen different, well-known Chinese dishes with complex, characteristic seasonings for the company's executives in the traditional manner, from which they chose four to bring to market: fish fragrant shredded pork, sweet and sour pork, diced chicken with chili, and red-braised beef. Yet even after much research and development, Ajinomoto's frozen versions of these Chinese dishes never took off in Taiwan's domestic market: after three years of declining sales, the company switched the factory over to making Japanese frozen dumplings for the Japanese market.

●   ●   ●

The introduction of frozen foods to Taiwan's domestic food market was predicated on widespread ownership of refrigerators, in which to store all these new frozen products. The 1977 Taipei housewives survey found that, by that point, ninety percent of urban households had a refrigerator. Yet refrigerators were still a new enough phenomenon that *Families* monthly magazine printed an article by journalist Yuan Minglun unveiling "The Secrets of Using Your Refrigerator." Yuan wrote about her brother and his new wife, who made their first major purchase together of a refrigerator when they started living in their own apartment, paying it off in installments. Their new appliance took pride of place next to the door, so that visitors could admire it. Prior to that moment, the young couple had subsisted on canned foods, buns, bread, instant noodles, and other dry goods, because when they returned home from work, all the nearby markets had long since closed. The couple would return to his parents' home on weekends to eat, making up for all the freshly cooked meals they hadn't eaten during the week.

Yet owning a new kitchen appliance also meant new regimes of care and responsibility. The young couple had to learn through experience not to pile too many food items in the freezer, impeding air circulation and proper freezing. If the drainage hole in the bottom of the refrigerator was blocked with sediment, potatoes would sprout in the vegetable drawer and scallions would blacken and wither. It also meant buying plastic bags, aluminum foil, and plastic lids for dishes to store food items properly so they would not mix their odors. Zheng Meiying, a home economics professor, cautioned, "Before going shopping, you should first have a look in the refrigerator and use up what you have left over in there and eat it. This will avoid your buying fresh foods, bringing them home and putting them in front of the shelf, with the old items getting squeezed to the back of each shelf." She therefore recommended thoroughly cleaning out the refrigerator every two weeks, and polishing the outside with leftover toothpaste, a method "both effective and economical."

New, processed food products and the ability to preserve fresh foods longer in the refrigerator went hand in hand with new ways of shopping for food items. While the 1977 Taipei housewives' survey found that most households had a refrigerator, more than half of the housewives, fifty-eight percent, still reported shopping for groceries every day. Most housewives shopped at traditional markets (*caichang*), with individual vendors selling everything from fresh vegetables to meats and seafoods. Consumers were not immediately attracted to the new supermarkets (*chaojishichang*) springing up everywhere around the city, which contained gleaming freezer cases full of frozen foods and large quantities of canned or otherwise processed foods. In an essay written for *Families* magazine in 1977, the author Xiao Hui explained why she continued to prefer shopping in her old familiar vegetable market over the shiny, new supermarket which had just opened next door. In the supermarket, "the environment is clean, the freezer glass cabinets have not a speck of dust, and the whole place is bright enough to dazzle. There is everything you could desire—vegetables, meats, fish—and the prices are reasonable." Yet it was devoid of shoppers. Meanwhile, the ordinary vegetable market a few steps away—dirty, crowded, noisy, smelly—was filled with customers.

The main reason Xiao Hui was drawn to the ordinary market was its abundance of human feeling (*renqingwei*): real, interpersonal interactions with familiar vendors with whom customers developed warm relationships. Many housewives, she reported, liked to bargain and comparison shop, determining the best prices and judging the quality of food items, feeling satisfied that they were getting a good deal. Familiarity bred comfort and confidence. "You know which stall's fish balls are the freshest and crispiest, which stall's *rousong* [dried pork floss] has just come out of the pan, which stall washes its vegetables the cleanest, which one has the most complete selection, and which meat counter has wild black boar from Yilan." Vendors might be persuaded to extend credit to regular customers, who had to wait until the end of the month to be paid or who might unexpectedly spend more in a given month to feed special house guests.

Beyond any financial advantages, however, it was the back-and-forth exchanges between vendor and customer that best gave expression to the warmth of human feeling that Xiao Hui prized. Familiar customers would be greeted like old friends, especially if they had not been seen for a while. A woman might say to her regular vendor, "Hey boss, have you got a few scallions today? Can you give me a few stalks?" And the vendor might generously stuff a few into her sack for free. Or he might respond, "Ah, sorry! No more scallions," yet substitute a small piece of ginger or a few hot peppers instead. Or she might complain, "Too expensive—can you make it a bit cheaper?" And he might respond, "Lady, no can do. There have been huge storms in the south, and the vegetables have been flooded over. There's no more veg! Ok, ok, you're an old customer. I'll give you a discount and I won't earn a penny."

Vendors were also often good cooks and could recommend different ways of preparing vegetables and meats. Some took orders by telephone and made deliveries, saving busy working women time and effort. The proprietress of one stall not only delivered vegetables, Xiao Hui recalled, she also made sure that "the vegetables that needed washing were already washed and everything that needed peeling was already peeled, saving me a lot of time when I was in a rush." It still moved her deeply to think about it. "The market is heavy on human feeling, but light on profit," Xiao Hui concluded. For all these reasons, she and many other housewives preferred the dirty and chaotic neighborhood market, where you could laugh and smile and feel welcomed by familiar old vendors, over the "neat and tidy supermarket, where you meet with a young miss with a cold face, just like the freezer."

Even if many (older) women preferred sticking to their familiar shopping habits, there was no shortage of younger consumers ready to embrace other technological innovations in the kitchen. Microwave ovens started to appear in Taiwan starting in the late 1970s, introduced as a kind of magical cooking machine. A 1979 Litton Corporation advertisement for its new microwave proclaimed, "With just the press of a button, the dishes come out by themselves!" The artist's fanciful rendering depicts a smiling woman standing behind what looks like a boxy, green cooking computer, poised to push one of its many buttons. On one side of the cooking computer stands an array of uncooked fresh vegetables—onions, peppers, carrots, cabbage, scallions—while a gleaming parade of beautiful, completed dishes rolls out the other side. Ads touted the way that microwaves were not only speedy ("Saving you three-quarters of the usual cooking time!"), but also clean ("No more smoke and oil, so you can be fashionably dressed in your kitchen!"), and versatile, cooking all kinds of Chinese, Japanese, and Western dishes.

Yet if there were any buttons being pressed, it was the way that advertisers targeted working women's nagging sense of guilt that they were not taking proper care of their families. The National Company boasted that their microwaves were "changing women's lives!" (Though obviously not changing them that much because women were still assumed to shoulder primary responsibility for making the family dinner every night.) "Get home at 6 p.m. and have a warm dinner ready by 6:30!" one ad banner reads. "If you are a career woman, you no longer need to feel guilty on behalf of your kids for going out to eat all the time, or for spending money on hiring kitchen help! No more feeling frustrated about eating dishes that do not suit your taste! So long as you have a National brand Quick Cooking Machine, there's no need to wave around a pan, or even think too much about it. In just a few minutes, you will have a table full colorful, aromatic, tasty dishes."

What is most striking about these early microwave advertisements is the way that the technology is marketed not simply as a convenient tool for heating leftovers or warming a cup of soy milk, but as a newer, cleaner, all-around *replacement* for gas ranges, able to handle a variety of challenging Chinese cooking techniques. The ads for Sampo's Heavenly Chef brand microwave, for example, boasted that it could "shallow-fry, stir-fry, steam, boil, stew, warm, or bake: it can do everything!" The logic of it did make a certain sense. After all, from the late 1950s to the late 1970s, propane gas tanks had steadily replaced other cooking fuels in Taiwan, such as wood charcoal, coal briquets, or kerosene. In her 1954 cookbook, Huang Yuanshan had advocated for the use of wood charcoal in a brazier, as opposed to coal or kerosene, because the resulting flame was most vigorous of the three fuels. Back then it was still typical to see housewives in Taipei's back alleys, "squatting on the ground fanning a brazier. Above the brazier rolled a thick smoke, which smudged both hands and got the eyes all red, polluting both the kitchen and the air." Even in 1962, when Fu Pei-mei made her debut on Taiwan Television, she was still lugging a charcoal brazier into the studio. But by 1970, Fu was appearing in print advertisements for a gas burner manufacturer, under the tagline, "Cooking is no longer an unrewarding chore!"

Why shouldn't, then, the microwave represent yet another welcome innovation for Chinese home cooks, one that would entirely replace gas ranges in smoky, oily kitchens with the powerful, scientific energy of a tidy, enclosed microwave oven? The microwave manufacturing industry certainly tried its best to convince Chinese women of the versatile culinary potential of microwave cooking. National established its own "Quick Cooking Institute" to teach women how to cook entire meals with their microwaves, and cookbook authors, like Elizabeth Huang of the Wei Chuan Cooking School, would soon follow suit, with an entire bilingual cookbook devoted to the subject of Chinese microwave cooking. An ad for a Litton microwave boasted that one could have a "complete" Chinese meal of four dishes, a soup, and a dessert on the table in only seventeen minutes, with the following menu and cooking times:

Fried beefsteak: 2 minutes

Stir-fried tomatoes and eggs: 2 minutes

Stir-fried spinach: 2.5 minutes

Fish slices with bean sauce: 3.5 minutes

Corn soup: 4 minutes

Coconut balls: 3 minutes

And if the family used precut frozen fish and vegetables, as Fu Pei-mei had suggested elsewhere, then the preparation time for each dish could be reduced even further.

The photograph in the Litton ad depicts a smiling father carrying a dish to the table in the raised palm of his hand, like a jovial waiter, while a smiling mother places another perfect dish on the table. The two children, a little boy and a little girl, sit at the dinner table, stretching out with their chopsticks to taste every dish. Yet of all the components of this visual tableau of familial and culinary perfection, perhaps the most astounding detail is the Peking roast duck. There it sits in the open microwave oven, gleaming with perfectly browned, delectably crispy skin. A microwave can cook many things, and even turn out a passable family dinner, but a perfectly roasted Peking duck? Yet even in this case, an avid Chinese microwave cookbook author like Helen Chao, who provided a microwaved Peking roast duck recipe to the *Washington Post* in 1984, insisted that such miracles were possible. (In truth, Chao's recipe did not entirely avoid the usual lengthy preparation, it merely shortened the overall cooking time by zapping the duck in the microwave first before a final roasting in a traditional oven.)

It was at the microwave oven that Fu Pei-mei drew her own culinary line in the sand. She, who could countenance retort pouches and instant ramen noodles, could not embrace microwave technology as a reasonable replacement for the gas range. (Her oldest daughter, Cheng An-chi, told me that her mother was not above sitting down to a simple bowl of instant ramen, especially if she was eating alone and had no one to cook for.) Though Fu grudgingly admitted in a 1992 interview that microwave ovens could be "cleaner," she was suspicious of the microwave's ability to generate enough heat—the all-important *huohou*, or fire-time—to cook food properly in a Chinese manner. "The procedures required for cooking genuine Chinese cuisine are very complicated," Fu insisted. "There can't be any shoddy work, and no inferior materials can be used, otherwise the color, aroma, and taste of the food will be lost." Speed and simplicity in Chinese cooking, in other words, did have its limits.

● ● ●

By 1992, Fu Pei-mei made the difficult decision to shutter her cooking school. She gave several reasons for doing so. For one, she wanted to spend more time with her husband, who was in poor health. But perhaps more practically, it had been getting harder and harder to fill her cooking classes. "Working women's attitudes have changed," Fu explained. "Most of them don't want to go into the kitchen to cook. Moreover, newly designed kitchens are all open plans, connected with the living room. They're afraid of the smoke and oil, and they don't feel like doing all that cleaning."

The wide range of options for eating outside the home in Taiwan also spelled the end of home cooking. At the start of the postwar era, there were few restaurants and little disposable income for eating out. Later in the 1970s and 1980s, as the economy prospered, there was a boom in high-quality restaurants offering regional Chinese cuisines, as well as growing interest in foreign foods, including Western-style fast-food chains. McDonald's opened its first branch in Taipei in 1984—on the same street that also boasted restaurants "serving Korean barbecue, Hong Kong-style seafood, Italian pasta, and Japanese-style coffee." Twelve years later, there were already 131 McDonald's franchises scattered around the island. But even before the arrival of McDonald's (transliterated in Chinese as *Mai-Dang-Lao*) in Taiwan, the taste for Western-style fast-foods was already long familiar: a copycat local version called *Mai-Dang-Le*, which sold hamburgers, French fries, and drinks, had busily served customers for more than a decade in front of the Taipei train station before a genuine McDonald's franchise finally opened in the city.

The response to Western or Western-style food, especially fast-food chains, varied largely by generation. Younger people seemed to love it, whereas older people either found it insipid or terrible. A 1984 article on the arrival of Western-style fast-food chains in Taiwan quoted a forty-year-old woman whose three school-aged children loved "fried chicken, hamburgers, sandwiches, milkshakes, and cola." She remarked, "Every time I see them wolf down their fried chicken and hamburgers, knowing that one portion will not be enough and they will need another, I think to myself, in matters of eating and taste, there is a generation gap between us." Another young man spoke for the fast-food fans of his generation, when he praised their speed of service and the benefit of knowing in advance the precise portion size, price, and taste. "It's not like Chinese food—even ordering is a bother, and sometimes when you just look at the name of a dish, you have no idea what it is. And for a lot of dishes, you have to wait half a day for them. It's a total waste of time."

●　●　●

It was clear on which side of the generation divide Fu Pei-mei found herself. In a 1997 interview, Fu explained that twenty years earlier there had not been so many places to eat out, and many people wanted to learn how to cook. However, at present she had observed that "opportunities for eating out have vastly increased, including a large number of Western foods and fast foods. Your average person isn't so picky about eating only Chinese food or hot foods. Now it's all just about convenience, especially for young people. Their tastes have become Westernized to a great degree. This has meant that fewer and fewer people want to learn how to cook." Fu was not opposed to fast-food as such—the industry's model of speed and convenience made sense in busy modern lives. It was instead the encroachment of *Western* fast-food on Chinese palates that she opposed.

Fu had determined to pivot away from her cooking classes toward what she considered a "better method for popularizing Chinese food"—working with food companies to make industrial food products. "In order to adapt to the needs of modern life, Chinese food must change its original cooking methods and transform into refrigerated food, frozen food, canned food, and the like." Even so, she insisted that such transformations should still "preserve the original taste." She was now putting all her energy into these efforts. "It's a pragmatic strategy," she admitted. "At least this will allow Chinese food to continue, and not be replaced entirely by Western food." One of her longest-running consultancies was her work for the Japanese restaurant chain Ringer Hut, which served a variety of Japanese and other Asian noodle dishes. Most of the ingredients for their Mixed Noodle dish—the pork, the wooden ear fungus, the pea shoots—all came from Taiwan, so Fu's job was to oversee their preparation for flash freezing before they were shipped to franchises all over Japan.

Although Fu wasn't teaching in person at her cooking school anymore, her television programs continued to bring her into people's living rooms, where she remained popular. She wanted to retire permanently from television in 1992, after thirty years on the air, but Taiwan Television executives convinced her to keep going. Fu herself attributed her longevity on television to "the frequently changing content, which had many things worth watching," as well as her own frank personality, which was "to say everything I know, and to do it without reservation." Her hands were quick, and her skills with the cleaver and heat-time were real. "My diligent efforts, my conscientiousness, my straightforward sincerity—I think after all of these years, audiences could all feel that." All her culinary skills were hard earned through years of experience, but perhaps by that point it no longer mattered: it was not audiences of housewives who were tuning in, as they had in the early decades, because they really wanted to learn how to make braised sea cucumber or bake a birthday cake, special dishes to please their families. By the end of her career, Fu had become such a television icon that viewers watched her for different reasons—as a kind of vicarious entertainment, as a kind of warm mother figure, to see what sort of delicious dish she would demonstrate that day—before they happily headed out to their favorite stall vendor to pick up a bowl of beef noodles, or even more conveniently, opened up a package of Fu's own instant ramen, to eat in their sparkling clean kitchens.

8

WHAT SHE PUT
ON THE TABLE

Publicity poster from the 2017 Taiwan Television dramatic
series, *What She Put on the Table*. The shorter actress on the
left (Sun Ke-Fang) carrying the shopping basket is in the role
of Fu's fictional housemaid, Ah Chun, while the taller actress
on the right (Amber An) stars as Fu Pei-mei.

IN 2017 A DRAMATIC TELEVISION SERIES BASED ON FU'S life made its debut in Taiwan. The Chinese title of the series was taken directly from Fu's autobiography, *Years of Five Flavors and Eight Delicacies* (*Wuwei bazhen de suiyue*), but the English title of the series was changed to *What She Put on the Table*. Set in the years before Fu's rise to fame, the most fascinating part of the series was the introduction of an entirely fictional character to the story: Fu's Taiwanese kitchen maid, Ah Chun, who becomes a crucial member of the household and a contributor to Fu's eventual television success. Images of the two actresses portraying Fu and Ah Chun adorn all the publicity posters for the series; the manga version of the drama was even packaged with two different collectible cards with Fu's portrait and Ah Chun's portrait.

In the television serial, it is Ah Chun who shows Fu how to wrap dumplings so they don't leak; Ah Chun who teaches her how to bargain with vendors in the market; Ah Chun who encourages her when she first sets out to teach cooking in her backyard tent; Ah Chun who finds a source for the yellow croaker for her when they can't be found anywhere else in the market. And, in the crucial moment at the television studio when Fu realizes she has forgotten her cleaver, it is Ah

Chun who saves the day by running to the cafeteria to procure a sub-stitute. Arguably, the "she" of the series' English title no longer refers to just Fu Pei-mei: it is instead what Fu *and* Ah Chun have put on the nation's collective table *together*.

For anyone familiar with contemporary Taiwanese politics, the decision to add the fictional figure of Ah Chun to Fu's story is more than just a tweak to allow for more dialogue and dramatic action between the two main actresses. It tacitly acknowledges that Fu's success story as an elite mainlander no longer suffices in the political and social context of contemporary Taiwan. While Taiwan was under Nationalist Party political control and martial law from 1949 to 1987, the decades since the 1970s have been a period of dramatic democrati-zation, with national popular elections and the rise of opposition polit-ical parties, such as the Democratic Progressive Party (DPP). During the same decades, in the realms of culture and society, there has been growing public consciousness and pride in a distinct Taiwanese iden-tity, often described by the term "nativization" (*bentuhua*), which has upended the long-standing hierarchy of mainlander dominance over the Taiwanese majority.

By placing Fu and Ah Chun together on the screen, the series pro-ducers were making a statement about the shared history of mainland-ers and Taiwanese in postwar Taiwan. The series website explains that "Ah Chun's life course is very much like a miniature version of that era's Taiwanese women. Though [Fu and Ah Chun] are born into entirely different circumstances and backgrounds, they come into contact and begin to grow accustomed to one another. By the end, they know and cherish each other, comparing notes to learn culinary skills from each other. They become life companions of mutual impor-tance." (In practice this means that they cry together a lot.)

After ten years together, Ah Chun prepares to leave the Cheng household because she is finally getting married. As the music swells, Fu says to Ah Chun tearfully, "Thank you for accompanying me on this journey.... How can I be alone in this kitchen without you? I won't be able to say, "Ah Chun help me boil the water. Ah Chun have you started the fire?" I won't have you to help me bargain at the market. No one will give me feedback on my dishes anymore." Ah Chun replies (also tearfully), "It's me who should be thanking you.... I have learned so much.... You always made me feel like part of the family." Notably, at this moment of heightened connection, Fu says "Thank you" to Ah Chun in Taiwanese, while Ah Chun thanks Fu in clear Mandarin, although until that point each woman has generally only spoken her own dialect.

Despite the television writers' attempt to draw the two women's experiences in parallel, it is the changes in Ah Chun's life that are most profound. She starts the series as an uneducated rural farm worker, squatting on the ground, hungrily scooping food into her mouth with a ham-fisted hold on a spoon. Along the way she learns to read, taught by a Taiwanese rice shop owner who is a Communist sympathizer. She eventually marries a mainlander who is a former Nationalist army soldier and now makes his living selling northern *jiaozi* (dumplings) and *mantou* (steamed buns). After she leaves the Cheng family to marry, Ah Chun becomes the successful proprietor of her own small restaurant (named "Mei's Delicacies," after Fu Pei-mei), which serves all of Fu's classic signature dishes, such as her dumplings (from northern China) and her squirreled fish (from Jiangsu)—all of which are mainlander specialties, not typical Taiwanese dishes, such as oyster omelets or pork belly buns.

This professed mutual regard, dramatic storyline, and happy ending for Ah Chun did not placate some viewers, who balked at Ah Chun's depiction. Taiwanese commentator Guan Renjian pointed out the inherent inequality of the two women's relationship, which was apparent even in the publicity photos for the series. Of the two actresses, "one is light-skinned, one is dark; one is tall, one is short—the tall one is even wearing high heels so that she appears to be even

taller. . . . One carries a leather purse the other carries a shopping basket. One wears a skirt and the other wears pants. Just guess—which of
these two is the mistress? Which is the maid? After seeing the photo,
there can't possibly be anyone who is going to get it wrong." Despite
their best efforts, the creators of the series could not erase and only
reinforced the hierarchical legacy of mainlander–Taiwanese relations, which irritated some viewers. A Taiwanese acquaintance of
mine was dismissive of both the television series and Fu's career,
when I told her about my research on Fu Pei-mei. "She means nothing
to me," she said scornfully.

•   •   •

When she first began teaching, Fu Pei-mei was not thinking about
Taiwanese cuisine or about a potential Taiwanese television audience.
Her motivation was to help her fellow mainlanders, who found themselves far away from home on a distinctive, tropical island. The available produce, everything from fruit and vegetables to meat and fish,
differed from what one might have eaten back home. Fu wanted to
help mainlanders learn which ingredients available in Taiwan could
be used to achieve their favorite, familiar regional flavors. "Back then,
almost all the friends and family around me were war refugees," Fu
recalled. "Nine out of ten couldn't cook. I thought that if I taught every
person how to cook the food of their own home province, this would
make every family happier." In the process, of course, many Taiwanese, such as Fu's teaching assistant Chen Yingzhou, who joined her
cooking school in 1971, also learned about distinctive mainlander
dishes and regional specialties. "I was a Taiwanese [*bensheng*] kid
from the countryside," says Chen, "and back then, we just ate our own
local dishes [*jiaxiangcai*]. As for banquet dishes from the eight great
Chinese regional cuisines, such as Shanghai, Fujian, Guangdong,
Sichuan, etc., we rarely saw them. So when Teacher Fu taught famous
dishes from each of China's major culinary regions, I really had my

eyes opened." Yet initially this culinary learning flowed in only one direction, outward from Fu: she did not start her cooking career by learning what dishes Taiwanese people were already eating or how they cooked available foods.

Her approach was not unusual at the time. Local Taiwanese culture, including its cuisine, was not regarded as refined or elegant by either mainlanders or by many Taiwanese themselves. "For decades after 1949, the regime in Taipei presented itself to the world as the true government of China, and society here was depicted as a repository of everything that was splendid about pre-Communist China," explain food writers Steven Crook and Katy Hui-wen Hung. "In food terms this meant celebrating foodways carried to the island in the late 1940s by refugee chefs and families, while ignoring those developed locally over hundreds or even thousands of years." My mother, ever the stalwart mainlander, maintains this prejudice against Taiwanese food. "We weren't used to eating Taiwanese tastes and even now I don't like Taiwanese dishes," she says. "They just seemed plain and tasteless to me, just boiled in water and not stir-fried." Whether or not one agrees with my mother's opinion, the lighter tastes of Taiwanese cuisine certainly contrasted sharply with the heavier, spicier, and saltier tastes of Sichuanese and northern cuisines to which my mother was most accustomed. Apart from home cooking in Taiwanese homes, most mainlanders experienced local Taiwanese food at best as street food snacks.

Fu Pei-mei was not unaware of the distinctions between mainlander and Taiwanese approaches to food. Nicki Croghan, the translator of the second volume (1974) of Fu's cookbook series, recalls that Fu wanted to get her cookbook out quickly to beat Huang Su-huei's bilingual cookbook, *Chinese Cuisine*, to the market. Like Fu's first volume, Huang's cookbook included recipes from different regions or cities of China, such as Sichuan, Canton, Shanghai, or Peking. But unlike Fu's first volume, Huang's cookbook also included numerous Taiwanese dishes. Huang herself was Taiwanese, the privileged daughter of the founder of the Wei-Chuan Foods Corporation, which had also established its own cooking school and publishing company. Fu's sense of rivalry was thus not merely a matter of market share: Fu seemed to feel that her own versions of mainlander recipes were more accurate than those of Huang, her Taiwanese competitor. "I think she felt that hers were the standard ones," recalls Croghan. "Their approaches were very different. The other one had more of a Taiwanese emphasis. Fu's cookbooks were more traditional foods from China without the influence of Taiwan."

A growing sense of Taiwanese pride and attention to Taiwanese cultural identity, including its language and cuisine, is intimately tied to democratization efforts and the rise in Taiwanese political power in the 1970s, 1980s, and 1990s. The Nationalist Party had declared martial law in Taiwan in 1949, which meant that opposition political parties were banned, while the government censored all media. Beyond the political realm, in order to bring a mixed nation of war refugees and former Japanese colonial subjects together, the Nationalist Party declared Mandarin as the national language, to be used exclusively in schools and mass media, while local dialects, including Hokkien and Hakka, were marginalized. The effect for native speakers of Hokkien and Hakka could be wrenching. To work in or lead a government agency required the ability to speak Mandarin, giving mainlanders an advantage in civil service and politics. Successful Taiwanese mastered both dialects, speaking Mandarin at school or work and Hokkien or Hakka at home, but many who could not become adept at Mandarin were excluded from advancement in government careers. Instead, it was left to Taiwanese to operate small businesses and prosper in the private economy.

Beginning in the 1960s, political activists, both Taiwanese and mainlanders, advocated for reforms, but these individuals were swiftly jailed or exiled. More coordinated efforts to challenge Nationalist hegemony in the national government took place in the 1970s. Although martial law banned the formation of new political parties, independent candidates could and did run successfully for local elections. These "Outside the [Nationalist] Party" (*dangwai*) candidates organized and coordinated their efforts, supporting one another's campaigns. A fierce government crackdown on a pro-democracy protest for human rights in Kaohsiung in 1979 (in which feminist activist Lu Hsiu-lien had participated) backfired, resulting in even greater public sympathy for democratic reforms. By 1986, the Democratic Progressive Party (DPP) was officially established by many of the opposition candidates banding together. The Nationalist government was forced to respond. Rather than crack down again and face more public backlash, the government loosened the reins by lifting martial law in 1987. Other democratic reforms would soon follow, including the first national elections for president in 1996.

Over these same decades of democratic reform, native champions of Taiwanese cuisine emerged, eager to advocate for its popular recognition and status. Lee Hsiu-ying began her restaurant Shin Yeh in 1977, with a determination to focus exclusively on ordinary Taiwanese home cooking. Critics of the time found it laughable: "How can you put ordinary home cooking on a restaurant table? If you want to eat home cooking, just eat at home. Why come to a restaurant?" Yet Lee persisted and eventually established a successful restaurant empire with four locations in Taipei, and another in Xiamen, located in Fujian Province on the Chinese mainland, in addition to assorted other restaurant interests. Shin Yeh is now the best known of several prominent, high-end restaurants specializing in local Taiwanese specialty dishes, and one branch of the restaurant recently received a Michelin star. Lee, too, has published several of her own cookbooks focused on Taiwanese cuisine.

As her career progressed, Fu also began to pay more attention to the eating habits of her Taiwanese neighbors. By the time she published the third volume of *Pei Mei's Chinese Cook Book* (1979), Fu had reconfigured the schema of Chinese culinary regions that she had described a decade earlier. Instead of focusing solely on the mainland cuisines of Sichuan, Canton (Guangdong), Jiangsu-Zhejiang, and northern China, Fu's third volume now added an additional section on Taiwanese cuisine, along with Hunanese and Fujianese cuisines. Fu explained that the culinary differences between Fujianese and Taiwanese cuisines resulted from Taiwan's distinctive history. While Fujianese dishes were represented most typically by the dishes of Fuzhou, Fujian's provincial capital, Taiwanese dishes had also been influenced by Japan, resulting from the island's fifty-year colonial occupation (1895–1945)—which Fu avoided naming explicitly. "In terms of taste, Taiwanese cuisine has been deeply influenced by Fujianese cuisine—elegant, fresh, and yet still emphasizing sweet and sour. Its cooking techniques have adopted Japanese traditions, using a lot of boiling, deep frying, and grilling, as well as considering the shape and color of dishes for serving food in order to heighten the aesthetic feeling."

Two decades later, Fu, assisted by her oldest daughter Cheng An-chi, finally wrote her own cookbook on Taiwanese dishes, *Delicious Taiwanese Cuisine: Traditional Tastes and Modern Trends* (*Meiwei Taicai: Guzaowei yu xiandaifeng*) (1998). Fu wrote in the preface that in the past ten years, she had wanted to seriously investigate Taiwanese cuisine from both a professional and personal interest, starting with its earliest beginnings to the latest new dishes, sharing what she had learned from having invited so many Taiwanese chefs and experts on her cooking program over the years. In so doing, Fu joined a growing trend in cookbook publishing in Taiwan starting in the 1990s, which was to move away from an emphasis on "Chinese" mainlander cuisines toward an emphasis on "Taiwanese" cuisine. The historian Pan Tsung-yi has memorably described this shift in cookbook publication as a turn from the "Fu Pei-mei era" of the 1960s–80s to the "Master Ah Chi era" of the 1990s to the present. "Master Ah Chi" is a nickname for Cheng Yen-chi, Taiwanese chef, cooking teacher, cookbook author, and television personality who made his name in the 1990s with a series of Taiwanese cookbooks and programs. (The prefix "Ah" is commonly added to a single character to create an informal nickname in Taiwanese or Cantonese.)

Food scholar Chen Yujen reminds us that Taiwanese cuisine has evolved and transformed over the course of more than a century from many different inputs. The concept of *Taiwan ryōri* (Jp.) first appeared in print during the Japanese colonial era (1895–1945), when it referred indiscriminately to fancier Taiwanese or Chinese dishes that Japanese were served at local banquets. Later, during the period of martial law under Nationalist rule, Taiwanese cuisine (*Taicai*) was generally considered by mainlanders like Fu Pei-mei as one of China's many regional cuisines. The then-current Chinese term for Taiwanese cuisine, *Taicai*, conformed to the two-character shorthand references for other Chinese regional cuisines, such as Sichuanese (*Chuancai*) or Cantonese (*Yuecai*) cuisines. But since democratization in the 1980s and 1990s, Taiwanese cuisine has been regarded as its own distinctive cuisine, with the full name of the cuisine, *Taiwancai*, reflecting this difference. Taiwanese cuisine incorporates foods of local Hokkien, Hakka, mainlander, and indigenous groups. It is also influenced by different sites and styles of consumption, emerging from restaurants, street food, and home cooking.

Not surprisingly, a very different perspective on Taiwanese cuisine can be found in a 2013 encyclopedia of Chinese regional cuisines published in the PRC, edited by Zhao Rongguang. In it, Taiwanese cuisine is classified as a subset of southeastern Chinese cuisine, and discussed alongside the cuisine of Hainan Province, since both islands occupy a similarly peripheral status in comparison to the Han core of China proper on the mainland. Instead of emphasizing the distinctive markers and unique historical influences on Taiwan's cuisine, Zhao

and his coeditors describe the migration of Fujianese and Cantonese to Taiwan in the seventeenth century, and their subsequent influence on Taiwanese foodways. Meanwhile, no mention is made of the
five decades of Japanese colonial rule over Taiwan in the early twentieth century. For these mainland scholars, cuisine is simply another
realm in which to make an implicit political claim about Taiwan's
connection—and ultimate belonging—to the PRC.

Despite her late efforts at local inclusion, Fu never became
known for her Taiwanese dishes and would more frequently invite
local experts to demonstrate Taiwanese cuisine on her cooking program. "I don't go to her cookbooks to learn about Taiwanese cuisine,"
says Kian Lam Kho, a contemporary food blogger and Chinese cookbook author. "Fu Pei-mei's cooking is not really 'Taiwan' cooking; it's
waisheng [mainlander] cooking. She was the first cookbook author
to write about *waisheng* or regional Chinese cooking. That's why
she's influential."

Yet not everyone maintains such a strict divide between mainlander and Taiwanese cooking. Food scholar Tiffany Liu grew up in a
middle-class Taiwanese family in Tainan. Her family migrated to Canada in 1993, when she was thirteen years old. While she understands
negative Taiwanese reactions to Fu as a mainlander, she doesn't share
those feelings because she says her family had positive relationships
with mainlanders. Her father's boss and mentor was a mainlander,
who treated him well. Her neighbors were northerners from Shandong, who fed her *baozi* (stuffed buns) and *jiaozi* (dumplings). Her
family's favorite restaurant in Tainan was Sichuanese. Later, she had
a boyfriend in Canada who came from a *waisheng* family from Shanghai, and his mother, a talented cook, taught her several Shanghainese
recipes, including sweet and sour fish, *caifan* (rice with salted pork
and greens), and *kaofu* (braised wheat gluten with bamboo).

Tiffany did not grow up with a strong political education. "My
family wasn't that politically engaged. We didn't talk about the dif-

ferences between *waishengren* and *benshengren*. Obviously, we knew
they spoke Mandarin with different accents, and we spoke Taiwanese
at home. We didn't think these differences were a big issue though." In
contrast, her younger brother, born fifteen years after her, had a very
different political education in school. "They talk a lot more about Taiwanese identity; they talk about 2–28. Now there's even a holiday on
2–28 to commemorate it." Tiffany is referring to the massacre known
as the February 28th Incident, which took place in 1947, when there
was a violent crackdown on anti-government protestors, with thousands of Taiwanese killed or jailed as political prisoners. In 1995, after
decades of silence surrounding the 2–28 incident, ROC President Lee
Teng-hui offered an official apology, initiating a major public reckon-
ing after decades of the Nationalist Party-led White Terror. Tiffany
herself was never taught about these things at school when growing up
in the 1980s, and only learned about them after she arrived in Canada.

Though she is now well aware of these political and social distinctions, they have not prevented Tiffany from enjoying mainlander
food or using Fu's cookbooks. She says her tastes were formed by her
maternal grandmother's Taiwanese cooking, as well as by her varied
experiences with mainlanders. Her grandmother was from a poor
Taiwanese farming family, and spoke no Mandarin, only Taiwanese
and Japanese. She lived next door to Tiffany's family in Taiwan and
often cooked meals for the children. "She cooked very *bensheng* [Tai-
wanese] dishes. I remember lots of stir-fried eggs with carrots, lots
of dried fish—because it was cheaper, never fresh or expensive fish—
pork rib soup, daikon radishes, sweet potato leaves, sweet potato rice
porridge." But Tiffany also learned how to cook mainlander food on
her own. She bought Fu Pei-mei's cookbook on Chinese home cooking when she returned to Taiwan for a visit in 2000, when she was
still in high school. At the time she had to take care of her younger sister in Canada because both of her parents had returned to Taiwan to
work. She assumed the cookbook was for overseas Chinese like herself

because it was bilingual. Eventually Tiffany acquired two more of Fu's cookbooks. She sees no contradictions in cooking and eating across the political divide: "I cook *waisheng* [mainlander] food and *bensheng* [Taiwanese] food."

● ● ●

My own memorable introduction to Taiwanese cuisine came late, in 2013, when I visited the island as part of a group of American scholars on a study trip sponsored by the ROC Ministry of Foreign Affairs. We toured the new National Museum of Taiwan History in Tainan, a city in the south of the island and a stronghold of nativist Taiwanese feeling. The beautiful new museum offers a dramatic study in contrasts to the National Museum of History in Taipei, the first museum to be established in Taiwan in 1955, after the Nationalist retreat from the mainland. While the exhibits and artifacts in the older museum in Taipei come largely from excavations on the mainland and venerate the glories of China's ancient past, the new museum in Tainan, which opened in 2011, celebrates the multicultural diversity of Taiwan's more recent past, including its native islanders and its years as an independent outpost of Ming loyalist pirates. Even the Japanese colonial period is not demonized as much as it is carefully examined as part and parcel of the island's history. I was impressed by the quality of the curation of the bilingual exhibits and their bold narration of a new history of Taiwan.

For lunch we went to a restaurant known for its fresh take on southern Taiwanese specialty dishes, such as *ta-a* noodles (a meat and seafood noodle dish meaning "shoulder pole," to indicate the way fishermen would carry and sell the noodles in the off-season) and *wha guey* (a savory rice pudding). I had never tasted any of these Taiwanese dishes before because I never ate them at home with my mainlander parents and we never visited Taiwan as a family. I was floored by how delicious each dish was and the care taken in their preparation. How could it have taken me so long to discover them?

During our visit, a young museum staffer reinforced this sense of Taiwanese pride and distinction when he told me, "I don't consider myself Chinese. I consider myself Taiwanese." That was the first time I had heard such a sentiment stated so plainly. Over the years, such feeling has grown, shared by more and more fellow citizens. According to a 2020 poll by National Chengchi University's Election Study Center, a record 67 percent of the population now considers itself "Taiwanese," whereas only 2.4 percent consider themselves "Chinese." Meanwhile, 27.5 percent consider themselves "Both Taiwanese and Chinese," a proportion that has steadily declined over the past thirty years. It makes sense that as time passes, the children and grandchildren of mainlanders will have less and less of a personal connection to Chinese identity and a stronger primary sense of identification with Taiwan. Nowadays, the term "Taiwanese" is not necessarily used exclusively to denote the subset of those of Hokkien and Hakka descent whose families have lived on the island for generations. It has become instead, for many, a national identity for *all* those on the island who find themselves increasingly in the shadow of their mainland PRC rivals.

To add even more confusion to the question of identity, many do have a mixed heritage, with one mainlander and one Taiwanese parent, or grandparents of different backgrounds. Perhaps there is no better-known exemplar of the complexity—and potential flexibility—of modern Chinese/Taiwanese identity than Jeremy Lin, the basketball player who set off the "Linsanity" craze during his startling 2011–12 season in the NBA, having been underestimated as an Asian American player all his life. His father's family, originally from Fujian, has lived in Taiwan for eight generations, since 1707. His maternal grandmother, on the other hand, was a mainlander born in Zhejiang

Province, who fled to Taiwan in 1949. Both of Lin's parents hold dual ROC–US citizenship, while Lin was born and raised in the United States. When asked by a reporter in 2013 for the millionth time how he would describe his identity, Lin laughed and side-stepped the issue, claiming all labels at once: "I have grandparents, great-grandparents from China. My parents were born and raised in Taiwan. I was born and raised in America. So there's a lot of history."

Making these distinctions has become ever more important for food writers and their audiences in the United States as well, as more people awaken to the delicious potential of the cuisines of Taiwan and to the careful historical distinctions required when discussing them. Cathy Erway, food writer, blogger, and podcast host, struggled to find a publisher for her cookbook on Taiwanese cuisine, *The Food of Taiwan* (2015). "Nobody wanted it for two years, because there was no precursor for this. There was just confusion . . . [and] some awkward conversations where they clearly didn't know what Taiwan was. 'Is it Thailand?' they would ask." Erway believes that the rise of a younger generation of prominent Taiwanese American cultural influencers—including Jeremy Lin, the fashion designer Jason Wu, and chef/television celebrity Eddie Huang—finally paved the way for publishers to understand the merits of her cookbook. "It's a cultural shift," she says of this growing awareness of Taiwanese identity as distinct from Chinese identity.

Erway purposely titled her cookbook *The Food of Taiwan*, rather than *Taiwanese Food*, to encompass the inclusion of mainlander dishes. "I wanted to make a book about everything that is found in Taiwan right now, and talk about all of those different influences that have made it what it is today, on the island." Erway's own maternal grandparents were mainlanders who arrived in Taiwan from Hunan Province in 1948, but her mother was born in Taiwan. She calls herself "American-born, half-Taiwanese." (Ironically, it is Erway's father, who is neither Chinese nor Taiwanese, who is the biggest fan of Fu

Pei-mei's cookbooks in her family. He discovered Fu's cookbooks as an undergraduate at Cornell and continues to cook from them today. He always uses exactly half a teaspoon of cornstarch in his shrimp and tomato sauce stir-fry, for example, "because that's what Pei Mei says.")

Another food writer, Clarissa Wei, who was born in Los Angeles, but now calls Taipei home, is much more forthright about her identity as a Taiwanese, not Chinese, American. Her family is originally from Tainan, in southern Taiwan, and her father is partly indigenous. Wei has also written a cookbook about modern Taiwanese cuisine. "The premise of my cookbook is that Taiwanese food is its own distinct cuisine and not a subset of Chinese food," says Wei. Compared with Fu Pei-mei's postwar moment, Wei argues, "you can't say that the food here is Chinese anymore, because people here would get offended and also because it has evolved so much from what it was during [Fu's] era." Part of her current project is to interrogate what Taiwanese identity means to her and those of her generation. In the past, growing up in Los Angeles, Wei just grouped herself with other Chinese Americans, simply because it was more expedient to explain her identity to people that way. At the time, she considered the categories Chinese and Taiwanese to be more or less "interchangeable."

But since relocating to Taipei, Wei has come to recognize herself as Taiwanese and Taiwanese cuisine as its own category, with its own subtropical ingredients, specific condiments, and culinary influences that extend beyond mainland China to include Japanese and indigenous cultures. "We are our own people, and I didn't necessarily think that way before," she says. For Wei, Tainan, the island's oldest city, not Taipei, is the real food capital of Taiwan. She finds that so-called Taiwanese restaurants in the United States are often "fixated on mainlander cuisines" and their owners often come from mainlander backgrounds. She is trying to learn to speak Taiwanese herself, to reclaim her roots, which she says many young people of her generation in Taiwan are trying to do. Yet although Wei has written a cookbook on Taiwanese cuisine for American audiences, what is perhaps most ironic is that few of her friends in Taipei actually cook for themselves at home. When apartment hunting, it was difficult for her to find any apartments that included kitchens. "Most people don't cook and if they get home-cooked food it's [from] grandma who lives at home," says Wei.

Though clearly not everyone will agree, being "Chinese" to me is not limited to a national label, but instead is expansive as a cultural one, potentially claimed by anyone of Han Chinese descent no matter where in the world they find themselves. Moreover, claiming this sense of Chinese identity is entirely distinct from agreeing with the political stances of the PRC and the Communist Party. Perhaps the best way to describe it is to use a phrase I once learned from one of my students. After college, I spent two years teaching English in the city of Changsha, in Hunan Province in the PRC. Frequently our students would chat with us during afternoon breaks to get more English practice. During one of these conversations, a bright and serious high schooler named Brandon proclaimed to me, "You are a daughter of the Yellow Emperor." The Yellow Emperor is the mythical founder of Han Chinese culture, and since the early twentieth century, it has been common to describe those of Chinese descent as his children.

This sort of misty Yellow Emperor language has been used strategically by both PRC leaders, such as Deng Xiaoping, and ROC leaders, such as Ma Ying-jeou, to bind together Chinese on both sides of the Taiwan Strait. Without question, the concept also has a potentially troubling tendency to overemphasize the significance of blood descent. But in my opinion, there's no reason that politicians should be allowed to overdetermine the scope and use of the phrase. It's the potential for connection rather than exclusion that seems most compelling to me. Calling me a daughter of the Yellow Emperor was simply a way for Brandon to articulate that bond, one he did not share with other white American teachers. That same connection can link me just as much to friends in Taiwan, Hong Kong, Singapore or around the world, whether they are Chinese Australians, Chinese Canadians, Chinese Germans, or Chinese Brazilians. And as in any extended family, there is plenty to argue and disagree about: not all members of the family get along or even wish to speak to one another. But above all else, more than land (too many scattered diasporas), more than language (too many dialects), more than history (too much Civil War), what connects all of us is food. If the Yellow Emperor ever held a feast in the heavens, we could never eat our way to the end of the table.

●   ●   ●

After almost twenty-five years on Taiwan Television, Fu finally got to headline her own show in 1987, *Fu Pei-mei Time* (*Fu Peimei shijian*), which was the first TTV program to be named after its host. The program, which aired for sixteen straight seasons, is the television series for which she is best remembered. The set was still spare and utilitarian by today's standards, with little more than two potted plants in the background and Fu standing behind a rigged-up countertop with her cutting board and cleaver. But at least now Fu was cooking on gas burners, while dish names and ingredient lists could be typed by computer to appear directly on television screens, rather than being written by hand on a chalkboard. Other updates included an unforgettably jaunty, tootling theme song (the 1969 hit, "Hot Popcorn," by Gershon Kingsley), composed entirely on a synthesizer. For Fu, the most welcome change was the program signboard with the title *Fu Pei-mei Time* hanging on the backdrop. After decades of hard work, she was justly proud of this accomplishment. "It was like America's Johnny Carson [or] Oprah . . . getting my own named 'show.'"

Though Fu was proud of having her own named television program, the honor was not quite what it seemed. For six years, *Fu Pei-mei Time* aired for five minutes a day, five days a week. The schedule was grueling for Fu, requiring her to come up with hundreds of new dishes to demonstrate in rapid sequence, with no repeats. The pressure was especially intense because she wanted to print a cookbook at the start of each season, for viewers to use as a guide to follow along with each program, which meant writing one hundred twenty recipes ahead of time and even more careful planning. She had to think very carefully about which ingredients to cut and which stages of the dish to prepare in advance, in order to show viewers the entire abbreviated process. She still had to haul in all the ingredients and equipment herself, now for tapings of ten episodes every two weeks. This meant juggling furiously to keep track of multiple ingredients, half-finished dishes, fully finished dishes, and requisite kitchen equipment and supplies. Luckily, she had the help of her oldest daughter, Cheng An-chi, and daughter-in-law, Theresa Lin, for much of this prep work. On camera, lack of time often prevented her from explaining techniques, and her hands often moved so fast the cameras could not keep up. Audiences were also not happy with the abbreviated format and wrote to complain that they did not even have time to write down the ingredients.

Fu continued at this breakneck pace for six years, demonstrating over twelve hundred dishes, but the effort exhausted her. By 1993, she had been on television for thirty years and wanted to retire at the top of her game. She had risen to the challenge of the short program format but did not have the energy to continue. Finally, after many negotiations with TTV executives and much arm-twisting, she agreed to continue making the program, but only if it returned to its earlier format of thirty minutes once a week. This gave Fu more time to plan each week's segment and allowed her to invite more guest chefs onto the program. Fu stayed at it for ten more years, before finally retiring in 2002, after four decades of continuous on-air appearances. Her right hand shook and at seventy-one, she was tired. "I am now going to start living for myself," she declared. She told her oldest daughter that in her next life, if she had a choice, she would want to become a fashion designer, not a cooking teacher—it was not nearly so exhausting, you could wear nice clothes and not get your hands splattered by oil, or constantly breathe in smoke.

Even after her retirement, Taiwan Television continued to air Fu's cooking program in syndication and in foreign markets. Fu herself had little time to enjoy her old age. She passed away from liver cancer two years later, in 2004. Immediately after her death, her legions of fans, many of whom were women, flooded newspapers with their memories of Fu and her profound impact on their lives. Some wrote from the perspective of their own struggles in the kitchen, attempting to satisfy their families with a variety of tasty dishes. Others recalled the deep impression Fu made when they watched her on television.

In a tribute written on the occasion of the tenth anniversary of Fu's death in 2014, Taiwanese food writer Chen Jingyi brings together all the various aspects of Fu's appeal: her reliably constant televisual self, the sense of vicarious nurturing that the food offered, and her presentation of regional mainlander specialties not often seen in Taiwan. Chen reminds us, too, that Fu's ascendancy took place during the very decades in which women entered the workforce in ever larger numbers in Taiwan.

> Coming home after school, the thing I used to do the most was to sit in front of the television to watch *Fu Pei-mei Time*. She was never late and never failed to show up. It was as if she was your own mother, cooking for you live. The ingredients would by the end be turned into a tasty-looking dish, and it was as if you yourself had eaten a plateful. You could then happily turn off the television and walk quickly into the street to eat some noodles.

In the absence of Chen's real mother, who was always working, Chen's college-aged older sister steps in as a surrogate. At one point, she makes "Beiping egg dumplings," which are not Taiwanese, but instead, as their name suggests, a northern mainlander dish. "I made it from *Pei Mei's Cook Book*," Chen's sister tells her. As her older sister's cooking skills grow, thanks entirely to reading Fu's cookbook, Chen is allowed to flip through it and order dishes from it. "Eventually those strange and distant tastes became part of our lives," Chen writes. "Fu Pei-mei, who was busy making dishes in Taipei television studio, could probably not have imagined that her every movement had captivated a little girl in an old apartment building in Tainan." Chen's nostalgia in remembering Fu represents not only a vivid bodily hunger, but more crucially, an emotional one. For Chen, and many others, the ultimate significance of Fu Pei-mei lies less in the actual dishes she made, and more in the memory of Fu as a warm and caring mother figure on television.

Ya-Ke "Grace" Wu is another Taiwanese woman with vivid memories of watching Fu Pei-mei on television. Grace was the middle child of five in a poor Taiwanese family, growing up in Taipei in the late 1970s and 1980s. Life was challenging for Grace's parents, who had little formal education and struggled to keep their household together. Her father spent two years in jail, and Grace's mother worked as a housekeeper and cook to keep the family afloat. Sadly, Grace's parents abused her and her siblings physically, verbally, and emotionally throughout their childhood and young adult years. With age, Grace now feels less anger than pity for her parents. "With the stress in their lives, that's the only way they knew how to treat their children."

Even as a child, Grace implicitly understood the hierarchy that divided mainlanders and Taiwanese, a difference reinforced by everything from the language they were allowed to speak in school to the lunches they brought from home. Schoolchildren were forbidden from speaking their native Taiwanese dialect in school, and Grace lived in constant fear of accidentally blurting out a Taiwanese word. Once, an unfortunate classmate slipped and said something in Taiwanese. His punishment was to wear a sign that said he was a dog. Kids from mainlander families also brought fancy lunches from home, balanced meals of chicken, rice, and vegetables, while Grace's lunchbox was often half empty, filled only with plain noodles.

Grace's grades were terrible; she came to school unwashed. She hated studying, and her teachers gave up on her. "I was the typical image of a *benshengren* [native Taiwanese] kid. Dirty uniform, crazy hair. I constantly forgot the books I needed to bring." She distinctly remembers getting called to the front of the classroom, while the teacher told the rest of the class, "Grace Wu will be a failure. She will not be successful. She will be at the bottom of society. This is an example you all need to learn from. You don't want to be like Grace." Grace felt the hurt and humiliation deeply, but she had no way to respond and no support at home.

In the midst of this tumult, Grace has vivid memories of watching Fu Pei-mei's show on the television. "I remember when I was in first or second grade, I would come home from school. I had a key to open the apartment by myself. My parents and other siblings wouldn't come back until after 7 or 8 p.m. There were a few hours that I was completely alone in the apartment." During those hours, Grace always watched Fu Pei-mei's cooking program. She thought of Fu as "that very elegant lady on TV," who existed in a world where every bowl, plate, and spoon had its place, and all the ingredients were neatly chopped and organized.

Yet it was not the food that left the deepest impression on Grace when she watched Fu Pei-mei on television—she doesn't actually remember any of the dishes Fu made. Rather, the program was a welcome respite from her chaotic family life. For Grace, Fu "represented a kind of energy outside of my reality."

> I wanted to have a life like Fu Pei-mei's.... Her world looked perfect, with no worries. They never suffered from hunger. They never had to worry about someone knocking on the door

at 3 a.m., using a weapon to threaten my father, asking for
money. Every time I watched her show, I always had a voice
in my mind that I'm going to get out of this chaos.... And for
some reason I knew that I could make my life different and
have the life that I wanted.

Against all odds, Grace did succeed. She left home at age fifteen to
study in a vocational nursing program, the cheapest and most direct
path she could choose out of her family. Afterward she worked as a
nurse for twelve years, including working night shifts for seven of
them, before coming to the United States to earn a PhD. She eventually became a professor of nursing at the University of North Carolina
at Chapel Hill.

It is only in hindsight that Grace now considers the larger political
implications of Taiwan Television and Fu's appearance on the channel. The adult Grace now recognizes that Taiwan Television "tried to
promote the positive image of people who came from mainland China.
Fu Pei-mei was very much being used for a political purpose in this
show." Yet at the time Grace had no idea about the "political battle"
between mainlanders and Taiwanese. She simply watched Fu's program with the rapt attention of a child, recognizing Fu as "this very
elegant lady on TV."

The story of modern Taiwan cannot be told without the mainland success story of Fu Pei-mei. Yet it also cannot be told without
the childhood memories of a young Taiwanese Grace, Fu's opposite in
almost every way. Their stories meet, but not in the saccharine con-
fabulation of the recent dramatic television series, which promotes a
false, feel-good relationship between mainlander Fu and the fictional
Taiwanese Ah Chun. The distance between Fu Pei-mei and Grace—in
terms of their relative social, economic, linguistic, and political
power—is very much part of the story. Grace's lonely childhood rec-
ollections, seen now from her perspective as a successful adult, cast

a nuanced shadow over any overly bright picture of Fu. Fu's flickering figure on the screen makes the deepest impression on us when we can also imagine young Grace watching her, spellbound, in a quiet moment to herself in an otherwise troubled household. She is captivated by Fu's calm energy and the vision of a distant future that young Grace can only dream of someday possessing.

KITCHEN CONVERSATION

The Novice

CHRISTY FU (NO RELATION TO FU PEI-MEI) IS THE mother of a friend. I was eager to interview her when I discovered that she had relied exclusively on Fu's cookbooks to learn how to cook after she came to the United States. She was born into a Hakka family in Miaoli County in Taiwan. Hakka is the second largest dialect group in Taiwan (fifteen percent), after Hokkien speakers (seventy percent). We had never met before our interview, and at the start, Christy seemed withdrawn and reserved. I wondered what, if anything, I might learn. But by the end of our two-hour conversation, Christy was open and relaxed, reminiscing about her late husband. There was so much more resilience and strength in this gray-haired, older Chinese woman than met the eye, and I was moved by the way she had created a life for herself and her family in the United States from humble beginnings. The experience reminded me of encountering Fu's own cookbooks for the first time—unless you get to know more about what is under the covers, you can't appreciate everything they contain.

Where were you born?

I was born in Miaoli, Taiwan. We are Hakka people and mostly we ate Hakka food. The food we ate was very plain, very light. Very basic. Salt, scallions, that sort of thing. My mother would make chicken soup and put in bamboo and *luobo* [daikon radish]. It was Hakka home cooking. Not as elaborate as Fu Pei-mei, with as many ingredients.

Did you speak Hakka at home?

When I was a child, we spoke Hakka. My parents were born and raised in Taiwan but they had gotten Japanese educations. Before I turned seven, at home they spoke Japanese. We had a lot of Japanese magazines, and we listened to Japanese radio stations. When I was about seven [*in 1957*], Taiwan's government stopped all of this overnight. No radio stations, no more magazines coming in. Everything was in Mandarin. When you went to school, they taught you Mandarin. They realized that my parents' generation was very resistant to learning Mandarin, even twelve years after the end of World War II. They just weren't willing to learn it. In the 1940s, they spoke Japanese. In the 1950s, they started to learn Mandarin to speak to their mainlander customers. They ran a hardware store. But they didn't speak it well because most of the time they spoke Hakka. In Miaoli everyone was Hakka.

How did you get the idea to come to the United States?

I went to nursing school in 1968. Everybody wanted to go to the United States at that time. Of our 58 nursing students, every single one chose to apply to the US. At the time the US had a law, if you were a skilled person, if you can get a job in the US, then you can apply for a visa.

What was the most difficult part about being in the United States?

I didn't really speak a word of English. That first year was hard. My mother later told me, if you were to look at your letters, that first year you really regretted going to America! All of my letters were full of complaints. I was lonely and I had no place to go because I couldn't drive. I watched a lot of Sesame Street programs. I learned basic English from there. I worked as a nurse's aide in a neurology department, with a lot of people who had had strokes. And they couldn't express themselves. Sometimes I could understand them, sometimes I couldn't. But in nursing you are doing basic stuff, feeding them, helping them get up, cleaning them, helping them walk. It didn't need a lot of speaking, so I got by OK.

Had you heard of Fu Pei-mei before you came to the United States? Had you seen her television program?

I never saw her television program before. I was too busy working as a private nurse to watch television. But I had heard of her name. Everyone knew her. I think I brought her first cookbook with me from Taiwan. But the second volume I know I bought here in the United States because the price tag is still on it! $8.95 from Goh's Market in Chicago.

When you first came to the United States, what did you miss the most about Taiwan?

Oh, the food, for sure. I think that's probably the reason why I went to Fu's cookbook. I missed the food. Not that I ate a lot of the cookbook style of Fu, but just the general cooking of Chinese food that I missed. When I was in Taiwan, I never cooked. Not one day. At home, my mother cooked. In college, I ate in the cafeteria or ate out. When I lived with my older sister in Taipei, she cooked. Back then [*in the United States*] you couldn't really go out to eat every night because there was no place for you to go. Besides the cost was so expensive, eating out all the time. So you had to learn to cook something for yourself.

How did you get started?

When I first started, I had no idea even how to cook meat. I didn't understand temperatures or how to prepare the meat. Then I read Fu's cookbook, and I learned you can use corn starch to marinate meat. I read her cookbook a lot, especially in the beginning. Looking at her cookbook, she had a beef and green peppers recipe. I would change the peppers for mushrooms or onions or broccoli. I learned the principles from her, like how to season things. And then slowly, I would substitute other ingredients and experiment with this and that.

Were there specific Hakka dishes that you missed that you couldn't make because they weren't in Fu's cookbook?

There were some ingredients that I couldn't get here. I couldn't get *jiucai* [garlic chives]. I couldn't get other vegetables that I really liked. Couldn't find them here. You couldn't even buy napa cabbage. Usually I was missing one or two kinds of ingredients, so I just had to prepare what I had, or add whatever I had. Whatever you made, the taste was not the same.

Was there a point in time where you felt, "OK, this now feels like home"?

Oh, it's never home.

Even now?

Even now I still miss Taiwan. I feel more comfortable in Taiwan. I visited two years ago with my children and grandchildren. I felt at ease. I had to look for places, but I knew what I was looking for, and I could get to places I wanted to go pretty easily. The food is more familiar. It's all convenient; you can eat anywhere. It's a smaller area.

When I was living in Taiwan, to get from my house to school I had to ride a bike. It took five or ten minutes. At the time, I thought, "Oh my god, that's so far." [*Laughs.*] One year when I went back to visit my parents, I walked from the Miaoli train station to my house. It didn't even take five or ten minutes. It wasn't even a quarter of Michigan Avenue [*in Chicago*]! I thought, "Oh my god, this is so short! How come I always thought it was so far away?"

9

A COOKBOOK IN
EVERY SUITCASE

(*L to R*) My older brother, myself as baby, my mother, and my older sister eating a Chinese American family dinner of hamburgers (without buns), baked potatoes, peas, and Jello salad. My father was behind the camera, as usual. Midland, Michigan, 1973.

WHEN I WAS A CHILD, IT WAS NOT UNCOMMON FOR my mother to single-handedly prepare a feast of seven or eight Chinese dishes for special guests. She would scour her cookbooks—including Fu Pei-mei's—for inspiration, creating a menu that was balanced carefully by color, ingredient, taste, and texture. Everything she made—shrimp with peas, braised pork ribs, tofu with diced vegetables, cold smoked fish, mushrooms wrapped in tofu skins, napa cabbage with dried shrimp, sticky rice cake with red bean paste, to name a few familiar dishes—required time, care, and multiple steps to complete, and their sheer variety meant hours of preparation, at least a day in advance. Chinese friends were always deeply appreciative, but it was non-Chinese guests who were the most impressed by my mother's cooking. This was a level of culinary skill and hospitality that they seem to have rarely encountered, but it was old hat for us. Home cooking by then had become a badge of honor for my mother, as it was for many of the other Chinese mothers in our community. Mrs. Lee, Mrs. Chang, Mrs. Tou, Mrs. Wang, known to us as "aunties," were all great home cooks, and we gladly devoured examples of their latest "signature dishes" (nashoucai) at family potlucks.

It's easy to forget that my mother's Chinese culinary expertise,

which seemed so natural to me as a child, was forged through failure. She still recalls the first time she tried to cook a proper Chinese
meal, for a group of ten librarians with whom she worked at Luther
College in Decorah, Iowa in 1966. All the women wanted to try Chinese food and there was no Chinese restaurant in the area, so they
begged my mother to cook for them. "You must be able to make Chinese food really well," they insisted. My mother was enthusiastic and
eager to please, so she agreed—even though she had little experience
in the kitchen, ate in the college cafeteria every day, and drank Tang
for breakfast. She remembers none of the other dishes she made, but
she still vividly recalls trying to make a soup out of *bianjian*—bamboo
cooked in salt water and then smoked dry—an expensive ingredient
that her mother had sent from Taiwan. "I wanted to take care of my
guests well," she said, "so I thought, 'I can't be stingy, I'll just use all
of it.'" She made the stock fresh from a whole chicken and then added
twenty-odd clumps of *bianjian*. "I just threw them all into the pot, like
this—*dong dong dong*," she gestures. At first she was too busy cooking
to eat with her guests, but finally she sat down to eat. When she tried
the soup, she was horrified. "It was so salty, like a whole carton of salt
had fallen into it! I said, 'Oh, no, no, no! This isn't what it is supposed to
taste like!' I felt so embarrassed." She had not known that she should
first soak the *bianjian* in several changes of water to remove the salt,
and that only a few clumps of the bamboo were needed, not twenty.
The *bianjian* had swollen up into a sodden, soggy, salty mess. "That,"
she concludes, "was my first formal cooking experience."

Starting in the 1970s, Fu Pei-mei's cookbooks arrived in the
United States, carried by students from Taiwan who had no desire
to leave behind their familiar comfort foods. It was often said that
all overseas students from Taiwan in those years brought with them
the same two items in their suitcases: a Tatung electric rice cooker
and a copy of Fu Pei-mei's cookbook. Indeed, both found spots on our
kitchen counter and cookbook shelf, where they became essential fix-

tures in our family kitchen. Although much has been written about the history of Chinese American restaurants, chop suey, and fortune cookies, few books have focused on the social world of Chinese American home cooking or family dinners. This seems strange to me, as most Chinese Americans encounter Chinese food regularly at home and not in restaurants. Beyond what Chinese food has meant for individual families, it has also been crucial ingredient in building Chinese American communities. Fu Pei-mei's cookbooks offer us a way to enter that world, as enduring symbols of diasporic Chinese culinary identity in the twentieth century.

● ● ●

It was my grandmother who sent my mother the first volume of Fu's cookbook from Taiwan, some years after she had arrived in the United States in 1963 to start a graduate program in library science at the University of Minnesota. "Why was that one special?" asks my mother. "Because it had color photographs. That was very different from other cookbooks. And it had Chinese and English, because sometimes the system of measurement was different between China and America." Unlike those who came to the United States later in the 1970s, my mother did not bring copies of Fu Pei-mei's cookbooks with her in her suitcase, because Fu had not yet written them. Instead, my mother brought with her Volumes 1 (1954) and 2 (1957) of Huang Yuanshan's Chinese cookbooks (*Yuanshan shipu*), from Taiwan's leading cookbook author of the 1950s, discussed in Chapter 2. Ultimately, though, my mother used Fu's cookbooks the most, thumbing through them before any dinner party and jotting down to-do lists. She eventually acquired all three volumes of Fu's signature series, as well as Volumes 1 through 3 of Fu's original mini-sized *Television Cookbooks*.

Although their publication dates are separated by only a decade, Huang and Fu's cookbooks belong to two different eras: black and white versus Technicolor, silent film versus the talkies. Huang's cookbooks are thin, flimsy softcovers—typical of old-school Chinese books—with only a few pages of simple brush ink drawings of cooking utensils in the first volume. In contrast, each of Fu's thick, hardcover cookbooks feature dozens of vibrant color photographs of finished dishes, along with photos of place settings, ingredients, and Fu's worldwide travels. Most importantly, Huang's audience was limited to readers of Chinese, whereas Fu's bilingual Chinese-English cookbooks could and did travel the world. For a non-Chinese reader, Huang's cookbooks do not beckon the eye with color photographs or odd English names for the dishes. In fact, I never noticed Huang's books on my mother's cookbook shelf growing up and didn't even realize that they *were* cookbooks.

There were other Chinese cookbooks published in the United States that my mother might have turned to at the time. Buwei Yang Chao (1889–1981) published *How to Cook and Eat in Chinese* in 1945. Chao was born in Nanjing and later trained in Japan as a medical doctor, but she gave up her practice after she married linguist Yuen Ren Chao in 1921. The couple emigrated to the United States in 1938, where Yuen Ren taught Chinese at Harvard, and then became a professor of linguistics at Berkeley. Buwei Yang Chao was the first to introduce Americans to Chinese dishes beyond the typical chop suey and chow mein fare popular in the United States at the time. She (or more accurately, her husband, who had edited their daughter's translation of the cookbook into English) is also credited with coining the English terms "stir-fry" and "potsticker." Pearl S. Buck, the Nobel Prize-winning author of *The Good Earth* (1931) and a friend of the Chaos, wrote in the preface, "There is not a dish in its pages which an American housewife cannot produce, without qualms over its difficulty." Chao's cookbook proved so popular that it was reprinted several more times in subsequent decades, with the second revised edition appearing in 1949 and the third revised edition in 1963.

Joyce Chen (Liao Jia'ai) (1917–94) was another Chinese émi-gré who gained fame in the postwar years as chef-owner of several Boston-area restaurants specializing in northern Chinese cuisine. She had moved to the United States from Beiping with her family in 1949, and she opened her first Joyce Chen Restaurant in 1958. Chen originally self-published *The Joyce Chen Cookbook* (1962) in a small run of six thousand copies, but it eventually sold more than seventy thousand copies nationwide after it was reprinted by J.B. Lippincott. Chen also appeared on a public television program on Chinese cooking from 1966–67, *Joyce Chen Cooks*, which was filmed on the very same WGBH set as Julia Child's *The French Chef.* Chen later patented her own line of flat-bottomed woks suitable for American electric ranges and developed a line of ready-made bottled Chinese sauces under the Joyce Chen Foods brand. Her impact on the American culinary scene has been recognized by the US Postal Service, which issued a com-memorative stamp in 2014 with her portrait in its series of Celebrity Chefs Forever Stamps.

But although Buwei Yang Chao and Joyce Chen have been justly celebrated for teaching American audiences how to cook Chinese food, neither of their cookbooks ever made their way onto my mother's cookbook shelf: she was not, after all, their intended audience. Chao and Chen were writing explicitly for English-speaking American (read: white) housewives, not Chinese-speaking diasporic ones, and the contents of their cookbooks reflect this. Both cookbooks contain a requisite section on how to use chopsticks, with detailed instructions and illustrations. Both contain shopping lists with Chinese characters for ingredients (with a tear-out version in Chen's cookbook), so that a reader could take the list directly to Chinatown and wave it under the nose of a Chinese shopkeeper to find the correct ingredients. "If you recognize from my description and pictures what you want, just point out to a clerk *I want some of that*," suggested Chen. "If no such things are in sight in the store, point out the items on your Chinese shopping

list and ask the clerk." Both cookbooks explain typically Chinese eating habits, with ample comparisons to American eating habits. Chao,
for example, admitted that after years of living abroad, she was always
conflicted as to whether she should slurp her hot soup or noodles in the
Chinese manner, or make as little noise as possible the American way.

For my mother, and other Chinese immigrants like her, it would
have been slightly perverse as native Chinese speakers to learn how to
cook Chinese food from recipes written in English, when enough linguistic labor had already been expended translating them into English
from Chinese. (Chen told her daughter that her cookbook had been
"written with blood, sweat and love," especially because of "struggling with my poor English.") Chen's recipes thankfully include the
name of every dish in Chinese characters, but Chao's recipes do not.
Chao's husband Yuen Ren had intentionally rendered many of the dish
names, such as "Sweet Peppers Stir Beef Shreds," "Cucumbers Stuff
Meat," or "Beef Emit-Silk," as ungrammatical, Chinese-sounding
English, "which he thinks Americans like better," Chao lamented.
Chinese readers of Fu's bilingual recipes, by contrast, could dispense
with such overt linguistic contortions and find exactly what they were
looking for: clear, easy recipes in Chinese for familiar home-cooked
dishes that would be welcome at the family dinner table.

For most American home cooks, Chinese food would only ever
be a curious novelty, something to prepare occasionally when entertaining guests to impress them with one's cosmopolitan tastes: it did
not represent an everyday approach to eating. Neither Chao nor Chen
were ever embraced as America's culinary darling in the same way
that Julia Child was, despite WGBH producers hoping for a cross-
over hit with Chen. (Publicity material even linked the two programs,
telling viewers, "Remember, you can watch Joyce Chen and still be
faithful to Julia.") Mainstream American television audiences (and
corporate sponsors) apparently did not consider a cooking program
with a Chinese woman speaking accented English and cooking only

Chinese food as television worth watching: Joyce Chen's program was canceled after only one season of twenty-six episodes. It would not be until 1982 that another Chinese individual, Chef Martin Yan, would be given the chance to host a cooking program on American television, finally breaking through to white audiences with his frenetic energy on *Yan Can Cook*.

In her own day, it was only Fu, with her forty-year career on Taiwan Television and dozens of cookbooks, who managed to achieve a stratospheric level of culinary success and influence in Taiwan that truly did rival Julia Child's, a goal that eluded Fu's Chinese contemporaries in the United States. One might even argue that Fu Pei-mei's cookbooks and fame traveled even further than Child's, escaping the borders of her home country, with a transnational audience inherently built into its bilingual platform. The different career trajectories of Chao, Chen, and Fu ultimately had nothing to do with their culinary skill, inherent talent, ambition, or even the so-called authenticity of their recipes. Instead, it had everything to do with the audiences that surrounded them: postwar American audiences were simply not yet ready or willing to embrace a Chinese woman as a culinary star. Because Fu addressed Chinese housewives, first and foremost, along with foreigners and overseas Chinese students, all of whom clamored to have a copy of her cookbook, she felt no special need to plead the case for Chinese food. It was a matter of course that readers would find these dishes delicious and want to cook them every day, or nearly every day, as part of a regular diet.

● ● ●

After finishing graduate school in Minnesota, my parents moved to the small town of Midland, Michigan, so that my father could take a job as a research chemist at Dow Chemical. Midland was a quintessential company town: my mother worked full-time as the supervisor of children's services at the Grace A. Dow Memorial Library; my brother, sister, and I attended the Herbert Henry Dow High School; our rival high schoolers, at Midland High, were known as the Chemics and represented by an atomic symbol mascot. The population of Midland was almost entirely white, including most of my school friends, my teachers, and my parents' coworkers. Although our professional and public lives took place in a white world, I felt that I had a secret Chinese double life, one which had nothing to do with my white peers. My family's primary social network was entirely Chinese, consisting of a dozen or so other Chinese families, whose fathers had also landed in Midland to work at Dow Chemical or one of its subsidiaries. This Chinese double life influenced our daily rhythms in a thousand tiny ways: living with grandmothers who spoke no English, greeting all family friends as "auntie" and "uncle," wearing slippers around the house, groaning about Chinese school on the weekend, storing huge bags of rice grains in the cupboard, and eating cooked rice every night for dinner.

The familiar squat white shape and black knob handle of our Tatung rice cooker, made grubby with years of use, was a fixture on countless Chinese American kitchen counters, including ours. Tatung started manufacturing electric rice cookers in Taiwan in 1960, and some time thereafter my grandmother sent one to our family. The characters which made up the company's name, 大同, were printed on the front of the rice cooker; for years they were some of the few Chinese characters I could reliably recognize. One of my regular kitchen tasks, once I got old enough, was to make rice for dinner after I came home from school, before my mother came home from work. The technology of a basic electric rice cooker remains the same today as it did sixty years ago. You measure out the desired amount of rice grains using a small plastic cup, fill the internal rice pot with water to the corresponding mark, and press a switch. When the water boils off and the rice is cooked, the internal temperature rises above 100 degrees Celsius and triggers the switch to turn off automatically. Perfectly cooked rice, every time. On days that I would ask for a second serving, my mother would joke and call me a "little rice bucket" (*xiaofantong*).

Socializing for us meant family potlucks with other Chinese families, always hosted at a different house, with a table for grown-ups and a table for kids. These potlucks included a rotating group of a dozen or more Chinese families: the Lees (of whom there were several unrelated families), the Wangs (ditto), the Tous, the Changs, the Chens, the Huangs, the Kaos, the Chows, the Suns, the Tiens, the Chaos, the Shihs, the Tongs, the Yues, the Chengs, and the indefatigable Auntie Luo. The potlucks, the mainstay of our family's social life, started before I was even born, right after my parents first arrived in Midland in 1966. "We got together almost every weekend to eat or to play mahjong," says my mother. Gatherings at the time took place at a local park because everyone was renting a house and did not have enough room to invite people over. Families would bring simple home-cooked dishes to share: stir-fried noodles, smoked fish, braised dishes. Along with the food, families, especially mothers, swapped ideas about how to get along in their new lives. "The environment was unfamiliar to everyone, so we could exchange information," my mother recalls. As recent immigrants, no one had any other family nearby to rely on, so they depended on each other instead.

Eventually, as the number of Chinese families expanded, someone suggested putting together an address list, with phone numbers, so people could contact one another easily. Later, in the 1970s, the informal group was given a formal name, the Tri-City Chinese Association (which included the mid-Michigan cities of Bay City and Saginaw and surrounding areas, along with Midland). Several times a year there were special celebrations involving the entire Chinese community, hosted by the Tri-City Chinese Association, which by then had a membership of eighty or ninety families. All these gatherings centered on food and eating, regardless of the occasion: bountiful Chinese New Year banquets at the Midland Community Center, a *zongzi* (sticky rice dumpling wrapped in bamboo leaves) picnic at Plymouth Park for the Dragon Boat Festival. Sometimes several families would go camping together at Houghton Lake or Higgins Lake. Even then, food was the highlight: our family would sleep in our pop-up Starcraft camper and everyone would savor my father's fruit pies around the campfire.

Eating together regularly with other Chinese families in Midland served as both an inspiration and an incentive to my mother to improve her own cooking. She distinctly remembers going to another woman's house for lunch in the early years. Therese Shih had invited my mother, my grandmother, who was visiting from Taiwan, and several other Midland Chinese aunties. When they all arrived in Therese's small apartment, they were confused. They saw no signs of food anywhere, nor any signs of preparation. "We whispered to each other, 'Didn't she invite us over for a meal?' Everything was spic and span. Very strange." Then Therese stood up and excused herself to go into the kitchen to cook, bringing out dish after delicious dish, which she had already semi-prepared. "We were so in awe!" my mother recalls. "Everything was so clean and then she just brought out all of these dishes. We thought, 'Oh! There's another way of entertaining!' Not messy like we did it."

With no local Chinese grocery stores in the area, families in Midland took trips to Detroit, Windsor, Ontario, and even Toronto (a six-hour drive away), to stock up on supplies. "You couldn't even buy soy sauce in Midland," remembers Auntie Jane Tou, who arrived in Midland with her husband James in 1965, the year before my parents. On those Toronto pilgrimages, we'd eagerly look for a dim sum restaurant, since dim sum wasn't available anywhere near us and wasn't anything you would attempt to make at home. We'd stuff ourselves silly, looking for the waitresses pushing the carts of our favorite snacks—radish cake, shrimp rolls, sesame balls, egg tarts. Afterward, we headed to the Chinese grocery stores. All Chinese grocery stores back then were *mama*-and-*baba* affairs, with the same familiar smell once you crossed the threshold: slightly stale, medicinal, mysterious, and occasionally fishy. The scent held the promise of haw flakes, white rabbit candy, and a renewed supply of my favorite, *rousong* (dried pork floss, which tastes much better than it sounds). Once, my parents bought a whole carton of fresh mangoes, which were unavailable in our local grocery stores in Midland. They covered the carton with a blanket and instructed me to sit on it in the car, so that we could sneak the fruit back over the border to Michigan.

Nor were there any Chinese restaurants in Midland or in any nearby towns when my parents first arrived. The lone exception was Rodeitcher's Chinese restaurant in Freeland, which as the name suggests, was not owned by a Chinese family. The original owner, Leo Rodeitcher (who had spent time in Alcatraz and was friends with Al Capone), hired a Chinese man to work in his household in the 1940s. Afterward, Rodeitcher added Chinese food to his restaurant menu, possibly making it the first Chinese restaurant in the state of Michigan. Auntie Tou recalls that the place served "American food—chop suey, fortune cookies, sweet and sour." Another Chinese restaurant later opened in Midland, the Shanghai Peddler, but that too was owned by a white man. Only in 1980 did Carl and Evangeline Chow become the first Chinese owners of a Chinese restaurant in Midland, Bamboo Garden. (Later, I found it odd to discover that a white high school friend's family went to eat there every week, as regular customers. My family hardly ever ate there, although the food was good—why would you pay for Chinese food in a restaurant when you could eat the same thing (or better) at home for less? Our family restaurant of choice was the steakhouse Ponderosa, with its all-you-can-eat salad bar.)

In the late 1960s, Auntie Tou, who had studied home economics in Taiwan, started teaching Chinese cooking classes through the adult education center in Midland. She continued to do so for more than twenty years and even wrote her own, self-published cookbook, *From a Chinese Kitchen* (1979). She was proud that her cookbook did not

depend upon specialized Chinese ingredients, which were so difficult
to source at the time. "Where do you find *haishen* [sea cucumber]?"
she asks. "Where do you find *jinzhen* [dried lilies], *mu'er* [wooden ear
fungus], or *xianggu* [dried mushrooms]? They had never even heard
of these things in Midland then. So, I tried to use local supermarket
ingredients to cook in a Chinese way. That's why people liked it." Her
recipe for fried rice, for example, included frozen mixed peas and carrots. Although she says the recipes in her cookbook were of her own
devising, when Auntie Tou was writing *From a Chinese Kitchen*, she
also consulted Fu Pei-mei's cookbook. She had asked her mother to
bring it with her when she came to visit from Taiwan. "I heard she
was famous," Auntie Tou remembers. "I just did it my own way in
the beginning. Later I looked at her cookbook as a reference. I didn't
really copy her exact method. But she has a good way of doing things."

In her early years in Midland, Auntie Tou recalls going to Midland's local grain elevator, Cohoon's, which sold wheat, beans, and
other grains. She was looking for dried soybeans so she could make
her own tofu, another unavailable staple. The mature yellow soybeans
were sold in the store as animal feed, so the man behind the counter
asked her, "What kind of animal are you raising at home?" She told him
she was actually buying them to make soybean milk. (Making soymilk
is the first stage of making tofu, after which it is mixed with a coagu-
lant and pressed, much like cheese.) "Soybean milk?" he responded.
"What's that?" None of this unfamiliarity discouraged Auntie Tou,
however. She is especially proud of the fact that she converted the
taste buds of even the most reluctant Americans. "In Midland, there
were some people who would say, 'I don't want to eat Chinese food.'
Have you ever met anyone like that? Especially in the early years.
They just wouldn't even touch it." She remembers one man who was
particularly against Chinese food, and later, after a cooking demonstration, returned to tell her that Chinese stir-fries had changed his
life, helping him eat more healthily without using butter. Another col-

lege student in one of her cooking classes told her that he had only ever eaten hamburgers, hot dogs and broccoli growing up. After taking her class, he said, "I open my refrigerator and can always find something to stir-fry." "This," Auntie Tou says, "is an accomplishment."

• • •

Non-Chinese tend to see and think of "Chinese Americans" or "Chinese immigrants" as a single, monolithic group with a shared history, but the people encompassed by this identity are extraordinarily diverse, shaped by distinct waves of migration. The first wave of Chinese migration to the United States was in the late nineteenth and early twentieth centuries, before and during the era of Chinese Exclusion (1882–1943). These nineteenth-century Chinese migrants overwhelmingly came from a single province of China, Guangdong Province (known in English as Canton), along China's southeastern coast. Astoundingly, historian Madeline Hsu writes that until 1960, "well over half of all Chinese in the United States came from [a] single county" in Guangdong Province, Toishan. Most were male and came as laborers in the mid-nineteenth century to California and other Western states, working in gold mines and building the transcontinental railroad. As those opportunities disappeared, some shifted to making a living as laundrymen, cooks, Chinese restaurant workers, or small grocery store owners. It was overwhelmingly Cantonese migrants who settled in America's Chinatowns, giving them their familiar culinary habits and sounds and inventing chop suey and chow mein for American palates. San Francisco's Chinatown, established in 1848, was the first in the country, but Chinatowns in other metropolitan areas soon followed: New York City, Boston, Philadelphia, Chicago, Los Angeles, Seattle, Portland, Honolulu.

Cookbook authors Grace Young and Ken Hom, whose families emigrated from Canton to the United States during the first half of the twentieth century, share this Cantonese culinary background.

Their cookbook memoirs, Young's *The Wisdom of the Chinese Kitchen: Classic Family Recipes for Celebration and Healing* (1999) and Hom's *Easy Family Recipes from a Chinese-American Childhood* (1997), are sprinkled with transliterations of Cantonese words and phrases (*jook* for "rice porridge," or *sik fan*, which literally means "eat rice" but is often used to mean, "Let's eat!"). Their memories, too, are intimately intertwined with their childhoods in urban Chinatowns. In Young's case, she grew up in San Francisco's Chinatown, where her parents cooked Cantonese food every day for her and her brother. "Whether it was a simple weeknight supper or a more elaborate weekend meal," Young writes, "my parents wanted us to know why, in all of China, the Cantonese were considered the best cooks." (As Young's recipes also demonstrate, out of all regional Chinese, the Cantonese have the strongest inclination to incorporate traditional Chinese medical concepts into their cooking, classifying foods as heating or cooling and using soups for healing.) Ken Hom recalls that the boundaries of Chicago's Chinatown were his entire world. When cooking, his single mother "stuck close to the Cantonese approach (none better!) and never attempted other Chinese regional styles."

Notably, both Young and Hom use the terms "Cantonese" and "Chinese" interchangeably, with the latter often standing in for the former. When Hom writes of his childhood, "We went only to Chinese-language movies; we read only Chinese magazines and newspapers; we ate foods prepared only in Chinese style," he actually means Cantonese movies, Cantonese magazines, Cantonese newspapers, and Cantonese foods. This almost unnoticeable substitution, in which Cantonese becomes Chinese, and vice versa, illustrates an important point—almost all Chinese immigrants, no matter where they come from, consider their own identity and experience as *the* definitive Chinese migration experience. For Young and Hom, this is natural: in the mid-century Chinatowns where they grew up, every Chinese person they encountered probably *was* Cantonese. So it makes sense for Young to recall her family's "Chinese kitchen," or for Hom to share recipes from his "Chinese American childhood."

But not all Chinese in the United States share this predominantly Cantonese background of first wave migrants. The second major wave of Chinese migration, which includes my parents, occurred in the immediate postwar decades, especially after 1965. The Chinese Exclusion Acts, federal legislation that by and large barred Chinese migration to the United States starting in 1882, were finally repealed in 1943, as the United States recognized that it needed to maintain a better footing with its wartime ally. Chinese migrants already in the United States were allowed to become naturalized citizens, while a tiny number of 105 new Chinese migrants were now legally allowed to arrive each year. Yet the greatest numerical and ideological shift in US migration policy came with the passage of the 1965 Immigration and Nationality Act, which did away with restrictive national quotas favoring northern and western European immigrants, replacing them instead with policies emphasizing family reunification and the recruitment of educated, skilled labor. This shift opened the doors of America to an increasing number of immigrants from Africa, Latin America, and Asia, as every country had a flat quota of 20,000 migrants per year. As Madeline Hsu has detailed, this shift from restrictive to selective immigration policies for Chinese and other Asian nationals over the course of the twentieth century was crucial in transforming fears of the "yellow peril" into new social myths about Asians as the "model minority."

Very few Chinese migrants in these mid-century decades came from mainland China itself, as mainland Chinese were not permitted to travel or migrate freely overseas after the Communist takeover in 1949. Instead, postwar Chinese migrants came from outside of mainland China, primarily from Taiwan, and to a lesser extent from Hong Kong (then a British colony) and Singapore (a newly independent city-state on the Malaysian peninsula with a majority population of Chinese descent). Because many of these postwar immigrants from Taiwan were also mainlanders, including my parents and all their friends, they spoke Mandarin, not Cantonese, as their primary language, and were accustomed to eating a different range of regional dishes. Between 1966 and 1975, more than 200,000 Chinese immigrants, mostly from Taiwan, were admitted into the United States, with another 125,000 arriving between 1976 and 1980. After the establishment of diplomatic relations with the PRC in 1979, mainland China was given its own separate allotment of 20,000 spots, and in the late 1980s, prior to the return of Hong Kong to PRC control in 1997, Hong Kong received its own annual quota of 20,000.

Most of these postwar Chinese immigrants were highly educated and skilled, coming to the United States to attain their graduate degrees in the hard sciences and engineering, such as my father pursuing his doctorate in chemistry. Moreover, these mobile, professional immigrants were no longer tied to traditional ethnic enclave Chinatowns within major cities, but rather scattered to the suburbs as their socioeconomic means and job opportunities allowed. Monterey Park, California, part of the sprawl of Los Angeles County, became the earliest and most prominent example of one such "suburban Chinatown" community in the 1980s, with a flourishing downtown business district nicknamed "Little Taipei." Other urban satellite Chinese communities in northern California and New York (such as Flushing in Queens) developed, attracting majority Asian populations in similar fashion. Other second-wave Chinese migrants—like my parents in Midland, Michigan—settled in small towns and cities across the Midwest and South, far from any coastal ethnic enclaves and large Chinese communities.

Fu Pei-mei's cookbooks accompanied immigrants from Taiwan to all the corners of the United States where they landed throughout the 1970s, 1980s, and 1990s. Alice Hsu, in Billings, Montana, explained to readers of the *Billings Gazette* that her favorite cookbook was Fu's first volume, from which she planned to select recipes to celebrate the Chinese New Year while far from other family and friends. Kevin Chien, manager of the Yellow Dragon restaurant in Bloomington, Indiana, named Fu's cookbook as one of his ten favorite books, along with *War and Peace, Gone with the Wind,* Sun Yat-sen's *Three People's Principles* manifesto, and *Foodservice Sanitation.* Grace Liu, owner of the Dynasty Restaurant in Williamsburg, Virginia, recommended that readers of her local newspaper bring along *Pei Mei's Chinese Cook Book* if ever stranded on a desert island: "It's very, very clear. It has all the Chinese names, the materials and the ingredients and a very good English translation. It has nice pictures too and covers all the regions and everything from first course to last course." Other Chinese cooking instructors and restaurant owners who had emigrated from Taiwan, such as Theresa Tang of Murfreesboro, Tennessee; Louise Teng of The Orient in Columbia, South Carolina; and Shan Fang of Soo Yuan in Calistoga, California, boasted of their training under Fu Pei-mei, at her Taipei cooking school.

Ming Tsai, award-winning chef, television personality, and cookbook author, grew up in a Chinese family that arrived in the United States as part of this second wave of Chinese migration from Taiwan. His paternal grandfather, a university official, fled to Taiwan from mainland China at the end of the Chinese Civil War, arriving indirectly from Macau in 1951. His father, Stephen, came to study at Yale and eventually found a job as an engineer at the Wright-Patterson Air Force Base in Dayton, Ohio. His mother, Iris, opened her own Chinese restaurant, the Mandarin Kitchen, in a Dayton strip mall, where Tsai learned about the restaurant business. On a 2014 episode of the PBS program *Finding Your Roots,* Tsai explained to host Henry Louis Gates, Jr., what it felt like to grow up in Dayton, a city with few other Chinese families: "Our family joke was, when we had the two or three Chinese families over to our house, we *were* Chinatown. [We were] always surrounded by food. All we did was cook and eat. And while we were eating dinner, we're talking about what are we eating next." Interestingly, for second-generation Tsai, his restaurant in Wellesley, Massachusetts, Blue Ginger, which first put him on the culinary map in 1998, was always known for its "East-meets-West" fusion cuisine, a branding and approach to cuisine that Tsai has never abandoned: none of his cookbooks or television programs have ever featured the word "Chinese" in their titles.

● ● ●

Although Fu Pei-mei was conscious of trying to write a cookbook that would be of some succor to overseas Chinese hungry for a taste of home, she could not have imagined all of the out of the way places in the United States where those suitcases carrying her cookbooks would land: Salem, Oregon; Calistoga, California; Bloomington, Indiana; Murfreesboro, Tennessee; Midland, Michigan; Dayton, Ohio; Williamsburg, Virginia; Columbia, South Carolina. Her dishes would help postwar migrants ease their homesickness, satisfy the demands of their hungry families, impress their friends, and build their communities. Those overseas readers might or might not be aware of Fu's fame as a television celebrity in Taiwan, but they would instantly recognize the bold red, blue, and green covers of her cookbooks, and the name PEI MEI emblazoned in capitals at the top. Their colorful packaging and compact bilingual presentation have allowed the cookbooks to evolve into the symbols of a specific mid-century version of Chinese culinary identity, one that can be passed down to the next generation. Fu Pei-mei's cookbooks have never been the only cookbooks on Chinese cuisine, but as the first bilingual cookbooks of their kind, they were the ones that best embodied that trans-Pacific journey, speaking to generations on both sides of the migration divide.

10

DISHES FOR A DIGITAL AGE

Dishes cooked by contemporary Fu Pei-mei fans, posted on Instagram for the Radical Family Farms Pei Mei Cookoff event (@radicalfamilyfarms, #rffcookoff, 2020). The dishes include (clockwise, from top left) Chris Young's Steamed Chicken with Green Onion; Linda Tay Esposito's Assorted Meat Soup in Winter Melon; Daphne Wu's Eggplant Sze-Chuan Style; and Lynn Chang's version of Fu's personal favorite, Sea Cucumber in Brown Sauce.

M Y MOTHER'S FIRST EXPERIENCE COOKING CHINESE food in Iowa reminds me of my own first attempt at cooking a Chinese meal for my host family in Germany, while studying abroad in college in the 1990s. Though it takes place three decades later, on another continent, and in another language, my story is filled with the same gendered cultural expectations on the part of outsiders and the same outsized optimism and desire to please on my part. "*Wir lieben chinesische Küche!*" enthused my host mother. So, *ja, natürlich*, I offered to cook a Chinese meal for them, to thank them for their kindness to me. At the time, however, I had little idea of how to cook anything, beyond some casual observations of my mother cooking at home. Moreover, the only Chinese ingredient my host mother had on hand was a tiny bottle of soy sauce. Still, I somehow believed that I would be able to conjure up something vaguely Chinese and tasty from nothing when the time came (how hard could it be?), only to realize when faced with the stove that no culinary miracle would save me.

I was mortified, and everyone tried to be polite about it, but the results—a valiant attempt at stir-fried beef—were terrible. That same summer, I tried cooking eggplant for myself for the first time, craving its purple, glistening skin, stir-fried with a garlicky sauce, which I had eaten so many times before. The soggy mass of oily, brown glop that resulted was barely edible, but I forced myself to finish it. I remember calling my mother long-distance from a phone booth after the eggplant incident to analyze what had gone wrong. That was the year that my mother first suggested I try some recipes from Fu Pei-mei's cookbook. I started with her recipe for Shredded Beef with Green Pepper, then made my own substitutions to cook a dish of chicken with red peppers. Only after I started writing this book did I realize that I was not alone in these early forays into Chinese cooking, guided by Fu's cookbook. When I would tell other second-generation Chinese and Taiwanese American friends that I was writing a book about Fu Pei-mei, they would say, "Oh yeah, we had her cookbooks too, growing up," or, "My mom gave me that cookbook." Along with oil splatters, the pages of Fu's cookbooks have absorbed all kinds of memories, and not just those of my own making. What seems most remarkable about Fu Pei-mei's durable legacy is the way she continues to appeal to fans in the second-generation, even in our digital age.

●   ●   ●

Denise Ho's father, an avid home cook who built a separate outdoor kitchen equipped with an open-flame burner and wok just for making Chinese food, gave her a used copy of *Pei Mei's Home Style Chinese Cooking* (1984) before she went to graduate school in the 2000s. Denise most appreciates its approachable, family style recipes and the bilingual format, which helps when shopping for ingredients. Yet Denise's general impression of Fu's cookbook as "old-fashioned" in its style, descriptions, photographs, and layout, suggests some of the barriers Fu's cookbooks face today in appealing to a new generation of Chinese home cooks. Compared to a contemporary Chinese cookbook author such as Fuchsia Dunlop, Denise says, for whom "everything is a poem, and you start salivating by the time she's done describing something," Fu's recipes are far more "practical and utili-tarian." Denise explains: "There's no ode to the food, there's no back-ground or historical context, no 'Here's my first experience walking along the streets and there were cleavers chopping, and this smell of something wafting in my direction.' There's nothing like that. It was just, 'Here's this food, here's a list of things, and here's how to make it.'" All the same, Denise still returns to Fu's recipes for dishes such as Three Cup Chicken (*sanbeiji*), Lion's Head Meatballs (*hongshao shizitou*), or Steamed Ribs with Rice Powder (*fenzheng paigu*).

At least one second-generation fan has attempted to bring Fu Pei-mei's recipes up to date. In 2009, Jaline Girardin started a blog called Pei Mei a Day, inspired by the movie *Julie and Julia*, which detailed writer Julie Powell's attempt to cook her way through Julia Child's *Mastering the Art of French Cooking* in a year. Jaline's goal for her blog was less deferential to Fu than pragmatic, "adapting recipes from her for the twenty-first century, where MSG and lard (two of PM's staples, along with hot oil) have both fallen out of favor." To make it easier on herself, Jaline didn't actually cook one Fu Pei-mei dish a day, but she did make several dishes per month. She stuck to the project for more than a year, documenting her trial of almost seventy dishes from Fu's cookbooks. Jaline received her copies of Fu's cookbooks from her mother, who emigrated to the United States from Taiwan for gradu-ate studies in the 1970s. Like Catherine Chen, Jaline's mother was not terribly interested in cooking and was more devoted to her career as a math professor, but she did regularly cook diced chicken with walnuts from one of Fu's recipes, which is still bookmarked in Jaline's copy. Jaline has always thought of Fu as the "cooking authority" of record, wondering to herself when preparing to cook a dish, "Let's see what Fu Pei-mei has to say about this."

Jaline's dish choices from Fu's cookbooks were idiosyncratic, reflecting her own preferences and personal circumstances. She never chose to make sea cucumber, for example, since she finds the taste and texture unappealing. As a graduate student at the time, Jaline also chose dishes that did not contain expensive ingredients (which excluded most seafood dishes), and dishes that would pack well for lunches. Jaline's favorite dish is what Fu calls Eggplant Sze-Chuan Style (*yuxiang qiezi*), also known as fish-fragrant eggplant. Jaline has made *yuxiang qiezi* so often that she calls it her "signature dish," her *nashoucai*. Only once was Jaline truly defeated in her cooking experiments with Fu's recipes, when she attempted to make *dan bing*, the pancakes used to wrap Peking duck and *mushu* pork. Jaline labeled the recipe difficulty level as "fiendish," mostly because Fu uses the traditional method of rolling out two pancakes at once, separated by a layer of oil, which are cooked together in a pan and then immediately pulled apart. (My northern Chinese father, in his culinary heyday, excelled at making *dan bing* for us in exactly this fashion.)

Jaline's blog not only served to document her own cooking experiments, but it also encouraged other fans to share their love for Fu's cookbooks. Mark's wife from Taiwan, who grew up watching Fu on TTV, was given Fu's three volume cookbook set by her best friend when she left for the United States. "Now that we are getting on in years, wife decided we should have the steamed chicken recipe on page 114 3–4 times per month," he writes. "She says Chinese will always be different from Americans because Chinese like vegi's fried & meat steamed, Americans like meat fried & vegi's steamed." Carol Yu received her copy of the first volume of Fu's cookbook from her godmother in the Philippines, who was herself a restaurant owner, when she got married in 1979. Dennis was introduced to Fu's first two volumes by a Chinese friend in 1977. He wrote to the address in the back of the book to see if he could purchase his own hardback copies and was surprised by the results. "I assumed I would receive a response from a secretary, however I received a handwritten letter from Fu Pei Mei stating that I could send the payment directly to her (either cash or check) including the shipping charge (either airmail or seamail). . . . I promptly sent a money order for $14.50 and received the books within a two week period. I have treasured both the cookbooks and her letter for all these years."

Fu achieved the ultimate digital status in 2015 when she was made the subject of a Google Doodle on what would have been her eighty-fourth birthday. Digital artist Olivia When drew Fu standing behind the counter on the set of her television show, *Fu Pei-Mei Time*, except in place of the show's title on the signboard was the search engine's familiar name. A silhouette of the camera and boom mike cut in from the side, while Fu is shown stirring a bowl of something with her chopsticks. A handy wok stands by (but strangely no cleaver or burners), along with two finished dishes, prawn slices with sour sauce and the Cheng family meat dish, and a heaping portion of rice. Fu is of course wearing a tidy apron, and her face is lined with grandmotherly wrinkles.

More recently, in 2020, Leslie Wiser, owner of Radical Family Farms in Sebastapol, California, launched a Pei Mei cookoff challenge online in an effort to sell her stash of nearly one thousand pristine out-of-print copies of the first volume of Fu Pei-mei's cookbook series. Wiser's mother is Taiwanese, and her enterprising German-Hungarian father had purchased his lot of Fu's cookbooks for $5 each in the mid-1980s. He had intended to sell them through magazine ads as part of a mail-order Chinese dry goods business, but the plan never took off. Instead, Wiser inherited the cookbooks, keeping them in storage over the years, and occasionally selling a few on eBay in college. Every time she moved, she lugged all fifty boxes of books with her, from Ohio to Indiana, back to Ohio, and finally to California. Now an organic farmer specializing in growing Asian heritage vegetables (@radicalfamilyfarms), Wiser came up with the idea of hosting an online Pei Mei cookoff to sell the rest of the cookbooks that she still had in her possession. She posted pictures of the cookbooks still in their original packaging from Taiwan, with their familiar bright red covers. "I'm not going to lie, it's hard to let go of these babies," she wrote on Instagram. "But I'm very thankful so many orders came in so Fu Pei Mei's legacy can spread across the US." Within a week, she had sold eight hundred cookbooks, at $75 per copy—a very reasonable price for these out-of-print classics. Meanwhile, participants in the cookoff joined from both the United States and England, and shared images of dishes they had cooked from Fu's cookbook—Steamed Chicken with Green Onion, Assorted Meat Soup in Winter Melon, Eggplant Sze-Chuan Style, and even Fu's favorite, Sea Cucumber in Brown Sauce (#rffcookoff).

• • •

There is a distinct difference between the way Fu's cookbooks are regarded today by Instagram foodies in the United States and the way that Fu's cookbooks are regarded in contemporary Taiwan. Ironically, among her overseas fans, many of whom have scant knowledge of the woman herself and her exceptional career, Fu's original cookbook can still serve as a living culinary document, with solid recipes for Chinese dishes that meet the needs of today's home cooks. Among her fans in Taiwan, perhaps precisely because they are more familiar with Fu's entire career, Fu's cookbook is treated as more of a relic of a bygone era. In 2013, for example, Andy Wu (Wu Enwen), a food television program host in Taiwan, published a Chinese cookbook which he called a "neo-classical salute to Madame Fu Pei-mei." In his cookbook homage to Fu, Wu offers updates on Fu's recipes, interspersed with his own observations on the dishes and excerpts from Fu's autobiography. His ultimate goal, he says, is to allow more readers to "become reacquainted with this contemporary legend." But Wu's reverence for Fu's reputation means that he does not interact with her as a culinary equal, treating her as merely one more potential source on Chinese cooking among many. Instead, he places her on a pedestal, beyond reproach or critique.

Cheng An-chi, Fu's oldest daughter, shares this nostalgic vision of Fu's cooking. The most notable example is her repackaging of Fu's recipes in her cookbook, *Mom's Dishes: Fu Pei-mei Hands Down the Taste of Family Happiness* (*Mama de cai: Fu Peimei jiachuan xingfu de ziwei*) (2014). In it, Cheng offers a selection of Fu's favorite recipes, including dishes she liked to perform on television, family favorites, dishes she invented, essential dishes taught at her school, and northern and southern dishes representing the regional background of Fu and her husband, as well as his Shanghainese coworkers. The copy on the front cover recalls Fu's impact on the postwar decades in which she lived: "During that era of simple, homely fare, Teacher Fu Pei-mei's cooking instruction let countless people gain happiness from their dinner tables." The recipes are largely the same as Fu's originals, with some minor edits, but all the photos have been updated, with food-stylist curated images similar to those that can be found in any contemporary cookbook. These changes may appeal to a domestic audience in Taiwan, but fans of Fu Pei-mei abroad don't necessarily want updated, repackaged versions of Fu's recipes with new covers; they want the mid-century retro feeling of the original red cover and the gaudy color photos. It is the physical heft of the original hardback, splattered with stains and smudges, that offers us the most direct connection with our culinary pasts, and with our own childhood memories.

The generation of women who originally grew up with Fu, learning how to cook from her through the television screen and her cookbooks, is now aging and passing away. I was deeply struck by this sense of the passage of time when I was in Taiwan conducting research in September 2014, which coincided with the tenth anniversary of Fu's death. Her three children, especially Cheng An-chi, had organized a special commemorative event in which three well-known restaurants in Taipei sold their versions of several of Fu's dishes, in a limited-time special offer for customers. The press conference kickoff was a spe-

cial "family reunion" banquet featuring a selection of these dishes;
Cheng An-chi had worked closely with the chefs at each restaurant to
ensure that they were making Fu's dishes in her mother's signature
style. Dian Shui Lou, a Jiang-Zhe style restaurant, had chosen Fu's
recipes for several famous dishes from Shanghai and Zhejiang, such
as deep-fried whole shrimp (*youbao xia*), sautéed crab with bean paste
sauce (*jiangbao qingxie*), and red bean paste pancakes (*dousha guo-
bing*). Chao Jiang Yan, a Chiu Chow style Cantonese restaurant, tack-
led several of Fu's Cantonese recipes, including classics such as sweet
and sour pork (*gulaorou*) and homestyle pan-fried noodles (*jiachang
liangmianhuang*), as well as a dish featuring Western flavors, baked
prawns smothered in cheese (*qisi ju mingxia*). The Taiwanese restaurant Shin Yeh did not offer its versions of Fu's Taiwanese recipes,
who of course was never known for her expertise in Taiwanese food.
Instead, the restaurant's founder and a close friend of Fu, Lee Hsiu-
ying, cleverly chose to offer a more personal selection of the Cheng
family's own favorite dishes: the Cheng family roast pork loin (*Cheng-
jia darou*); "firewood bundle" duck soup (*chaiba yatang*), so-called
because the main ingredients are chopped into matchsticks of equal
lengths then tied together in a tidy bundle with a length of dried gourd;
and deep-fried custard fritters with sesame (*zhima guozha*).

No one at the event even pretended that Fu's dishes were *au
courant*, catering to contemporary tastes. On the contrary, they
were appealing precisely because they evoked the culinary past and
reminded diners of how people had eaten in Taiwan forty or fifty years
earlier. Publicity posters urged diners to "savor the original taste of
Teacher Fu's famous classic dishes." In her remarks at the time, Cheng
An-chi said that these dishes "remind us of the taste of Chinese food
in our parents' time," underscoring a sense of generational difference.
Ironically, because cooking and eating in Taiwan have changed so
dramatically over the past several decades, it is impossible to see Fu's
cookbooks as timeless there: they are instead poignant reminders of a

fleeting culinary past. The mainlander restaurants that built Taipei's reputation as a postwar culinary mecca and that imparted Fu with her own authority as an expert in various Chinese regional cuisines are slowly dying away as younger diners favor international tastes and seek out novel dining experiences.

Meanwhile, overseas, Fu Pei-mei has not aged in the pages of her cookbook, or rather, has aged directly into a kind of mid-century retro cool. Even today her cookbooks are still useful for their methodical instructions on how to cook a wide range of standard Chinese dishes, especially for those who already possess a basic knowledge of cooking. From there, it isn't difficult to adjust the ingredients and seasonings to whatever you happen to have on hand or whatever suits your own tastes, a kind of adaptive cooking practice that Fu herself always preached. More than one user has echoed the sentiment expressed by Fu's daughter Cheng An-chi: "Many people would say if you just follow her recipes step-by-step, even if the results aren't always one hundred percent, they'll at least reach eighty percent." Cookbook reviewer and blogger Jon Tseng put it this way in his review of Fu's best-known cookbook series in 2012: "The recipes actually do work! That's a big danger, particularly for cookbooks of a certain age. . . . I can also defer to my mother on this one—having cooked from Volumes I and II for over twenty years she can certainly say they work."

● ● ●

In the United States, the most recent wave of Chinese migration has occurred since the 1980s, in the wake of post-Mao reform and prosperity in mainland China. The People's Republic of China began allowing out-migration of its citizens again in 1977, and since then ever-greater numbers of mainland migrants have come to the United States. By 2018, mainland China was the origin of the greatest number of new immigrants coming to the United States, with 149,000 that year, followed by India (129,000), Mexico (120,000), and the Philip-

pines (46,000). At the same time, the general improvement of economic conditions in Taiwan has meant that fewer students have been
lured away to settle permanently overseas. (The number of students
coming from Taiwan to study in the United States from 2010–20 aver-
aged only 22,438 per year for the decade.)

Mainland Chinese immigrants in this most recent wave fall at
both ends of the socioeconomic spectrum. One group consists of
working-class migrants, some of whom may be undocumented and
arrive with little knowledge of English. Without other marketable
skills, they often must make their living by working in Chinese restaurants, as cooks, waitstaff, busboys, and delivery workers, or alterna-
tively in garment shops or construction work. A 2019 Pew Research
Center report estimates that thirteen percent of all Chinese living in
the United States live in poverty, with an even higher percentage, fifteen percent, of foreign-born Chinese living in poverty. Another group
of recent Chinese immigrants consists of highly educated and skilled
workers, often coming to the United States for undergraduate or graduate studies. As a group, Chinese immigrants in 2018 were "more than
twice as likely to have a graduate or professional degree" when compared to the general population of arriving immigrants or when compared to US-born populations.

What is most striking about the current generation of working-
class Chinese immigrants is that, like the nineteenth and early twentieth century generation of predominantly Cantonese immigrants
that came before them, most of today's Chinese restaurant workers
come from a single province, and even a single region in that province:
Fujian Province, particularly from the areas around the provincial
capital of Fuzhou. Fujianese not only now own the majority of Chinese restaurants in this country; they also run the support networks
(employment agencies, bus routes, ancillary businesses to buy phone
cards and wire money home) for the entire Chinese restaurant industry. Fujianese have become the largest subethnic group in New York

City's Chinese enclaves, for example, replacing the earlier dominance of the Cantonese.

In my classes on Chinese food history at the University of North Carolina at Chapel Hill, I have had several students whose first-generation Fujianese parents have toiled in the family's Chinese restaurant for years, all in the hopes that their second-generation college-educated children will become high-earning, white-collar professionals. The hours are long, requiring much precious time away from the family, and the work is exhausting. As Hannah Jian, the daughter of Fujianese restaurant owners in Greensboro, North Carolina, explained to one of my students, for her parents, "owning a restaurant is the last resort. If you don't do well at school, you're gonna be a restaurant owner and you're gonna do this for the rest of your life."

Understanding Chinese migration as a series of distinct waves helps to explain why I did not recognize myself in books by Chinese American authors from earlier generations, which I read as a teenager, during my adolescent search for examples of what it meant to be Chinese American. Jade Snow Wong's acclaimed autobiography, *Fifth Chinese Daughter* (1950), details her life growing up during the Depression in her father's overall factory in the middle of San Francisco's Chinatown as she tries to find her way toward an independent life, working as a housemaid to put herself through college and as a secretary in a shipyard office during World War II. Our differences were not only temporal and socioeconomic; they were also linguistic and regional. Her family's Cantonese roots, her father's Christian beliefs, her parents' traditional values and inability to speak English, their working-class San Francisco Chinatown existence—these all described a world very far from my own. My own parents spoke Mandarin and had white-collar careers as a research chemist and a librarian, which required daily communication in English; we lived in a small corner of mid-Michigan surrounded by a white majority. Cantonese was essentially a foreign language to us, one that I associated only with going to Chinese restaurants in big cities, such as Toronto.

Today I wonder how the most recent third wave of Chinese immigrants from the mainland and their children will respond to my parents' and my own second wave story. Our chapter in the Chinese American story of migration immediately precedes theirs, but do they see points of resonance—living among majority white communities in far-flung corners of the United States, the struggle to reconcile Chinese and American aspects of one's identity, the irrefutable bonds of family? Or do they see only irreconcilable differences, given the vastly different political histories of China and Taiwan and disparate paths of labor and migration that our families have tread? One of my former students, Jacky Zheng, is the son of Fujianese immigrants who owned a small Chinese restaurant in Wilmington, North Carolina. When Jacky talks about what his parents sacrificed to give him the opportunities in life they never had, he says, "Symbolically, the restaurant represents how my family wrote our story in America and carved out a place for ourselves." I admire Jacky's insistence on his parents' labor as a tremendous act of will, from which they have crafted a sense of national belonging, rather than waiting for it to be handed to them. Yet I wonder if Jacky and Hannah see me as part of *their* story. Their relationship to Chinese food—as a basic, material means of survival, not just as a prominent marker of home and Chinese identity—is bound to have its own unique contours, ones that may or may not coincide with my own.

No one can claim to speak for all Chinese American experiences— let alone all Asian American ones—across all time. They are simply too diverse, shaped by language, region, religion, gender, generation, sexuality, socioeconomic status, politics, and geographic location. I am struck by the idea, suggested by the title of historian Erika Lee's book, of the "making and remaking of Asian America." Each generation of Asian migrants must discover anew for itself (or even each migrant for him or herself) how to form or navigate relationships to their own ethnic identities and homelands, to other racial groups, to the social relations that sustain them, and to the system of laws or societal assumptions that constrain their actions. Although Lee encourages Asian American readers to see the "significant similarities and connections" of their historical experiences, she admits that "Asian Americans with long roots in this country may wonder what they have in common with today's recent arrivals. Similarly, new Asian immigrants and their descendants may not think that the histories of earlier Asian Americans are relevant to their own experiences. But they should.... Both the diversity and shared experiences of Asian Americans reveal the complex story of the making and remaking of Asian America. There is not one single story, but many."

Rereading Jade Snow Wong's 1950 memoir now as an adult, there are scenes I do readily recognize—and all of them involve food. Wong describes how she learned to cook rice properly at the age of six, rinsing until the grains ran clear, adding enough water to cover her knuckle joints, and waiting for the pot to boil and then steam, without ever lifting the lid. At eleven, she learns to shop for groceries at various Chinatown purveyors, such as the fishmonger, the butcher, the vegetable stand, and the dry goods store. While in college, she lives and works at the dean's house, and invites her group of girlfriends (all of whom are Asian or Asian American, along with one white girl), over for a home-cooked Chinese meal, making egg foo young and tomato-beef. Having distinguished herself in this way, the dean asks her to cook a Chinese meal for an esteemed group of visiting musicians. Wong's family, which has never before shown the slightest interest in any of her college activities, is suddenly stirred into action: her father and mother decide on a simple, workable menu, her father acquires freshly made chicken stock from a restaurant for the soup and gathers all the kitchen equipment she will need, her mother goes over all of the detailed instructions for cooking each dish, her older brother drives over all of the necessary pans, pots, utensils and ingredients to the dean's house, and her younger sister accompanies her to help her cook the whole meal and clean up afterward. The event is a success, in no small part because of the support of her entire family. I recognize the unspoken elements of this episode: the pride entangled in presenting Chinese food to foreigners, the desire to feed guests well, and the willingness of her entire family to pitch in, as a tangible manifestation of their love.

This is why, I think, that food is such a fundamental anchor of Chinese American identity. It is a bind that stretches across different immigrant generations, even as other ethnic markers, such as language fluency or cultural awareness, recede. As a perceptive undergraduate once observed to me, food is the only thing that he, a second-generation kid with parents from Taiwan, and a new immigrant fresh-off-the-boat have in common: "You don't know the language, history, or culture—that's all gone. But you can both sit down at the table and eat the same things." In other words, even after the Cantonese or Mandarin or Taiwanese is forgotten, the language of food remains. Fu Pei-mei, Jade Snow Wong, my parents, my students, and I may have come of age at very different historical periods, in distinctive national, political, and social contexts, speaking different dialects of Chinese or none at all. But I'd like to imagine that we could still all sit down at the same table and enjoy a Chinese meal together, over steaming bowls of rice (or noodles, or buns, or pancakes) and a delectable feast of endless dishes. Pull up more chairs to the Yellow Emperor's table—it extends not only across geographies and national boundaries; it also passes into the past and future, into generations unknown.

●   ●   ●

Viewers hungry for footage of Fu Pei-mei now have the chance to see for themselves how she wielded her cleaver with speedy finesse or handled boiling hot oil in the wok. Since 2017, Taiwan Television has uploaded almost seven hundred and fifty episodes of Fu's last and most widely known cooking series, *Fu Pei-mei Time* (*Fu Peimei shijian*) to YouTube. Fu estimated that she taught more than four thousand dishes across her sixteen years on the show, which broadcast more than fourteen hundred episodes. (Julia Child's cooking program, *The French Chef*, meanwhile, consisted of only two hundred and one episodes across nine seasons.) Prior to that moment, the only Fu Pei-mei videos available on YouTube were those that had been dubbed into Tagalog for rebroadcast on a Philippines television station, uploaded by a Filipino fan. The episodes, which originally aired in Taiwan in the 1980s and 1990s, are all in Chinese and not subtitled in English, but this has not prevented viewers from all over the world from tuning in. Comments from viewers are written not only in traditional Chinese (used in Taiwan and Hong Kong) and simplified Chinese (used in the PRC, Malaysia, and Singapore), but also in English, Spanish, Thai, Tagalog, Japanese, and Korean. The most popular episode by far is Fu's demonstration of scallion braised duck with 693,058 views, but several others, including her episodes on hot and sour soup (263,469), Hunanese cured meat (190,576), and scallion braised sea cucumber (178,500), have also garnered hundreds of thousands of views.

It remains to be seen whether these recent digital updates will keep Fu Pei-mei relevant for a new generation of viewers, especially in Taiwan, where so many fans connected with her originally through her years of television appearances. Those under age thirty won't have seen Fu live on television and most of her cookbooks are now out of print. Thus the 2017 Taiwan Television dramatic series, *What She Put on the Table*, added another plotline set in the contemporary period. The plotline involves the grandson of Fu's fictional Taiwanese kitchen maid, Ah Chun. Chuan Bao, her grandson, finds an old VHS videotape of *Fu Pei-mei Time* in his grandmother's cupboards and says, "Who? I've never heard of the name." After learning more about his grandmother's past, Chuan Bao decides to revive the fortunes of her restaurant, which had specialized in Fu Pei-mei's signature dishes. He learns to cook—not directly from his grandmother, who is temporarily incapacitated in the hospital—but by watching videos of *Fu Pei-mei Time* on his tablet device.

Chuan Bao is not alone. Perhaps the most noticeable difference between my mother's generation of Chinese home cooks and my own are the greater numbers of men in the kitchen, who are taking on some or even all their family's regular cooking duties. In my own family, although my mother was responsible for the everyday cooking and stir-frying, my father was the sous chef, responsible for chopping all the vegetables and meat, as well as washing dishes. As a northerner, however, my father also made all the flour-based specialty dishes in our family, such as dumplings (*jiaozi*), red bean paste buns (*doushabao*), plain steamed buns (*mantou*), pancakes for *mushu* pork (*xiaobing*), and his signature scallion pancakes (*congyoubing*). He also dabbled in making soymilk and undertaking various pickling projects. As it turns out, among all the siblings and spouses in the second generation, it is my non-Chinese husband who is most likely to keep alive the culinary traditions of my father's flour-based specialties. When we met, my husband was already a dab hand at making homemade pasta, bread, pie crusts, and pizza dough, so it has not been a huge stretch for him to expand his repertoire to include numerous tutorial sessions with my father on achieving the perfect layers of flakiness in a scallion pancake or the perfect level of crispiness in a potsticker. He shares with my father a scientific mindset when cooking and continually tinkers with recipes and procedures until achieving desired results. Working together, the two of us have made strides in our collective effort at making steamed buns for our own children: he makes the dough for buns and rolls out the skins, while I make the meat fillings and fold them for the most attractive and delicious results.

My friend Harrison Huang best represents this new generation of male Chinese home cooks. He is the most talented, dedicated, and obsessive Chinese home cook I know, male or female. He has opinions about everything, from the proper filling for a vegetarian *jiaozi* to which brand of kitchen knives he will deign to use. He has recently explored a passion for the varieties of Chinese vinegars and their myriad uses, one of his many obsessions. He argues that the way that most Asian Americans think about their food heritage is far too narrow. His sister, for example, will say, "Oh, that's not the Chinese food I had when I grew up," equating her personal experience with a broader definition of Chinese food. "Somehow your own individual experience becomes the boundary for some notion of cultural identity or cultural character." But for Harrison, "being Chinese is so much bigger than that, so much bigger than what you have experienced. It can't be limited to your own lifetime. . . . You have to be able to imagine a community that's broader than yourself." Harrison's convictions are compelling. China is too big, its regional foodways too broad, deep, diverse, and complex, that it would take several lifetimes to ever learn it all. It puts into perspective my own personal search to transmit a Chinese culinary identity to my children, as but one small wrinkle in an immense culinary story. It is humbling to know that no matter what culinary techniques I might someday learn or master, I will only ever know one tiny corner of the vast culinary traditions that comprise Chinese food.

●   ●   ●

More than any other Chinese culinary figure of the twentieth century, the emergence of Fu Pei-mei signaled a new era of modern Chinese cooking, distinct from its traditional past. Her impact was both domestic and global in its reach, centered on the role of women in feeding their families, and shaped by a raft of new kitchen technologies, industrial food processing techniques, and mass media. She not only introduced the range of China's regional specialties to new middle-class housewives in Taiwan via television and multiple cookbooks; she also traveled the world as the Republic of China's self-appointed culinary ambassador, ensuring that millions would associate her name with authentic Chinese home cooking.

As the most successful of a postwar generation of female Chinese cookbook authors, Fu Pei-mei acknowledged and supported the central role of women in the daily task of feeding their families. This responsibility generally fell upon women's shoulders, regardless of whether they considered themselves housewives or career women, and Fu wanted to do everything she could to make their lives easier and their families happier. Fu Pei-mei both reflected and shaped the expectations of the new, middle-class housewife, who, in addition to braising sea cucumber and wrapping dumplings, was eager to learn how to bake birthday cakes and banana bread. Women in Taiwan were curious about the ways in which their new Sichuanese, Fujianese, Hunanese, Shanghainese, northern and other regional neighbors were eating, and they wanted to serve their families nutritious, novel foods they would love. Fu's intimate connection to her female audience was distinct from the centuries of male-authored Chinese food writing that preceded it, which was more concerned with the discerning taste of the gentleman eating the food than with the cook whose hands happened to make it. Meanwhile, within Fu's own domestic relationship with her male chauvinist husband, in which she ceded to him financial control and did not challenge his position as the ultimate decision-maker within the family, she still carved out the operational freedom to devote herself to a flourishing career outside the home, entirely of her own making.

Fu's success in disseminating modern Chinese cooking techniques was built upon the rise of mass media, particularly television, and shaped by the spread of new kitchen and food technologies, which Fu embraced. Beyond Taiwan, Fu endeared herself to television audiences in Japan and the Philippines, who loved her skilled approach to Chinese home cooking. Fu collaborated and consulted with a range of food purveyors interested in either capturing Chinese tastes for mass consumption or capturing the Chinese market for foreign food products, including China Airlines, the Ringer Hut restaurant chain in Japan, Uni-President's line of instant ramen, and the Australian Meat and Livestock Association. The rise of the supermarket, refrigerator, gas stove, and electric rice cooker eliminated the need for daily shopping at the traditional market and cooking over charcoal braziers, and dramatically expanded the possible range of dishes to make by extending natural seasons and improving food preservation. In Taiwan, it became possible to eat out every day, with the sudden proliferation of vendors, restaurants, night markets, and the overall postwar abundance of food.

Most significantly, Fu Pei-mei went global with Chinese cooking in a way that is still unmatched by any other contemporary Chinese cookbook author, thanks to her visually appealing, bilingual Chinese–English cookbooks. She managed to attract audiences at home in Taiwan while reaching out to new, foreign audiences with growing appetites for Chinese food, both in Asia and around the world. Fu's cookbooks also traveled the world in the suitcases of students from Taiwan going overseas, as portable totems of Chinese culinary identity in a new era of global migration. Her attempts to promote the international profile of the Republic of China and to serve as its self-appointed culinary ambassador mark some of Taiwan's earliest efforts at gastrodiplomacy, undertaken in a climate of shifting Cold War alliances.

Today's generation of Chinese food bloggers and vloggers may be unaware of Fu Pei-mei's legacy and her pioneering role as the first global Chinese cooking instructor of the twentieth century. But she paved the way for all of those who would follow, and today's Chinese food media stars stand in her shadow. "I don't dare say whether I've achieved success or not," Fu wrote as she looked back over her career, "but I have certainly devoted my entire life and exhausted all my efforts trying my best to develop the culinary arts in the East and the

West." Past and present, Fu and today's food media stars are part of the same sprawling, continually evolving story of Chinese cuisine as it has spread around the world in the modern era. Although it seems as if each of us must discover for ourselves the tricks of proper wok seasoning and the secrets of dumpling wrapping, in truth we never really make a dish from scratch. We are always channeling culinary knowledge accumulated through our cookbooks and travels, through countless meals and family observations. With each dish we create, whether for the first time or the hundredth, we write ourselves into that story, one dish at a time.

Epilogue

DUMPLINGS FOR ALL

"What is your favorite kind of Chinese food?" bar graph chart
by Penelope King (Age 7, First Grade), Spring 2019.

THIS BOOK BEGAN WITH A FREEZER INVENTORY LIST from my mother, and it ends with this bar graph from my daughter. My daughter is enrolled in a unique dual language immersion program in her public school and spends half of her day learning in Mandarin. When she was in the first grade, her class took a poll on their favorite Chinese foods. The results were as follows: Rice—4 / Dumplings—10 / Noodles—8 / Buns—4 / Spring Rolls—5. Dumplings by a landslide!

But the bar graph was not even the best demonstration of the class dumpling craze. At one point, my daughter asked if she could bring dumplings to school for lunch. I was shocked—never in a million years would I have considered bringing to school anything in my lunch besides a sandwich to avoid embarrassment, and her question made me realize how very different her grade school experience has been, with so many other Asian American peers. I stifled my surprise and tried to ask her neutrally why she wanted them in her lunch. She shrugged her shoulders and said another child had brought dumplings, they looked good, and she wanted to bring some for lunch too. That she was so matter of fact and unconcerned about her request struck me deeply. Dumplings are normal for her. Fu Pei-mei would no doubt prefer that I wrap those dumplings by myself, taking care not to use the same chopsticks to fill as I do to seal. I'm working on it, but for now, I'm happy enough if my daughter is willing to eat the frozen version.

For someone like me, the arc of Fu's story, from domestic disaster to culinary competence—a story that was repeated for so many middle-class women of Fu's generation—is a refreshing reminder that good Chinese home cooks are made, not born. Eating home-cooked Chinese food need not just be a matter of nostalgic memory, but it *can* be a daily reality, even for a second generation, with enough practice and patience. My own goals in the kitchen are ambitious, but not impossible. To start, I'd like to expand my current culinary repertoire beyond "scrambled eggs with" (scrambled eggs with ham, scrambled eggs with tomatoes, scrambled eggs with spinach, etc.), fried rice, noodle soup, and the occasional *mapo* tofu. Moreover, I want to speed up my cooking for weeknights, to see if I can turn out one main dish and one vegetable dish in the time it takes to cook a pot of rice—a handy culinary yardstick suggested by my friend Harrison as a general weeknight cooking guideline. I have had the time and freedom to experiment with more elaborate dishes over the months sheltering at home during the pandemic, relying on a combination of cookbooks, online searches, and last-minute phone calls to my mother. I have tried my hand at dishes such as sweet and sour spareribs, pork belly with pickled mustard greens, stir-fried lotus root, and winter melon soup. Most of all, I want my children to discover their own favorite Chinese dishes, things that they will remember me preparing for them with TLC, which will someday join my family's pantheon of irreplaceable home-cooked dishes, next to my mother's hot and sour soup and my father's scallion pancakes.

A central motivation for writing this book has been to consider how and what I want my own children to eat. It matters to me deeply that my children enjoy Chinese food, even as I struggle to learn how to make it, because refusing it would be a rejection of everything I hold dear about my family. As I grow older, I realize that of all the things that my parents did to raise my siblings and me, the act that humbles me most was the way they managed to put a home-cooked dinner on the table, day in and day out, without fuss or fail, even while they both worked full-time. Every night we had at least two or three dishes to eat, usually a quick stir-fry of whatever was at hand, and another dish of leftovers from the day before. Sometimes my mom experimented with American food, like meatloaf, or my dad made spaghetti with a jar of Ragu sauce. I don't remember dinner being any terribly burdensome thing—groceries were procured, food was cooked, dishes were washed. Now, as a working parent myself, I can finally see the passive construction of that last sentence, something I never grasped as a child. Home-cooked meals did not magically appear on our dinner table every night, but required regular, ongoing planning, coordination, and action on the part of my parents to make it happen. The best way I can think of to honor their efforts is to commit to more home-cooked meals for my own family, on days when I don't feel like it, as much on the days when I do.

Food remains an essential way my parents, now in their eighties, continue to communicate their loving care for me, their adult daughter, a love which now encompasses my husband and children. My parents and I live in different states, and we don't see each other as much as I would like, especially when the coronavirus pandemic grounded visits with elderly relatives to a halt. Yet even when we could visit in person, our relationship, like any other parent–adult child relationship, can be complicated. Words easily become tangled, and arguments rise quickly (my sister once nicknamed our family car the Bickermobile)—especially between my parents and me. We hug only when we arrive and when we depart, and even then it is hard to do so without wanting to cry—these days their bodies feel so light and fragile. At their ages, I never know if it's the last time I'll see my parents, and there's so much we all want to say, but words can only express so much. That is why we share snapshots of Chinese dishes we have made in quarantine, from my mother's vegetarian steamed buns, to my father's noodles with braised beef tendons, to my latest experiments with steamed daikon radish cake or sticky rice stuffed lotus root. To others it may seem like we are just exchanging foodie pics, but to those who speak the language of food, we know better. Every dish speaks. Take care of yourselves. I love you. Thank you for everything you have done for me. Fu Pei-mei would be proud.

Acknowledgments

Though cooking a meal may seem like a solo act, in reality meals are never truly made by one person working alone. Writing a book is much the same. It requires financial, logistical, intellectual, and emotional support to go from a vague idea to a finished product that you can actually hold in your hands.

The writing and research of this book was generously supported by a Henry Luce Foundation and American Council of Learned Societies Program in China Studies Postdoctoral Fellowship (2014–15), a University of Texas at Austin Institute for Historical Studies Research Fellowship (2016–17), the Carolina Women's Center Faculty Scholar Program (2017–18), a National Endowment for the Humanities Public Scholars Grant (2021), and a University of North Carolina (UNC) Institute for Arts and Humanities Faculty Fellowship (2023). The UNC History Department, UNC Carolina Asia Center, and UNC Asian American Center also provided funds for a book manuscript workshop. My sincere thanks to all these institutions for their financial and logistical support; all of the viewpoints expressed in this book remain solely my own.

Thank you to the generous librarians and staff at the National Central Library of Taiwan and the UNC Chapel Hill Libraries, where

I conducted the bulk of my research. UNC's Hsi-chu Bolick was marvelous, cheerfully answering every question, tracking down difficult to find sources, and suggesting others that came her way. The Schlesinger Library at Harvard University also generously supplied scans of sources. Thanks to Wen-Li Yeh and Fashion Chou for arranging access to Taiwan Television, where I spent several weeks in 2014 watching videos of Fu's cooking programs before they were available online.

Scholarly and public audiences at the following institutions gave generous feedback and shared their enthusiasm for my project: Academia Sinica in Taipei; University of Texas at Austin Institute for Historical Studies Research; University of Michigan Liberthal-Rogel Center for Chinese Studies; Emory University; University of Toronto; University of Texas Rio Grande Valley; University of California, Davis; Association for Asian Studies; Association for the Study of Food and Society; North American Taiwan Studies Association; and the North Carolina Taiwan Professional and Scholarly Society. Participants in the 2017 Culinary Nationalism in Asia conference and the 2022–23 UNC Institute for Arts and Humanities Faculty Fellows also offered feedback on specific chapters in this volume. My thanks to all for their ideas and suggestions.

In particular, I'd like to thank my cohort of UNC IAH Faculty Fellows, including Janet Downie, Oswaldo Estrada, Shakirah Hudani, Heidi Kim, David Lambert, Chérie Ndaliko, Antonia Randolph, Eliza Rose, Ana Maria Vinea, Ben Waterhouse, and Brett Whalen, who thoughtfully commented on parts of the manuscript and encouraged me to go forth. Food studies colleagues around the world, including Dan Bender, Yujen Chen, Wendy Jia-chen Fu, Jakob Klein, Seungjoon Lee, Jeffrey Pilcher, Krishnendu Ray, Françoise Sabban, Jayeeta Sharma, Pin-tsang Tseng, and James Watson, have inspired me with their work and scholarly generosity. Hearty thanks to Seth Garfield, Madeline Hsu, and Courtney Meador for making my stay in Texas both warmly welcoming and intellectually productive.

Sincere thanks to my agent, Lucy Cleland, who worked with me for more than a year to polish the book proposal and then deftly sealed the deal. Huge thanks go to my editor, Melanie Totoroli, whose patient good sense has helped give shape to the book. Beibei Du prepared a database of all online episodes of Fu Pei-mei's videos and transcribed several interviews; Daniele Lauro hunted down and translated Japanese sources for me in Tokyo; Gabriel Moss designed the map; Annabel Brazaitis helped with the logistical details of production. My thanks to all of you for bringing the manuscript ever closer to book form.

I am deeply grateful to all the people I interviewed, whose words pepper the pages of this book. I was not able to include material from every interview I conducted, but this does not diminish my appreciation for the time everyone took to speak to me. Without their stories and insights, this book would be much the poorer: John Chen, Sean Chen, Chen Yingzhou, Andrew Coe, Nicki Croghan, Christina Cruz, Lawrence David, Jennifer Dearth, Michael Drompp, Cathy Erway, Wendy Jia-chen Fu, Jaline Girardin, Denise Ho, Hsiang Julin, Frank and Paula Hsu, Harrison Huang, Wendy Hubiak, Kian Lam Kho, Jenny Kim, Ellen Huang King, Stanley S. T. King, Lee Hsiu-ying, Lee Lin-huei, April Lee, Nancy Lee, Theresa Lin (Lin Huiyi), Tiffany Liu, Angie Ma, Oscar Ma, Carolyn Phillips, Françoise Sabban, James Tou, Jane Tou, Edna Tow, Linus Tsai, Luke Tsai, Maika Watanabe, Leslie Wiser, Ya-Ke "Grace" Wu, and Angie Yuan. Others provided some of the crucial textual and visual sources used in this book: "Cybie" Fang Ling, Dominic Meng-hsuan Yang, the late Frank Zeck, Jr. Joanna Handlin Smith generously mailed me copies of other mid-century cookbooks she acquired in Taiwan.

In particular, I'd like to extend my deepest thanks to Fu Pei-mei's three children, Cheng An-chi (Angela), Cheng Mei-chi (Maggie Hsu), and Cheng Hsien-hao (Michael), whose support for this project and generosity in sharing their memories and photographs of their mother made this book possible. I'd also like to give special thanks to the wonderful women who were the subjects of the extended Kitchen Conversations, Catherine Chen, Christy Fu, Huang Minlin, as well as Susanna Foo, whose story appears elsewhere in the book. Their life stories as working women and mothers, who met every challenge with aplomb, continue to serve as an inspiration to me.

I have deeply appreciated the support of my colleagues in the UNC History Department, which I have been fortunate enough to call my professional home for the past seventeen years. Many have heard me talk about my research in our departmental colloquium, a wonderful sounding board for knotty questions in one's manuscript. Several colleagues read and commented on drafts or chapters of my work at different stages, and I thank them warmly for their time and insights: Karen Auerbach, Flora Cassen, Emma Flatt, Heidi Kim, and Katie Turk. My thanks also to Molly Worthen, who exchanged weekly check-ins with me during our mutual year of research leave. A huge shout-out to Kathleen DuVal, who has been a great role model, mentor, and friend. Kathleen first encouraged me to try writing a book for a public audience, then followed her words with action, offering feedback on the proposal and connecting me to her agent.

A special thank-you goes to commentators who read a draft of the entire manuscript and participated in the book manuscript workshop: Yujen Chen, Eileen Chow, Wendy Jia-chen Fu, Jakob Klein, and Luke Tsai. Wen-hsin Yeh has supported and championed my work for my entire career, including writing countless letters, putting me in touch with her extensive contacts in Taiwan, reading and commenting on the manuscript, and participating enthusiastically in the book workshop. It has meant everything to have your continued guidance and encouragement through these many years. My whole-hearted thanks to all these colleagues for their time and input; any remaining infelicities in the text remain my own.

I am especially grateful for the ongoing, weekly support of my writing group, which originated as part of the National Center for Faculty

Development and Diversity 2019 Summer Bootcamp. A shout-out to Janice Pata, Cabeiri Robinson, and Theresa Runstedtler: four years, ladies, and still going strong! Other friends and family generously commented on the entire manuscript despite their busy schedules: Erica Johnson, Laura King, Stuart White. Many dear friends, all amazing women in their own right, have sustained me through writing and life in general: Karen Auerbach, Flora Cassen, Sara Chaganti, Charlotte Cowden, Wendy Jia-chen Fu, Stefanie Griffin, Stephanie Heit, Denise Ho, Wendy Ma Hubiak, Jenny Kim, Betsy Lee, Tina Ong, Avani Pendse, Berta Rodriguez, Claire Lasher Tetlow, Edna Tow, Maika Watanabe, Sandy Yu, and Angie Yuan. I am so grateful to have all of you in my corner.

Finally, my deepest gratitude goes to my family. Thank you to my parents-in-law, Michael and Margaret King, for their love and support. Thank you to my brother, Todd King, for all of his sage advice, even though the cover is not scratch-and-sniff. Thank you to my sister, Laura King, for her sharp-eyed guidance on all things visual. I could not ask for better siblings; this shared history is yours, too. Enormous thanks go to my mother, Ellen Huang King, whose presence and story undergird this entire book. Thank you, Ma, for everything you have ever done for me, which represents so much more than I can express in words. This book is ultimately a celebration of the life you and Ba built here together. Sadly, my father Stanley S. T. King passed away before he could see this book in print, but his beloved scallion pancakes live on in memory and in deed. We miss him terribly. My biggest thank-you goes to my loudest cheering section, Ian, Penelope, and Hamish, who happily traveled with me to far-flung places, all in search of the best bowl of noodles ever. Ian, thank you for cooking countless meals and washing so many dishes, for paddling as hard as you can to keep our canoe afloat, and for encouraging me always to just kick the can down the road. Penelope and Hamish, thank you for your cartoon Fu Pei-mei book cover, pictures of jumping toast, and most enthusiastic hugs. You have all given me the best reasons ever to keep trying to perfect those dumplings.

Notes

IN THE FREEZER, READY TO EAT

xxii **Zhonghua:** The term *Zhonghua* itself is not immune from political manipulation and intense debate. In May 2022, Taiwan's former vice president Lu Hsiu-lien (whose early feminist beginnings are profiled in Chapter 5) proposed the formation of a commonwealth economic relationship between China and Taiwan, under the banner of "One Zhonghua." See Jason Pan, "Former VP Lu Suggests Taiwan–China Federation," *Taipei Times,* May 8, 2022, https://www.taipeitimes.com/News/taiwan/archives/2022/05/08/2003777892.

CHAPTER 1—EXILE AND ARRIVAL

3 **unwanted house guest:** Fu Pei-mei, *Wuwei bazhen de suiyue* [*Years of five flavors and eight treasures*] (Zhonghe: Juzi chuban youxian gongsi, 2000), 53.

3 **ka-clunk:** Chinese often described the sound of a typewriter as *"gada-gada-gada."* See Thomas S. Mullaney, *The Chinese Typewriter: A History* (Boston: MIT Press, 2017), 30–31.

4 **"Some of the machines":** Fu, *Wuwei,* 53.

4 **same callus:** Fu, *Wuwei,* 53.

4 **"I no longer needed":** Fu, *Wuwei,* 53.

4 **typewriter girl:** Mullaney, *Typewriter,* 173.

4 **work as a typist:** Fu, *Wuwei,* 55.

4 **pinched existence:** Pin-tsang Tseng, "The Wartime Regime and the Development of Public Diet in Taiwan (1947–1950s)," *Journal of Chinese Affairs* 47:2 (August 1, 2018), 113–136. https://doi.org/10.1177/186810261804700205.

5 **"I didn't know anything":** Fu, *Wuwei,* 55.

6 **"a piano, Tianjin carpet":** Fu, *Wuwei,* 26.

7 **lifelong Japanophile:** Fu, *Wuwei,* 34.

7 **his death eight years later:** Fu, *Wuwei,* 37.

7 **only Chinese student:** Fu, *Wuwei,* 30–31.

7 **oyakodon:** Fu, *Wuwei,* 36.

8 **"conscientious, punctual, and collaborative":** Fu, *Wuwei*, 113–114.

8 **self-criticisms:** Fu, *Wuwei*, 47.

8 **"wandering years":** Fu, *Wuwei*, 43.

9 **"Like the little donkey":** Fu, *Wuwei*, 45–46.

9 **between one and two million:** The exact number of mainlander refugees that fled to Taiwan is difficult to calculate. While the number of mainlander civilians in Taiwan was counted as 640,072 in the 1956 census, the number of military personnel was kept secret. See the discussion on population in Dominic Meng-Hsuan Yang, "The Great Exodus: Sojourn, Nostalgia, Return, and Identity Formation of Chinese Mainlanders in Taiwan, 1940s–2000s," Ph.D. diss. (University of British Columbia, 2012), 50–61.

10 **"The ordinary hard-drinking revelers":** Translation of Yuan Mei's "Chuzhe Wang Xiaoyu zhuan" [Biography of Chef Wang Xiaoyu] from Arthur Waley, *Yuan Mei: Eighteenth Century Chinese Poet* (New York: Grove Press, 1956), 52–53.

11 **"trained" at least two cooks:** F. T. Cheng, *Musings of a Chinese Gourmet* (London: Hutchinson, 1954), 30.

11 **"man of taste":** Cheng, *Musings*, 29–30.

11 **"neither religion nor learning, but food":** Lin Yutang, *My Country and My People* (New York: Reynal and Hitchcock, 1935), 337.

11 **"In the cooking of ordinary things":** Lin, *My Country*, 341.

12 **"ugly to look at":** Qi Rushan, *Qi Rushan huiyilu* [*Qi Rushan memoirs*] (Beijing: Baowentang shudian, 1989) [orig. pub. 1956], 262.

12 **cicada wing cut:** Qi, *Qi*, 263.

13 **"They never pay attention":** Qi, *Qi*, 263.

13 **"like a dragonfly flitting":** Xia Chengying, in *Yuanshan shipu dierce* [*Yuanshan's cookbook, vol. 2*], vol. 2 by Huang Yuanshan (Taipei: Sanmin shuju, 1957), 14.

13 **"no time to taste":** Qi Rushan, "Qi Rushan xiansheng xu" [Preface by Mr. Qi Rushan], in *Yuanshan shipu*, vol. 1 by Huang Yuanshan (Taipei: Sanmin shuju, 1954), 15.

14 **"good old days of Peking":** Cheng, *Musings*, 47.

14 **"trip to the Arctic":** Lin Yutang, "The Art of Cooking," in Lin Tsuifeng and Lin Hsiangju, *Cooking with the Chinese Flavour* (London: William Heinemann, 1957) [orig. pub. 1956], xii.

14 **"acting as a fastidious":** Lin, "Art," xii.

14 **"man has driven himself":** Lin, "Art," xiii.

15 **"draw up sharp":** Lin, "Art," xi–xii.

17 **1956 registry:** Data from Table 13.5 in Lin Tongfa, *1949 da chetui* [*1949's great withdrawal*] (Taipei: Lianjing chuban shiye youxian gongsi, 2009).

17 **male mainlanders outnumbered:** Joshua Fan, *China's Homeless Generation: Voices from the Veterans of the Chinese Civil War, 1940s–1990s* (New York: Routledge, 2011), 64.

17 **local Taiwanese women to marry:** Fan, *Homeless*, 65.

17 **no in-laws to care for:** Fan, *Homeless*, 85.

17 **beef noodle soup:** Cathy Erway, *The Food of Taiwan: Recipes from the Beautiful Island* (New York: Houghton Mifflin Harcourt, 2015), 135–137; Steven Crook and Katy Hui-wen Hung, *A Culinary History of Taipei: Beyond Pork and Ponlai* (Lanham, MD: Rowman and Littlefield, 2018), 55.

18 **"if we go":** Huang Minlin, author interview, January 29, 2021.

18 **conditions of hyperinflation:** Tsong-Min Wu, "From Economic Controls

to Export Expansion in Postwar Taiwan: 1946–1960," RIETI Discussion Paper Series 16-E-028 (March 2016), https://www.rieti.go.jp/jp/publications/dp/16e028.pdf.

19 **some twenty thousand civilians:** Estimates of deaths range from 18,000 to 28,000. Thomas J. Shattuck, "Taiwan's White Terror: Remembering the 228 Incident," Foreign Policy Research Institute, uploaded February 27, 2017, https://www.fpri.org/article/2017/02/taiwans-white-terror-remembering-228-incident/.

19 **public discussion of the event:** Yang, "Great Exodus," 10.

19 **"We lost everything in China":** Catherine Chen, author interview, August 16, 2019.

19 **elderly mother and parents-in-law:** Fu, *Wuwei,* 41.

20 **"I always put something extra":** Pai Hsien-yung, "Glory's by Blossom Bridge," *Taipei People: Chinese–English Bilingual Edition,* ed. George Kao, trans. Pai Hsien-yung and Patia Yasin (Hong Kong: Chinese University Press, 2000), 270.

21 **"endless turmoil and anguish":** Pai Hsien-yung, dedication page, *Taipei People.*

21 **"incapacitated by nostalgia":** Pai Hsien-yung, "The Wandering Chinese: The Theme of Exile in Taiwan Fiction," *The Iowa Review* 7:2/3 (Spring–Summer 1976), 205–206.

22 **"That's what impressed me most":** Nicki Croghan, author interview, March 7, 2023.

CHAPTER 2—MAKING A HOME

25 **"How could anyone eat these *jiaozi*":** Fu Pei-mei, *Wuwei bazhen de suiyue* [*Years of five flavors and eight treasures*] (Zhonghe: Juzi chuban youxian gongsi, 2000), 60–61. All details and quotes in this and following two paragraphs from the same source.

27 **newlyweds had been introduced:** Fu, *Wuwei,* 58–60.

27 **Kaohsiung office:** Fu, *Wuwei,* 62.

27 **"Can't you change it up":** Fu, *Wuwei,* 88.

28 **"I don't care a fig":** Fu, *Wuwei,* 88.

28 **tried to watch various street food vendors:** Fu, *Wuwei,* 88–89.

28 **"Cooking has to have some love in it":** Fu Pei-mei, radio interview (ca. 1983), Zhongguo guangbo gongsi, AM006 B102–0112, Collection of the National Central Library, Arts and Audiovisual Center, Taipei.

29 **"I had a husband who loved me":** Fu, *Wuwei,* 19.

29 **"never considered adoption":** Julia Child with Paul Prud'homme, *My Life in France* (New York: Knopf, 2006), 94.

29 **"This is a book for the servantless American":** Simone Beck, Louisette Bertholle, and Julia Child, *Mastering the Art of French Cooking* (New York: Knopf, 1961), vii.

31 **"love may lead to differences of opinion":** Nancy Lee Swann, *Pan Chao: Foremost Woman Scholar of China* (New York: The Century Co., 1932), 83–89.

32 **"small" and "large family household":** Susan Glosser, *Chinese Visions of Family and State, 1915–1953* (Berkeley: University of California Press, 2003).

33 **"Do all of the housework yourself":** Gao Junyin as quoted in Constance Orliski, "The Bourgeois Housewife as Laborer in Late Qing and Early Republican Shanghai," *Nan Nü* 5, no. 1 (2003): 56–57.

33 **"Don't entrust all your housework":** As quoted in Helen M. Schneider, *Keep-*

ing the Nation's House: Domestic Management and the Making of Modern China (Vancouver: UBC Press, 2012), 55.

34 **1947 cartoon:** Wu Yu, "Jiating zhufu de yi ke" [Lesson for a housewife], *Zhongyang ribao,* November 27, 1947.

34 **"Wanted: Maid":** Classified advertisement, *Zhongyang ribao,* February 10, 1950. My thanks to Dominic Meng-hsuan Yang for generously sharing this source.

35 **"Anytime you get three housewives":** "Jiajia you ben nan nian de jing; jiating zhufu tan 'xianü'" [Every family has its own kind of problem: Housewives talk about housemaids], *Zhongyuan* 5 (July 1964), 3.

35 **a succession of thirteen maids:** Ye Man, "Taiwan nüpu qunxiang" [A collective portrait of Taiwan's female servants] in *Ye Man sanwenji* (Taipei: Shuiniutushu, 2010), 237.

36 **"they had all been happy before":** Ye Man, "Taiwan nüpu," 239.

36 **"I never saw my own relations":** Ye Man, "Taiwan nüpu," 240–241. All quotes in this paragraph from the same source.

36 **"the same dish that satisfies":** "Zhongdeng jiating renkouduo; jiyao jingji you yao jinshan jinmei; seweixiang yao jubei xianü nanwei" [Large middle-class family, demanding economical yet also flawless, colorful, fragrant, tasty (meals); Making it hard for the housemaid], *Zhongyuan* 5 (July 1964), 7. It is unclear from the tone of the article whether the reporter interviewed an actual family or if this story is entirely fabricated. All quotes in this paragraph from the same source.

38 **"tremble with fear":** "Huang Yuanshan," Baike, accessed June 2, 2022, https://www.baike.com/wiki/%E9%BB%84%E5%AA%9B%E7%8F%8A?view_id=3k8rmy2ljjc000. All details in this paragraph from the same source.

38 **"When a household has lots of people":** Huang Yuanshan, "Sancong side yu jiazheng" [Three followings, four virtues, and household management], *Jiazheng jiaoyu tongxun* 1:2 (May 1958), 8.

39 **Qi Rushan moved in:** "Huang Yuanshan," Baike.

39 **"personally responsible for going into the kitchen":** "Huang Yuanshan," Baike. All quotes in this paragraph from the same source.

39 **"father-in-law would then taste it":** "Huang Yuanshan," Baike.

41 **"At the time I didn't understand":** Fu, *Wuwei,* 39.

41 **tremendous guilt:** Fu, *Wuwei,* 41.

41 **"male chauvinist":** Fu, *Wuwei,* 58–60.

41 **"It was only because of this":** Fu, *Wuwei,* 194–195.

42 **in-laws and a housemaid:** Cheng An-chi, author interview, May 19, 2014.

42 **boarding school:** Cheng, interview.

42 **"spread out her big circle skirt":** Cheng An-chi, *Mama de cai: Fu Peimei jiachuan xingfu de ziwei* [Mom's dishes: Fu Pei-mei hands down the taste of family happiness] (Taipei: Juzi wenhua, 2014), 105.

42 **"ghost to push a millstone":** Fu, *Wuwei,* 89.

42 **one *liang* of gold was worth:** Wu Wanru, "Fu Pei-mei de pengren suiyue" [Fu Pei-mei's years of cooking], *Jiangyi* 20, no. 4 (January 1997): 67.

43 **minimum wage:** "The History of Enacting and Adjusting the Minimum Wage Policy," Ministry of Labor Republic of China (Taiwan), last modified September 20, 2022, https://english.mol.gov.tw/6386/6394/6402/26387/.

43 **"chefs had the same problem":** Fu, *Wuwei,* 89–90.

43 **"The master would not even":** Fu, *Wuwei,* 177.

44 **With gusto they ate:** Fu, *Wuwei,* 90.

44 **"bring a bunch of random strangers":** Fu, *Wuwei*, 94.

44 **first class had eight students:** Fu, *Wuwei*, 94. My thanks to Yujen Chen for pointing out their wealthy Taiwanese background.

44 **Bolero Western Restaurant:** "Guanyu Bolilu canting" [About Bolero Restaurant], Bolero Western Restaurant website, accessed February 27, 2023, https://bolero1934.com.

45 **"Everyone wanted to learn how to cook":** Fu, *Wuwei*, 95.

45 **housewives in Taiwan grew curious:** The desire of housewives in Taiwan to learn how to cook these unfamiliar regional dishes mirrors the situation in India described in Arjun Appadurai's classic article on cookbook writing from the 1960s to the 1980s. Arjun Appadurai, "How to Make a National Cuisine: Cookbooks in Contemporary India," *Comparative Studies in Society and History* 30:1 (1988), 3–24.

45 **My aunt encountered:** Huang Minlin, author interview, January 29, 2021.

45 **"every table in our house was covered":** Wu, "Fu Pei-mei," 67.

45 **"When I just started, I had no experience":** Weng Yumin, "Fu Peimei: Geile women sishinian xingfu de ren" [Fu Pei-mei: Giving us forty years of happiness], *Jiangyi* 28, no. 4 (January 2001): 31–32.

46 **"I'd tell the students not to make the same mistakes":** Fu, *Wuwei*, 94.

46 **"who has never failed?":** Fu, *Wuwei*, 94.

KITCHEN CONVERSATION—THE HOUSEWIFE

This transcript has been edited and condensed for clarity from the author's interview with Huang Minlin, January 29, 2021. Original interview in Chinese, all translations are my own.

CHAPTER 3—SQUIRRELED FISH ON THE SMALL SCREEN

55 **one of Fu's favorite dishes:** Cheng An-chi, *Mama de cai: Fu Peimei jiachuan xingfu de ziwei* [Mom's cooking: Fu Pei-mei hands down the taste of family happiness] (Taipei: Sanyoushu, 2014), 10.

55 **supply all the ingredients:** Fu Pei-mei, ed., "Tangcu songshu yu" [Sweet and sour squirreled fish], *Dianshi shipu*, vol. 1 (Taipei: Dianshi zhoukan she, 1965), 55.

56 **three children and her mother:** Fu Pei-mei, *Wuwei bazhen de suiyue* (Tapiei: Juzi chuban youxian gongsi, 2000), 107.

56 **forgotten to bring her cleaver:** Fu, *Wuwei*, 107–108.

56 **"You were in such a rush!":** Fu, *Wuwei*, 108.

57 **invited to return:** Fu, *Wuwei*, 108.

57 **Delia Smith . . . Elinor Schildt:** Huang Yumei, "Di-li-ya shi-mi-si: ta shi Yingguo 'Fu Peimei'" [Delia Smith: She is England's Fu Pei-mei], *Lianhe Bao*, January 24, 1996; Shen Yi, "Ai-li-nuo: Fenlan de Fu Peimei" [Elinor: Finland's Fu Pei-mei], *Lianhe Bao*, November 21, 1996.

58 **more than three dozen culinary experts:** Fu Pei-mei, ed., *Dianshi shipu*.

58 **elegant Madame Chiang Kai-shek:** *Dianshi zhoukan* 2 (October 22, 1962), front cover and inside front cover.

58 **five hours of programming per evening:** "Benzhou jiemu" [This week's program schedule], *Dianshi zhoukan* 8 (December 3, 1962), 42–45.

58 **broadcasts only reached viewers:** "Taiwan dianshi gongsi guangboshoushiqu yutu" [Taiwan Television broadcasting reception area map], *Dianshi zhoukan* 8 (December 3, 1962), 4.

58 **signal was strengthened:** "Taishi boyang xitong yanshen dao zhongnan bu" [TTV's broadcasting system extends into central and southern regions], *Dianshi Zhoukan* 157 (October 11, 1965), 46–47.

58 **only three thousand television sets:** "Yazhou geguo dianshi guangbo diantai tongjibiao" [Table of television transmitter-receivers for Asian countries], *Dianshi zhoukan* 2 (October 22, 1962), 4.

58 **one-third of households owned:** Ti Wei and Fran Martin, "Pedagogies of food and ethical personhood: TV cooking shows in postwar Taiwan," *Asian Journal of Communication* 25:6 (2015), 638.

58 **1975, almost three-quarters:** Wei and Martin, "Pedagogies," 638.

59 **Song Jiajin:** Song Jiajin, "Mama de chengfa" [Mother's punishment], *Dianshi zhoukan* 56 (November 4, 1963), 4. All quotes in this paragraph from the same source.

59 **Model 14T-511:** Advertisement, *Dianshi zhoukan* 1 (October 10, 1962), back cover.

59 **"long-legged older sister":** Chen Taizhou, "Changtui jiejie" [Long-legged older sister], *Dianshi zhoukan* 65 (January 6, 1964), 51.

59 **special dust cover:** Zhang Bingling, "Huode le zhili ceyan guanjun jiang" [Winner of the Intelligence Quiz Champions Award], *Dianshi zhoukan* 68 (January 27, 1964), 47.

60 **5,000 yuan:** Wu Wen, "Sannian de jixu," [Three years of savings], *Dianshi zhoukan* 62 (December 16, 1963), 49.

60 **my mother earned:** Ellen Huang King, personal communication with the author, March 18, 2023.

60 **minimum wage in 1964:** "The History of Enacting and Adjusting the Minimum Wage Policy," Ministry of Labor Republic of China (Taiwan), last modified September 20, 2022, https://english.mol.gov.tw/6386/6394/6402/26387/.

60 **three years' worth of his family's savings:** Wu, "Sannian."

60 **borrowed 400 yuan from each:** Li Lingzhi, "Zui pianyi de yule" [The cheapest entertainment], *Dianshi zhoukan* 61 (December 9, 1963), 52.

60 **"between education and entertainment":** Luo Chaoliang, "Dianshi jiemu" [Television programming], *Dianshi zhoukan* 1 (October 10, 1962), 18.

60 **"Mr. TTV":** Ding Zongyu, "TTV," *Dianshi zhoukan* 57 (November 11, 1963), 32–33.

61 **cup of hot tea . . . "I can miss a meal":** Chen Xiuqin, "Yuan yu dianshi tongzai" [I want to be with the television], *Dianshi zhoukan* 59 (November 25, 1963), 44.

61 **young sailor no longer wasted money . . . "It has become my best friend":** Fan Xianglin, "Wo de zhiyou" [My best friend], *Dianshi zhoukan* 60 (December 2, 1963), 20.

61 **"women's program":** Luo, "Dianshi," 19.

61 **December 1962:** "Benzhou jiemu" [This week's program schedule], *Dianshi zhoukan* 11 (December 24, 1962), 2–4.

61 **"elite women and intellectual classes":** Si Ci, "Jieshao funü jiating jiemu zhuchiren Sun Bufei xiaojie" [Introducing the host of the women's program, Miss Sun Bufei], *Dianshi zhoukan* 6 (November 19, 1962), 32.

61 **featured on Wednesday evenings:** "Benzhou jiemu" [This week's program schedule], *Dianshi zhoukan* 8 (December 3, 1962), 43.

61 **"don't forget about whatever you are cooking":** Yu Fei, "Chao huashui" [Stir-fried fishtails], *Dianshi zhoukan* 18 (February 11, 1963), 10.

62 **"my old man":** Wu Shuyuan, "Tianxia yitong" [One nation under all], *Dianshi zhoukan* 262 (October 16, 1967), 9–10.

62 **squirreled fish . . . sea cucumber . . . shrimp with kidneys and cashews:** Yu
Fei, "Tangcu songshu yu" [Sweet and sour squirreled fish], *Dianshi zhoukan* 10
(December 17, 1962), 14–15; Yu Fei, "Hongshao haishen" [Braised sea cucum-
ber], *Dianshi zhoukan* 13 (January 7, 1963), 13; Yu Fei, "Xiaren shuangyao"
[Shrimp with kidneys and cashews], *Dianshi zhoukan* 17 (February 4, 1963), 11.

62 **TTV executives:** "'Dianshi cai' ming bu xuchuan" [TV dinner: Not just an
empty word], *Dianshi zhoukan* 18 (February 11, 1963), 10.

62 **dragon-phoenix legs:** Sun Hai, "Jieshao yidao xinnian jiayao: longfeng tui,"
[Introducing a delicious dish for New Year's: Dragon-phoenix legs], *Dianshi
zhoukan* 15 (January 21, 1963), 11.

62 **Milky Way fish lips soup:** Yu Fei, "Yinhe yuchun" [Milky Way fish lips soup],
Dianshi zhoukan 12 (December 31, 1962), 48.

62 **spicy carp . . . roast pork . . . braised quail eggs:** Yu Fei, "Ladouban liyu" [Sich-
uanese spicy carp], *Dianshi zhoukan* 7 (November 26, 1962), 47; Ah Mei, "Jiating chashao" [Cantonese roast pork], *Dianshi zhoukan* 25 (April 1, 1963), 4; Yu
Fei, "Hongpa chundan" [Braised quail eggs], *Dianshi zhoukan* 9 (December 10,
1962), 38.

63 **cooking columns for two newspapers:** Pan Peizhi, "Zixu" [Preface], *Pan
Peizhi shipu*, vol. 1 (Taipei: Jiwen shuju, 1965), 2–3; Pan Peizhi, "Qianyan"
[Foreword], *Pan Peizhi shipu*, vol. 2 (Taipei: Jiwen shuju, 1966), 2.

63 **lemon pie, raisin pudding . . . country soup:** Yu Fei, "Ningmeng paibing"
[Lemon pie], *Dianshi zhoukan* 8 (December 3, 1962), 47; Yu Fei, "Putaogan bud-
ing" [Raisin pudding], *Dianshi zhoukan* 14 (January 14, 1963), 10; Ren Fang,
"Xiangxia nongtang" [Country soup], Dianshi zhoukan 41 (July 22, 1963), 3.

63 **Smooth Sailing:** "Yifan fengshun" [Smooth sailing], *Dianshi zhoukan* 22
(March 11, 1963), 7.

63 **grandmother took a cooking class:** Ellen Huang King, author interview, January 24, 2017.

63 **Huang Yuanshan's cookbooks:** Huang Yuanshan, *Yuanshan shipu* [*Yuanshan's
cookbook*], vol. 1 (Taipei: Sanmin shuju, 1954); *Yuanshan shipu*, vol. 2 (Taipei:
Sanmin shuju, 1957); *Yuanshan dianxinpu* [*Yuanshan's snacks and desserts cookbook*] (Taipei: Sanmin shuju, 1956); *Yuanshan xicanpu* [*Yuanshan's Western food
cookbook*] (Taipei: Sanmin shuju, 1960).

63 **Seattle and Chicago:** Huang Yuanshan, "Dianshi pengtiao biaoyan ji"
[Notes on television cooking demonstrations], *Zhongguo yizhou* (November
13, 1961), 17.

63 **father-in-law . . . husband . . . passed away:** "Huang Yuanshan," Baike zhishi,
accessed November 17, 2021, https://www.easyatm.com.tw/wiki/%E9%BB%8
3%E5%AA%9B%E7%8F%8A.

63 **"made me feel the worst":** Huang Yuanshan, "Zixu" [Preface], *Yuanshan shipu*,
vol. 3 (Taipei: Sanmin shuju, 1964), 3.

64 **Sun Bufei:** Si Ci, "Jieshao funü jiating jiemu zhuchiren Sun Bufei xiaojie"
[Introducing the host of the women's program, Miss Sun Bufei]," *Dianshi zhoukan* 6 (November 19, 1962), 32.

65 **"we get heaps of letters praising her":** Ah Mei, "Qianceng gao" [Thousand-
layer cake], *Dianshi zhoukan* 40 (July 15, 1963), 5.

65 **"extreme conscientiousness":** Ah Mei, "Qianceng gao."

65 **"famous dishes of each province":** "Shuiguo naidong" [Chilled fruit milk],
Dianshi zhoukan 42 (July 29, 1963), 52.

65 **"accurate recipes and ingredients":** "Shuiguo naidong."

65 **"qualified and competent":** "Shuiguo naidong."

65 **"Teacher Fu Pei-mei":** Mi-guo, "Liaoli qimeng dangran shi *Fu Peimei Shijian*" [Of course my cooking enlightenment came from *Fu Pei-mei Time*], *Lianhe bao,* July 31, 2011.
65 **"symbol of traditional, orthodox":** Wei and Martin, "Pedagogies," 641.
66 **"point out all of the secrets":** Ah Mei, "Haoyou niurou" [Beef with oyster sauce], *Dianshi zhoukan* 38 (July 1, 1963), 8.
66 **"When they lost track of time":** Fu, *Wuwei,* 109.
67 **"chop and explain, cook and explain":** Ai-ya, "Kan Fu Peimei shaocai," [Watching Fu Pei-mei cook], *Lianhe bao,* January 25, 2009.
67 **"What if the spatula":** Ai-ya, "Kan Fu Peimei."
67 **never any rehearsals ... single set of ingredients ... one chance:** Cheng An-chi, author interview, May 19, 2014.
67 **nail protruding from the set:** Shao Zheng, "Tu yu wen" [Words and pictures], *Dianshi zhoukan* 140 (June 28, 1965), 47.
68 **"excellent enunciation":** Ah Mei, "Haoyou niurou."
68 **"standard Mandarin, Japanese, Taiwanese":** "Shuiguo naidong."
68 **"not so good at speaking standard Mandarin":** Fu, *Dianshi shipu,* 3.
68 **dishes from a different province:** Fu, *Wuwei,* 108–109.
69 **dishes by main ingredient:** Fu, *Wuwei,* 110.
69 **"Their ovens are many times more":** Qi Rushan, "Qi Rushan xiansheng xu" [Preface by Mr. Qi Rushan], in Huang, *Yuanshan shipu,* vol. 1, 14.
69 **"with regard to Western desserts":** Yu Fei, "Ningmeng."
70 **egg pudding, birthday cake:** Fu, *Dianshi shipu.*
70 **"Mix ½ c. lard":** Fu, "Xiangjiao mianbao" [Banana bread], *Dianshi shipu,* vol. 1, 174.
70 **surge in the number of Western bakeries:** Fu, *Wuwei,* 110.
71 **store that specialized in baking equipment:** Fu, *Dianshi shipu,* 190.
71 **Taiwan imports more than ninety-nine percent of its wheat:** Chiou Mey Perng and Andrew Anderson-Sprecher, "Taiwan Grain and Feed Annual Report 2018," USDA Foreign Agricultural Service, March 30, 2018, https://apps.fas.usda.gov/newgainapi/api/report/downloadreportbyfilename?filename=Grain%20and%20Feed%20Annual_Taipei_Taiwan_3-30-2018.pdf.
71 **one hundred sixty Chinese recipes:** Fu, *Dianshi shipu.*
71 **a fifth to a third of all the recipes:** Fu Pei-mei, ed., *Dianshi shipu* [The Television Cookbook], vols. 1–3 (Taipei: Dianshi zhoukan she, 1965, 1968, 1970).
71 **"Cut your food up":** Huang Yuanshan, *Yuanshan xicanpu* [Yuanshan's Western food cookbook], (Taipei: Sanmin shuju, 1960), 37.
72 **"difficult to make the dish":** Sun Hai, "Jieshao yidao."
72 **"Yesterday, Fu Pei-mei said":** Meng Lei, "Linju lianyi hui" [Neighborhood get-together], *Dianshi zhoukan* 261 (October 9, 1967), 14–15. All quotes in this and following three paragraphs from the same source.
74 **"It used to be that Mrs. Zhao":** Li Lingzhi, "Zui pianyi de yule" [The cheapest entertainment], *Dianshi zhoukan* 61 (December 9, 1963), 52.

CHAPTER 4—FOR THE SAKE OF FOREIGN READERS

79 **"I had no way to describe":** Fu Pei-mei, *Wuwei bazhen de suiyue* [Years of five flavors and eight treasures] (Zonghe: Juzi chuban youxian gongsi, 2000), 126–27.
80 **"That day I nearly fainted":** Fu, *Wuwei,* 126.
80 **"reading it until I could recite":** Mi Guo, "Liaoli qimeng dangran shi *Fu Pei-*

mei Shijian" [Of course my cooking enlightenment came from *Fu Pei-mei Time*], *Lianhe bao*, July 31, 2011.

84 **Mold San-Sze Soup:** Fu Pei-mei, *Peimei shipu* [*Pei Mei's Chinese Cook Book*], vol. I (Taipei : Fu Peimei, 1969), 30–31.

84 **Mold Pork in Brown Sauce:** Fu, *Peimei*, vol. I, 24–25.

85 **"Of all U.S. activities":** "MAAG—Saga of Service," *Taiwan Review*, June 1, 1966, republished on Taiwan Today, https://taiwantoday.tw/news.php?unit =4&post=6910. Numbers of servicemen and families stationed in Taiwan also from this source.

86 **"skillfully compiled and up-dated recipes":** Dorothy McConaughy, "Foreword," in Fu, *Peimei*, vol. I, 1.

86 **"Chinese and foreign ladies have hoped to buy":** Fu, *Peimei*, vol. I, 2.

86 **Yvonne Zeck:** Yvonne Zeck photograph albums, private collection. I am indebted to the late Frank Zeck, Jr. for allowing me access to his mother's albums and mementos from Taiwan.

87 **Zeck's black-and-white photos:** Zeck photograph albums.

88 **"I had not studied English":** Fu, *Wuwei*, 126.

88 **"Chinese cooking techniques have long surpassed":** Qi Rushan, "Qi Rushan xianshengxu" [Preface by Mr. Qi Rushan], in Huang Yuanshan, *Yuanshan shipu*, vol. 1 (Taipei: Sanmin shuju, 1954), 14–15.

88 **1993 article:** Fu Pei-mei, "Zhongguo pengtiaofa ji qi jishuxing yu yishumian" [The art and techniques of Chinese cooking], in *Diyijie Zhongguo yinshi wenhua xueshu yantaohui lunwenji* (Taipei: Zhongguo yinshi wenhua jijinhui, 1993), 213–23.

89 **"To write the recipes in English":** Fu, *Wuwei*, 126.

89 **"Dear Mrs. Zeck":** Yvonne Zeck papers, private collection.

90 **"Nicki" Croghan:** Monica "Nicki" Croghan, author interview, March 7, 2023. All quotes and details in this paragraph from the same source. I have been unable to find more information on the translator of the third volume in the series, Nancy Murphy.

91 **"Chinese cuisine is divided into large sections":** Fu, *Peimei*, vol. I, 2.

91 **later Chinese cookbook authors:** Florence Lin, *Florence Lin's Chinese Regional Cookbook* (New York: Hawthorn Books, 1975); Deh-Ta Hsiung, *Chinese Regional Cooking* (New York: Mayflower Books, 1979).

91 **cooking method:** Huang Yuanshan, *Yuanshan shipu* [Yuanshan's cookbook] (Taipei: Sanmin shuju, 1954).

91 **main ingredient, dish type:** Huang Yuanshan, *Yuanshan shipu erji* [Yuanshan's cookbook, second volume] (Taipei: Sanmin shuju, 1957).

91 **season:** Wang Yuhuan, *Jiating shipu daquan* [Family recipe collection] (Tainan: Chengguang chubanshe, 1964).

91 **"for the sake of foreign readers":** Fu, *Peimei*, vol. I, 2–3.

91 **"difficulty of buying ingredients":** Fu, *Peimei*, vol. I, 3.

92 **"seaslugs":** John Burns, "Peking Drafting Best Chefs to Prepare Delicacies for U.S. Visitors," *New York Times*, February 19, 1972.

92 **potential guide for Americans:** Theresa Lin, author interview, November 11, 2014.

92 **originally featured:** Haiming Liu, "Chop Suey as Imagined Authentic Chinese Food: The Culinary Identity of Chinese Restaurants in the United States," *Journal of Transnational American Studies* 1:1 (2009), 1–25.

92 **Fu's version features:** Fu, *Peimei*, vol. I, 162–163.

93 **"Looking at a map of mainland China"**: Fu, *Peimei*, vol. I, 6.

93 **"typical of my country"**: Fu, *Peimei*, vol. I, 8.

94 **Huang Su-huei** : Huang Su-huei, *Zhongguocai* [Chinese Cuisine], (Taipei: Wei-Chuan Publishing, 1972).

95 **Judy Getz:** Barbara Wolfe, "She Studied Chinese Cooking with Taiwan's Julia Child," *Courier-Post*, August 1, 1973. All quotes in this and the following paragraph from the same source.

96 **Ruth Aston:** "Maine Woman Cooks in Taiwan," *Bangor Daily News*, April 25, 1967.

96 **Val Sterzik:** Julie Micheal, "Julie's Jottings," *Petoskey News-Review*, November 21, 1977.

96 **Midge Jackson:** Dianne Strahan, "Food for thought," *Tyler Courier-Times*, June 17, 1987.

96 **Ed Faist:** Josephine Bonomo, "With Wok in Hand," *The Herald-News*, November 23, 1977.

96 **Bruce Borthwick:** Betsy Anderson, "Political Science Teacher Doesn't Limit His Vistas," *Battle Creek Enquirer and News*, October 12, 1975.

96 **Michael Drompp:** Michael Drompp, author interview, May 17, 2021. All quotes and details in this and following four paragraphs from the same source. See also coverage of Drompp's culinary skills acquired through Fu's classes in Lisa Jennings, "Wok-king in Memphis: Scholar Feasts Body and Mind," *The Commercial Appeal*, January 12, 1994.

99 **"advance the friendship"**: McConaughy, "Foreword."

99 **"cooking is a vital part of a country's culture"**: Fu, *Wuwei*, 133.

100 **slogan quickly goes viral**: Gavin Yeung, " 'Love Our People Like You Love Our Food': How Overseas Asians Are Fighting Racism with Food," *Tatler*, March 30, 2021, https://www.tatlerasia.com/dining/food/hk-how-overseas-asians-are-fighting-racism-through-food.

CHAPTER 5—MUST A HOUSEWIFE FORGET HERSELF?

105 **"symbols of industriousness," "abilities and graceful bearing"**: Huang Beilang, "Linlangmanmu, huasefanduo: Fu Peimei de weiqun dazhan," [A feast for the eyes, a wide variety of designs: Fu Pei-mei's major apron exhibit], *Lianhe bao*, January 20, 1977.

105 **measurements and sewing instructions:** "Fu Peimei de weiqun shijie" [Fu Pei-mei's apron world], *Jiating yuekan* (March 1977), 105.

106 **"tradition of 'men manage the outer' "**: Lu Hsiu-lien, *Xin nuxing zhuyi* [New Feminism] 4th ed. (Taipei: Qianwei chubanshe, 1990), 124.

106 **"We support struggles toward gender equality"**: Kate Cairns and Josée Johnston, *Food and Femininity* (London: Bloomsbury, 2015), 5.

107 **feeding the family:** Marjorie L. DeVault, *Feeding the Family: The Social Organization of Caring as Gendered Work* (Chicago: The University of Chicago Press, 1991).

107 **poem:** Chu Honglian, "Fu Peimei de 'lishi' weiqun' " [Fu Pei-mei's historical aprons], *Zhongguo shibao*, January 21, 1977. Translation is my own.

107 **"in her everyday life":** Fu Pei-mei, *Wuwei bazhen de suiyue* (Taipei: Juzi chuban youxian gongsi, 2000), 38.

107 **Meng Jiao:** Poem translation is my own.

108 **"I never thought about it back then":** Fu, *Wuwei*, 60.

108 **"It's not like I can't take care of you":** Cheng An-chi, author interview, May 19, 2014.

109 **"had the authority and the money":** Fu, *Wuwei*, 63.

109 **"This is money that you earned yourself!":** Fu, *Wuwei*, 63.

109 **20,000 yuan:** Fu, *Wuwei*, 63.

109 **"It was *mianzi*":** Arthur Zich, "Taiwan Tastes: Munching One's Way Through the Other China," *Islands Magazine* (Mar–Apr 1999), 105.

110 **"she had exhausted her dowry":** "Woking Ambassador," *Taiwan Today*, originally published September 1, 1992, https://taiwantoday.tw/news.php?post=25 268&unit=20,29,35,45.

110 **"study to make up for any deficiencies":** Huang Tong, "Pengzhe huangjin xue chuyi" [Offering up gold to learn the culinary arts], *Fandian shijie* 6 (2011), 12. All quotes in this paragraph from the same source.

111 **"I had not one ounce of regret":** Fu, *Wuwei*, 75.

111 **Lu Hsiu-lien:** Biographical details from Hsiu-lien Lu and Ashley Esarey, *My Fight for a New Taiwan: One Woman's Journey from Prison to Power* (Seattle: University of Washington Press, 2016), 48.

112 ***Semiotics of the Kitchen:*** "Martha Rosler—Semiotics of the Kitchen, 1975," uploaded October 8, 2017, YouTube, https://www.youtube.com/watch?v=ZuZy mpOIGC0.

112 **"importance of cooking to women surpasses":** Fu Pei-mei, *Dianshi shipu* [*The Television Cookbook*] (Taipei: Dianshizhoukan she, 1965), 2.

112 **"woman-to-woman":** Friedan as quoted in Jocelyn Olcott, *International Women's Year: The Greatest Consciousness-Raising Event in History* (New York: Oxford University Press), 9.

113 **Conference organizers had invited:** Doris T. Chang, *Women's Movements in Twentieth-Century Taiwan* (Urbana: University of Illinois Press, 2009), 86.

113 **"I was the first one to ask":** Lu, *My Fight*, 52.

113 **"Taiwanese women have different cultural reference points":** Lu, *My Fight*, 70.

114 **"dark side of society":** Lu, *My Fight*, 70.

114 **"encourage cooperation and division of labor":** "Yijia zhi zhuye yao hui zhu, qiekan laofu shouyi ruhe" [A master of the house must also be able to cook: see how your old man's skill compares], *Lianhe Bao*, February 22, 1976.

114 **"We welcome husbands and wives":** "Yijia zhi zhuye."

114 **two Chinese dishes:** "Yijia zhi zhuye."

114 **"no longer be the sole territory of women":** "Nanshi pengtiao haocai" [Men cook good dishes], *Lianhe Bao*, March 7, 1976.

114 **a thousand spectators:** "Nanshi pengren bai yao fenchen: yi jia zhi zhu wuwei tiaohe" [Gentlemen cooks in a profuse display: one family cooks five flavors in harmony], *Lianhe Bao*, March 8, 1976.

114 **dishes cooked by the winners:** "Liang Xuan Xiao Qing jinyinshuangqiu, gegedoufu shouzu shicuo" [Liang Xuan and Xiao Qing's gold and silver balls; losing one's head over fragrant tofu], *Lianhe Bao*, March 8, 1976.

115 **original tune:** For a recording of the original song, see "Zhi yao wo zhang da" [Just let me grow up], Taiwan yinsheng 100 nian, National Museum of Taiwan History, https://audio.nmth.gov.tw/audio/zh-TW/Item/Detail/bcf4eeac-aeaa -45cf-86c5-c0d3b3ba688b.

115 **"Who says a gentleman stays away from the kitchen?":** "Gege baba jin chu fang: zheng zhu jian chao yangyang qiang" [Older brother and dad go into the

kitchen: steaming, boiling, pan-frying, stir-frying—they can do it all], *Lianhe Bao*, March 4, 1976.

116 **Fu had praised the artist Zhang Jie's:** "Liang Xuan."

116 **"Some wives think":** Chen Changhua, "Zhang Jie tan zuocai: shi yi zhong xiangshou" [Zhang Jie talks about cooking: it's a type of enjoyment], *Lianhe Bao*, March 2, 1976.

116 **"Tea Talk on Women":** "Shiwu wei jiechu nuxing jiang changtan chenggong yinsu" [Fifteen prominent women will speak openly about the factors of success], *Lianhe Bao*, March 5, 1976. All quotes in this paragraph from the same source.

117 **Madam Weiwei:** Weiwei furen, "Liangxing jiaose duitiao huodong" [Swapping roles of the two sexes events], *Lianhe Bao*, March 8, 1976. All quotes in this paragraph from the same source.

118 **"Do you wish that your own married life":** "Jiehun yihou xilie zuotanhui" [After Marriage symposium series], *Jiating yuekan* 10 (July 1977), 19.

118 **"I'm not making excuses for men":** "Jiating zhufu yiding yao 'wangwo' ma?" [Must a housewife forget herself?], *Jiating yuekan* 10 (July 1977), 16.

118 **Mr. Hu Qingheng stood up:** "Jiating zhufu yiding yao 'wangwo' ma?", 18.

118 **"Must a housewife forget herself?":** "Jiating zhufu yiding yao 'wangwo' ma?", 16–17. All quotes in this paragraph from the same source.

120 **Susanna Foo:** Susanna Foo, author's interview, June 3, 2020. All quotes and details in this and following five paragraphs from the same source.

123 *Philadelphia Inquirer*: The original review did not actually call Susanna's restaurant the "best Chinese restaurant in Center City," as Foo stated during our interview. Reviewer Elaine Tait did, however, praise Foo's "modern and eclectic style." Elaine Tait, "A Worldly Style of Chinese," *Philadelphia Inquirer*, November 1, 1987.

123 **"I designed an apron":** Lu, *My Fight,* 83–84. Lu's quotations in this paragraph from the same source.

124 **apex of her political career:** In recent years, Lu's political status has dimmed, tarnishing her feminist historical legacy. Her views have demonstrated "virulent homophobia and racism," as one reporter put it, "providing the perfect illustration of how many of yesterday's revolutionaries have become today's reactionaries in contemporary Taiwan." See Brian Hioe, "Annette Lu illustrates how yesterday's revolutionaries are today's reactionaries in contemporary Taiwan," https://newbloommag.net/2019/09/20/annette-lu-conservative -shift/. For an analysis of Lu's political legacy as vice president, see Wen-hui Anna Tang and Emma J. Teng, "Looking again at Taiwan's Lu Hsiu-lien: A female vice president or a feminist vice president?" *Women's Studies International Forum* 56 (May–June 2016), 92–102.

KITCHEN CONVERSATION—THE WORKING MOM

This transcript has been edited and condensed for clarity from author's interview with Catherine Chen, August 16, 2019.

CHAPTER 6—CULINARY AMBASSADOR TO THE WORLD

133 **feasted on pea sprouts:** Raymond Sokolov, "The Menus at Peking Banquets Didn't Do Justice to the Foods," *New York Times*, February 26, 1972.

134 **"approximating the dishes served"**: "Two Dishes Served in the Great Hall," *New York Times*, February 26, 1972.

134 **"Julia Child of Chinese cooking"**: Raymond Sokolov, "Pei-Mei's Cold (and Hot) Salads," *New York Times Magazine*, July 25, 1971.

134 **James Soong**: James Soong, "Foreword," in Fu Pei-mei, *Wuwei bazhen de suiyue* [Years of five flavors and eight treasures] (Zonghe: Juzi chuban youxian gongsi, 2000), 17. All quotes in this paragraph from the same source.

137 **Yoshiko Yamaguchi**: Weng Yumin, "Fu Peimei: geile women sishinian xingfu de ren," [Fu Pei-Mei: A person who has given us forty years of happiness], *Jiangyi* 28:4 (January 2001), 32.

137 **sent Fu to a Japanese elementary school**: Fu, *Wuwei*, 19.

137 **"to propagandize for Chinese culture"**: "Fu Pei-mei de wuwei bazhen de suiyue" [Fu Pei-mei's years of five flavors and eight treasures], *Jiating Yuekan* no. 240 (November 2000): 79.

137 **foreign journalists**: Cheng An-chi, *Mama de cai: Fu Peimei jiachuan xingfu de ziwei* [*Mom's dishes: Fu Pei-mei hands down the taste of family happiness*] (Taipei: Sanyoushu, 2014), 9.

137 **"person-to-person diplomacy"**: Fu, *Wuwei*, 133–134. All quotes in this paragraph from the same source.

138 **"A revolution is not a dinner party"**: Mao Zedong, "Report on an Investigation of the Peasant Movement in Hunan," March 1927. *Selected Works of Mao Zedong*, vol. 1. https://www.marxists.org/reference/archive/mao/selected-works/volume-1/mswv1_2.htm.

138 **"pay close attention to the well-being"**: Mao Zedong, "Be concerned with the well-being of the masses, pay attention to methods of work," January 1934. *Selected Works of Mao Zedong*, vol. 1. https://www.marxists.org/reference/archive/mao/selected-works/volume-1/mswv1_10.htm.

138 **six-month food supply in twenty days**: Gene Hsin Chang and Guanzhong James Wen, "Communal Dining and the Chinese Famine of 1958–61," *Economic Development and Cultural Change* 46, no. 1 (October 1997): 5.

138 **cookbook for communal canteens**: *Gonggong shitang pengrenfa* [*Cooking methods for communal cafeterias*] (Shanghai: Shanghai yinshi fuwu gongsi, 1959). Subsequent quotes in this paragraph from the same source.

139 **"People's canteens are great!"**: "The Commune's Dining Hall Is Powerful, the Dishes Are Deliciously Made. You Eat Like You Wish, Production Ambitions Are Rising" *Chineseposters.net*, accessed November 9, 2021, https://chineseposters.net/posters/e16-204. The translation of the poster text in the chapter is my own.

139 **"near-total eclipse"**: Sasha Gong and Scott D. Seligman, *The Cultural Revolution Cookbook* (Hong Kong: Earnshaw Books, 2011), 9.

140 **exhibition material for international book fairs**: Fu, *Peimei*, vol. II, 2.

140 *Cookbook for the Masses*: *Dazhong caipu* [Cookbook for the masses] (Beijing: Qinggongye chubanshe, 1973).

140 **"Our country has five thousand years"**: Fu, *Peimei*, vol. I, 2.

141 **"Our China position will not support"**: "Conversation Between President Nixon and the Ambassador to the Republic of China (McConaughy)," National Archives, Nixon Presidential Materials, White House Tapes, Oval Office, Conversation No. 532–17, June 30, 1971, https://history.state.gov/historicaldocuments/frus1969–76v17/d136.

141 **the rest of the body voted**: UN General Assembly, 26th session: 1976th ple-

nary meeting, Monday, October 25, 1971, New York. Resolution 2758, ¶477, https://digitallibrary.un.org/record/735611?ln=en.

142 **"peaceful, affluent, and happy environment"**: Fu, *Peimei*, vol. II, 2.

142 **"just over $3 billion"**: "Conversation," National Archives.

143 **"At present, it is only in Taiwan"**: Fu, *Peimei*, vol. III, 3.

145 **Food Logistics Training Center**: Fu, *Wuwei*, 101.

146 **"hodgepodge picture"**: Fu, *Wuwei*, 102.

146 **9 × 15 cm tray**: Fu, *Wuwei*, 155.

146 **cashew chicken, oil-dripped chicken, or red-braised beef**: "Huahang gongying daodi Zhongguocai, tiaohe dianding youlao Fu Peimei" [China Airlines to provide authentic Chinese dishes, Fu Pei-mei works to harmonize their cooking pots], *Lianhe Bao*, November 4, 1973.

146 **"didn't understand Chinese food"**: "Huahang."

147 **fingers were too beefy**: Fu, *Wuwei*, 156.

147 **"Do something for your country!"**: Fu, *Wuwei*, 151–2.

147 **"English newspapers in the Philippines"**: Hong Liante, "Fu Pei-mei pengren zhi lü de shouhuo" [Cooking travels: Fu Pei-mei's harvest], *Zhongguo shibao*, June 24, 1972.

148 **"color of the bean paste"**: Da Fang, "Pengtiao dashi Fu Peimei" [Culinary ambassador Fu Pei-mei], *Jiating yuekan* 20 (May 1978): 18.

148 **"overseas Chinese living in the Philippines"**: Hong, "Fu Pei-mei."

149 **"native ingredients as substitutes"**: "Fu Pei-mei fu Fei chuanshou Zhongguocai" [Fu Pei-mei goes to the Philippines to teach about Chinese food], *Jingji ribao*, May 6, 1972.

149 **one hundred rolling pins**: "Fu Pei-mei," *Jingji ribao*, May 6, 1972.

149 **"They like to eat meat in large pieces"**: Zhong Lizhu, "Fu Peimei dao Aozhou chuanbo Zhongguo chi de yishu" [Fu Pei-mei goes to Australia to transmit the art of Chinese food], *Jiating yuekan* 100 (January 1985): 107–110.

149 **"Australian shadow"**: Zhong, "Fu Peimei." All quotes in this paragraph from the same source.

150 **Society pages**: Carmen Perez, "Day and Night," *Manila Daily Bulletin*, May 28, 1972; uncredited photo of "Chinese Cook Fu Pei Mei," Society Section, *Philippines Daily Express*, May 28, 1972.

150 **middle state powers**: Shannon Haugh et al., eds., special issue on gastrodiplomacy, *Public Diplomacy Magazine* 11 (2014).

152 **graphic visualizations of Taiwanese identity**: Anne Quito, "A quirky passport design contest evokes Taiwan's search for national identity," *Quartz*, August 25, 2020, https://qz.com/1891180/covid-19-caused-taiwan-to-redesign-its-passport/.

152 **Cha House**: "Welcome to Cha House," Cha House, accessed November 9, 2021, https://www.chahouseusa.com.

152 **Möge TEE**: "About," Möge TEE, accessed November 9, 2021, https://mogeteeusa.com/.

153 **Fu never drank bubble tea**: Cheng An-chi, personal communication with author, July 6, 2023.

CHAPTER 7—DINNER IN SEVENTEEN MINUTES

157 **"like long dragons"**: Fu Pei-mei, *Wuwei bazhen de suiyue* [Years of five flavors and eight treasures] (Zhonghe: Juzi chuban youxian gongsi, 2000). 159. All quotes and details in this paragraph from the same source.

158 **small research lab**: Fu, *Wuwei*, 158.

158 **"When I wrote the recipes":** Fu, *Wuwei*, 161.
158 **"Colors would fade":** Fu, *Wuwei*, 159.
158 **"our tongues had long ago":** Fu, *Wuwei*, 159.
159 **"Starting in ancient times":** Fu, *Wuwei*, 164.
159 **"If you could package tasty":** Fu, *Wuwei*, 160.
159 **"That's what society needs now":** "A Woking Ambassador," *Taiwan Today*, https://taiwantoday.tw/news.php?post=25268&unit=20,29,35,45, originally published in *Taiwan Review*, September 1, 1992.
160 **needs of younger housewives:** Fu, *Wuwei*, 129.
161 **"Unlike the previous generation":** Fu Pei-mei, *Dianshi shipu disance* [*The Television Cookbook, vol. 3*] (Taipei: Dianshi zhoukan she, 1970), 1.
161 **"All of her energies":** Chu Honglian, "Fu Peimei nushi he sucheng Zhongguo-cai," [Fu Pei-mei and speedy Chinese food], *Zhongguo shibao*, July 26, 1971. All quotes in this paragraph from the same source.
162 **first domestic company . . . instant ramen noodles:** Lin Zhengzhong, et al., "Paomian, yi chi 57 nian" [We've eaten instant ramen for 57 years], *Lianhe xinwen wang*, August 25, 2015, https://udn.com/upf/newmedia/2015_vist/08/20150825_noodle_03/index.html.
163 **"I would have to tackle issues or topics":** Fu, *Wuwei*, 160–161.
163 **collaborated on developing:** Fu, *Wuwei*, 162. See a copy of Fu's original hand-written notes for the Man-Han beef noodle recipe in Zhang Zhesheng, "Fu Pei-mei yu Manhan Dacan" [Fu Pei-mei and Man-Han Imperial Feast], January 8, 2019, *Yahoo Travel*, https://yahoo-twtravel-beefnoodles.tumblr.com/post/181831740332/%E5%82%85%E5%9F%B9%E6%A2%85%E8%88%87%E6%BB%BF%E6%BC%A2%E5%A4%A7%E9%A4%90.
163 **US$3 million in sales:** Jim Hwang, "Three Minutes to Go," *Taiwan Today*, accessed November 10, 2021, https://taiwantoday.tw/news.php?post=12808&unit=8,29,32,45, originally published in *Taiwan Review*, June 1, 2007.
163 **six different varieties:** Zhang Zhesheng, "34 nianqian, Fu Peimei zhidao yanfa de 'Manhan dacan' sushimian shangshi" [34 years ago, the Man-Han Imperial Feast instant noodles, guided by Fu Pei-mei in R&D, hit the market], Facebook, February 15, 2017, https://m.facebook.com/zhangzhesheng/posts/10155038377789531/.
163 **second generation improvement:** Zhang, "34."
164 **entire automated assembly line from Japan:** Fu, *Wuwei*, 163.
164 **Luke Tsai:** Luke Tsai, author interview, May 15, 2019. All quotes in this paragraph from the same source.
164 **orange juice concentrate, fish sticks, and turkey TV dinners:** Laura Shapiro, *Something from the Oven: Reinventing Dinner in 1950s America* (New York: Penguin Books, 2004), 10–20. Interestingly, the American Frigi-Dinner company even offered mid-century consumers a frozen "Chinese platter," with egg rolls, fried rice, and chicken chow mein. Shapiro, 18.
165 **"When you bring up frozen vegetables":** Fu Pei-mei, "Lengdong shucai zenme chao?" [How do you stir-fry frozen vegetables?], *Jiating yuekan* 23 (August 1978): 118.
165 **per capita consumption of frozen foods:** "Fast, Fresh and Fancy," *Taiwan Today*, https://taiwantoday.tw/news.php?post=22451&unit=12,29,33,45, originally published in *Taiwan Review*, September 1, 1992.
165 **Ajinomoto:** Fu, *Wuwei*, 167–168.
166 **ninety percent of urban households:** Liao Rongli, "Zhufu de ershisi xiaoshi" [The 24 hours of the housewife], *Jiating yuekan* 11 (August 1977): 44.

166 **"The Secrets of Using Your Refrigerator"**: Yuan Minglun, "Shiyong bingxiang aomiao" [The secrets of using your refrigerator], *Jiating yuekan* (January 1977): 95. All details and quotes in this and the following paragraph from the same source.

167 **fifty-eight percent, still reported shopping**: Liao, "Zhufu," 44.

167 **"the environment is clean"**: Xiao Hui, "Caichang li de renqingwei" [The human feeling of vegetable markets], *Jiating yuekan* 12 (September 1977): 126–127.

167 **"fish balls"**: Xiao Hui, "Caichang."

168 **"Hey boss"**: Xiao Hui, "Caichang." All quotes in this and the following paragraph from the same source.

169 **"With just the press of a button"**: Litton Microwave Cooking, advertisement, *Jiating yuekan* 28 (January 1979): 121.

169 **"Saving you three-quarters"**: Sampo Heavenly Chef microwave, advertisement, *Jiating yuekan* 36 (September 1979): 151.

169 **"No more smoke and oil"**: Litton Microwave Cooking, advertisement.

169 **"changing women's lives!"**: National microwave, advertisement, *Jiating yuekan* 34 (July 1979): 127.

169 **"Get home at 6 p.m."**: National microwave, advertisement, *Jiating yuekan* (January 1980): 129.

169 **"If you are a career woman"**: National microwave, advertisement (July 1979).

170 **"shallow-fry, stir-fry, steam"**: Sampo Heavenly Chef microwave, advertisment.

170 **advocated for the use of wood charcoal in a brazier**: Huang Yuanshan, "Preface," *Yuanshan shipu* [Yuanshan cookbook], vol. 1 (Taipei: Sanmin shuju, 1954), 20.

170 **"squatting on the ground"**: Dan Li, "Wasi: chufang de zhujue" [Gas: the kitchen's leading role], *Jiating Yuekan* (February 1977): 116–117.

170 **"Cooking is no longer"**: Hotai Miaomiao gas burner, advertisement, *Dianshi zhoukan* 417 (October 5, 1970), back cover.

170 **"Quick Cooking Institute"**: National microwave, advertisement, *Jiating yuekan* 45 (June 1980): 133.

170 **Elizabeth Huang**: Elizabeth Huang, *Microwave Cooking Chinese Style* (Taipei: Wei Chuan Cooking Institute, 1988).

171 **"Fried Beefsteak"**: Litton Microwave Cooking, advertisement, *Jiating yuekan* (March 1980): 127.

171 **microwaved Peking roast duck recipe**: Gail Forman, "New Wave Microwave," *The Washington Post*, February 1, 1984, https://www.washingtonpost.com/archive/lifestyle/food/1984/02/01/new-wave-microwave/959e1c5a-593d-49ac-90eb-de8f640f9883/.

171 **sitting down to a simple bowl of instant ramen**: Cheng An-chi, author interview, September 17, 2014.

172 **"The procedures required"**: "Woking Ambassador."

172 **"Working women's attitudes have changed"**: Fu, *Wuwei*, 100–101.

172 **"serving Korean barbecue"**: David Y. H. Wu, "McDonald's in Taipei: Hamburgers, Betel Nuts, and National Identity," Chapter 3 in *Golden Arches East*, ed. James L. Watson (Stanford, CA: Stanford University Press, 2006), 115. Originally published in 1997.

172 **131 McDonald's franchises**: Wu, "McDonald's," 121.

173 **Mai-Dang-Le**: Xiang Qiuping, "Xishi liansuo canting lianlian tuichu: chi de yishu mianling kaoyan" [Western-style chain restaurants keep appearing: The art of eating is put to the test], *Jiating yuekan* 88 (January 1984), 55–64.

173 **"fried chicken, hamburgers"**: Xiang, "Xishi." All quotes in this paragraph from the same source.

173 **"opportunities for eating out"**: Wu Wanru, "Fu Peimei de pengren suiyue" [Fu Pei-mei's years of cooking], *Jiangyi* 20:4 (January 1997), 71.

174 **"In order to adapt to the needs"**: Wu, "Fu Peimei," 71. Subsequent quotes in this paragraph from the same source.

174 **Ringer Hut**: Fu, *Wuwei*, 165.

174 **"frequently changing content"**: Fu, *Wuwei*, 120. All quotes in this paragraph from the same source.

CHAPTER 8—WHAT SHE PUT ON THE TABLE

180 **manga version**: Zuo Xuan, *Wuwei bazhen de suiyue* (Taipei : Yuandongli wenhua shiye youxian gongsi, 2017).

180 **"Ah Chun's life course"**: "Renwu jieshao: Lin Chun" [Cast of characters: Lin Chun], *What She Put on the Table* series website, accessed July 20, 2021, https://www.ttv.com.tw/drama16/Qseries/WhatShePutOntheTable/cast.asp?PID=3.

180 **"Thank you for accompanying me"**: *What She Put on the Table*, episode 6, aired August 18, 2018, on Taiwan Television. As of 2021, the entire series is available for streaming on Netflix.

181 **"one is light-skinned"**: Guan Renjian, "Tamen weishenme kongju Taiyu gonggong dianshitai?" [Why are they scared of a Taiwanese language public television station?], *Newtalk*, October 5, 2017, https://newtalk.tw/news/view/2017–10–05/99619.

182 **"Back then, almost all the friends"**: Weng Yumin, "Fu Peimei: Geile women sishinian xingfu de ren" [Fu Pei-mei: giving us forty years of happiness], *Jiangyi* 28, no. 4 (January 2001): 28–35.

182 **"I was a Taiwanese kid"**: Chen Yingzhou, author interview, September 29, 2014.

183 **"For decades after 1949"**: Steven Crook and Katy Hui-wen Hung, *A Culinary History of Taipei: Beyond Pork and Ponlai* (Lanham, MD: Rowman & Littlefield, 2018), ix.

183 **"We weren't used to eating Taiwanese tastes"**: Ellen Huang King, author interview, January 24, 2017.

184 **"hers were the standard ones"**: Monica "Nicki" Croghan, author interview, March 7, 2023.

184 **required the ability to speak Mandarin**: Shelley Rigger, *Why Taiwan Matters: Small Island, Global Powerhouse* (Lanham, MD: Rowman & Littlefield, 2011), 28–30.

185 **"How can you put ordinary home-cooking"**: "Renwu zhuanfang: Shinyeh 100 sui Ah-ma—Li Xiuying Dongshizhang" [Profile of Shin Yeh's 100-year-old Amah and the Chairman of the Board, Li Xiuying], Genzhe dongshizhang qu lüxing, [Traveling with the Chairman of the Board], accessed February 22, 2021, https://www.taiwanviptravel.com/articles/shinyeh-founder/.

186 **"In terms of taste, Taiwanese cuisine"**: Fu Pei-mei, *Peimei shipu* [Pei Mei's Chinese Cook Book], vol. III, (Taipei: Fu Peimei, 1979), 269.

186 *Delicious Taiwanese Cuisine*: Fu Pei-mei, "Xu" [Preface], in Fu Pei-mei and Cheng An-chi, *Meiwei Taicai: guzaowei yu xiandaifeng* (Taipei: Taolue chuban, 1998).

186 **"Fu Pei-mei era"**: Pan Tsung-yi, "Fu Peimei yu Aji Shi zhi wai: Zhanhou Taiwan de shipu chuban qushi yu bianqian" ["Beyond Fu Pei-mei and Master

Ah-chi: Trends and changes in postwar Taiwan cookbook publishing"], *Journal of Chinese Dietary Culture* 16, no. 1 (2020): 115–177.

187 **Chen Yujen:** Chen Yujen, "Taiwanese Cuisine and Nationhood in the Twentieth Century," in *Modern Chinese Foodways*, edited by Wendy Jia-chen Fu, Michelle King, Jakob Klein (forthcoming). See also Chen Yujen, *"Taiwancai" de wenhua shi: Shiwu xiaofei zhong de guojia xian* [A cultural history of "Taiwanese cuisine": The manifestation of nation in food consumption] (Xinbeishi, Taiwan: Jingji chuban shiye, 2020).

187 **2013 encyclopedia:** Zhao Rongguang, ed., *Zhongguo yinshi wenhua shi* [The History of Chinese Dietetic Culture], 10 vols. (Beijing: Zhongguo qinggongye chubanshe, 2013). Taiwan appears in the fifth volume, on the Southeast Region.

188 **"I don't go to her cookbooks":** Kian Lam Kho, author interview, February 8, 2021.

188 **Tiffany Liu:** Tiffany Liu, author interview, December 10, 2020. All quotes and details from this and following two paragraphs from the same source.

191 **2020 poll:** Wu Po-hsuan and William Hetherington, "Record number identify as 'Taiwanese,' poll finds,", *Taipei Times*, July 5, 2020, https://www.taipeitimes.com/News/front/archives/2020/07/05/2003739375.

191 **"I have grandparents":** "Jeremy Lin 林書豪: "Chinese, Taiwanese, and American" Heritage—Ethnicity—Nationality," uploaded on February 16, 2013, YouTube video, 0:48, https://www.youtube.com/watch?v=tKslZGjGam0.

192 **"Nobody wanted it":** Cathy Erway, author interview, June 1, 2019. All quotes in this paragraph from the same source.

192 **"I wanted to make a book":** Erway, interview.

192 **maternal grandparents:** Cathy Erway, *The Food of Taiwan: Recipes from the Beautiful Island* (New York: Houghton Mifflin Harcourt, 2015), 13.

192 **"American-born, half-Taiwanese":** Erway, *Food*, 19.

193 **"that's what Pei Mei says":** Erway, interview.

193 **cookbook about modern Taiwanese cuisine:** Clarissa Wei with Ivy Chen, *Made in Taiwan: Recipes and Stories from the Island Nation* (Simon Element, 2023).

193 **"Taiwanese food is its own distinct cuisine":** Clarissa Wei, author interview, November 11, 2021. All quotes in this and the following paragraph from the same source.

195 **"America's Johnny Carson":** Fu Pei-mei, *Wuwei bazhen de suiyue* (Taipei: Juzi chuban youxian gongsi, 2000), 118.

195 **schedule was grueling:** Fu, *Wuwei*, 117–119. All details in this paragraph from the same source.

196 **wrote to complain:** Cheng An-chi, author interview, May 19, 2014.

196 **Her right hand shook:** Cheng An-chi, author interview, September 17, 2014.

196 **"I am now going to start living for myself":** Cheng An-chi, author interview, September 17, 2014.

196 **fashion designer:** Cheng An-chi, author interview, September 17, 2014.

197 **syndication:** Cheng An-chi, author interview, September 17, 2014.

197 **"Coming home after school":** Chen Jingyi (Chen Shala), "Guoxiaoshi, wo shi suowei de 'yaoshi ertong'" ["When I was in elementary school, I was a 'latchkey kid'"], Facebook, September 15, 2014, https://www.facebook.com/permalink.php?story_fbid=10152190683721116&id=558946115. My thanks to Fang Ling (Cybie) of Shin Yeh Restaurants, Taipei, for sharing this Facebook post. All quotes in this paragraph from the same source.

198 **Grace Wu:** Ya-Ke "Grace" Wu, author interview, September 1, 2020. All of Wu's quotes in this and following five paragraphs from the same source.

KITCHEN CONVERSATION—THE NOVICE

This transcript has been edited and condensed for clarity from the author's interview with Christy Fu, May 13, 2021. Original interview in Chinese and English, all translations are my own.

CHAPTER 9—A COOKBOOK IN EVERY SUITCASE

212 **first time she tried to cook:** Ellen Huang King, author interview, January 24, 2017. All quotes and details in this paragraph from the same source.

213 **"Why was that one special?":** King, interview.

214 **"There is not a dish in its pages":** Pearl S. Buck, "Preface," in Buwei Yang Chao, *How to Cook and Eat in Chinese*, 3rd ed. (New York, Vintage, 1963) [orig. 1945], xviii.

215 **sold more than seventy thousand copies:** Niu Yue, "Carrying on a Chinese food legacy," *China Daily USA*, uploaded April 2, 2015, http://usa.chinadaily .com.cn/world/2015-04/02/content_19985670.htm.

215 *I want some of that:* Joyce Chen, *The Joyce Chen Cookbook* (New York: J. B. Lippincott, 1962), 5.

216 **slurp her hot soup:** Chao, *How to Cook*, 13.

216 **"written with blood":** Chen, *Joyce Chen*, 221.

216 **"which he thinks Americans like better":** Chao, *How to Cook*, xxii.

216 **"Remember, you can watch Joyce Chen":** Dana Polan, "Joyce Chen Cooks and the Upscaling of Chinese food in America in the 1960s," Open Vault from GBH, accessed February 25, 2022, https://openvault.wgbh.org/exhibits/ art_of_asian_cooking/media.

219 **"We got together almost every weekend":** King, interview. All quotes in this and following two paragraphs from the same source.

220 **"You couldn't even buy soy sauce":** Jane Tou, author interview, July 2, 2021.

221 **Rodeitcher's:** Deborah Brown, "Rodeitcher's sale brings history of storied past and its famous visitors," MLive.com, updated January 21, 2019. The 1940 census records show one Chinese man, Sing Lum, age 38, living in the Rodeitcher household in Freeland. Sing Lum in the 1940 Census, Archives.com, accessed March 9, 2022, http://www.archives.com/1940-census/sing-lum-mi -121164349.

221 **"American food—chop suey":** Tou, interview.

221 **adult education center:** Tou, interview. All quotes and details in this and the following paragraph from the same source.

223 **"well over half of all Chinese in the United States":** Madeline Hsu, *Dreaming of Gold, Dreaming of Home: Transnationalism and Migration Between the United States and South China, 1882–1943* (Stanford University Press, 2000), 3.

224 **"Whether it was a simple weeknight supper":** Grace Young, *The Wisdom of the Chinese Kitchen: Classic Family Recipes for Celebration and Healing* (New York: Simon & Schuster, 1999), xiii.

224 **"stuck close to the Cantonese approach":** Ken Hom, *Easy Family Recipes from a Chinese–American Childhood* (New York: Alfred A. Knopf, 1997), 11.

224 **"We went only to Chinese-language movies":** Hom, *Easy*, 5.

225 **tiny number of 105:** "Milestone Documents: Chinese Exclusion Act (1882)," National Archives, https://www.archives.gov/milestone-documents/chinese -exclusion-act#:~:text=In%201943%2C%20when%20China%20was,the%20 right%20to%20seek%20naturalization.

225 **flat quota of 20,000 migrants per year:** "Historical Highlights: Immigration and Nationality Act of 1965, October 3, 1965" United States House of Representatives, https://history.house.gov/Historical-Highlights/1951–2000/ Immigration-and-Nationality-Act-of-1965/.

225 **Madeline Hsu:** Madeline Y. Hsu, *The Good Immigrants: How the Yellow Peril Became the Model Minority* (Princeton: Princeton University Press, 2015).

226 **Between 1966 and 1975:** Hsiang-shui Chen, *Chinatown No More: Taiwan Immigrants in Contemporary New York* (Ithaca, NY: Cornell University Press, 1992), 6.

226 **separate allotment of 20,000 spots:** Kenneth J. Guest, "From Mott Street to East Broadway: Fuzhounese Immigrants and the Revitalization of New York's Chinatown," *Journal of Chinese Overseas* 7 (2011): 29.

226 **"suburban Chinatown":** Timothy P. Fong, *The First Suburban Chinatown: The Remaking of Monterey Park, California* (Philadelphia: Temple University Press, 1994).

226 **Alice Hsu:** Joyce Michaels, "Chinese Year of the Sheep," *The Billings Gazette* (Billings, MT), January 25, 1979.

227 **Kevin Chien:** James Keeran, "The 10 Best: What 10 Books Do You Think Everybody Ought to Read to Be Culturally Well-Rounded and World Knowledgeable?" *The Pantagraph* (Bloomington, IL), April 24, 1994.

227 **Grace Liu:** Prue Salasky, "Required Reading: Need a Good Cookbook? Here Are a Few 'Necessities,'" *Daily Press* (Newport News, VA), June 6, 1996.

227 **Theresa Tang:** Carole Shelton, "Students Prepare a Variety of Chinese Dishes in Class," *The Daily News-Journal* (Murfreesboro, TN), February 15, 1984.

227 **Louise Teng:** Bill McDonald, "Year of the Rat Feast for Kids," *The State* (Columbia, SC), March 14, 1996.

227 **Shan Fang:** Mary Wallis, "Napa Valley Chef Teaches Home Cooking China Style," *The Napa Valley Register* (Napa Valley, CA), August 22, 1990.

227 **arriving indirectly from Macau:** Transcript, "The Melting Pot," *Finding Your Roots*, Season 2, Episode 5, aired October 21, 2014, https://search.alexander street.com/preview/work/bibliographic_entity%7Cvideo_work%7CC2804315.

227 **engineer at Wright-Patterson:** Liesl Schillinger, "Ming's Thing: How to Become a Celebrity Chef," *The New Yorker*, November 15, 1999, 61.

227 **"Our family joke was":** Transcript, "The Melting Pot."

CHAPTER 10—DISHES FOR A DIGITAL AGE

232 **Denise Ho:** Denise Ho, author interview, August 22, 2019. All quotes in this paragraph from the same source.

233 **"adapting recipes from her for the twenty-first century":** Jaline Girardin, Pei Mei a Day, "Mission," accessed March 30, 2022, https://peimei.wordpress .com/about/.

233 **"Let's see what Fu Pei-mei has to say":** Jaline Girardin, author interview, September 18, 2015.

233 **never chose a sea cucumber dish:** Girardin, interview.

234 *yuxiang qiezi*: Pei Mei a Day, recipe for Eggplant Sze-chuan Style.

234 *dan bing*: Pei Mei a Day, recipe for Dan Bing.

234 **Jaline's blog:** Pei Mei a Day, "Mission," from Mark (December 31, 2011) and (February 22, 2015), Carol Yu (June 10, 2012), Dennis (May 17, 2015).
235 **Google Doodle:** Google Doodles Archive, October 1, 2015, https://www.google.com/doodles/pei-mei-fus-84th-birthday.
235 **Leslie Wiser:** Luke Tsai, "Why a Small Sebastopol Farm Has 1,000 Copies of This Iconic, Out-of-Print Chinese Cookbook," Eater.com, November 17, 2020, https://sf.eater.com/2020/11/17/21570459/radical-family-farms-fu-pei-mei-chinese-cookbook-taiwan-cook-off.
235 **Every time she moved:** Leslie Wiser, author interview, June 15, 2023.
236 **"I'm not going to lie":** Radical Family Farms, Instagram post, November 20, 2020.
236 **Within a week, she had sold eight hundred:** Wiser, interview.
236 **shared images of dishes:** Radical Family Farms, Instagram, #rffcookoff.
236 **Andy Wu:** Wu Enwen, *Jingdian chongxian: Wu Enwen yujian Fu Peimei* [Andy Wu's neo-classical cookbook: A salute to Madame Fu Pei-mei], (Taipei: Sikuaiyu wenhua youxian gongsi), 12.
237 *Mom's Dishes:* Cheng Anchi, *Mama de cai: Fu Peimei jia chuan xingfu de ziwei* [Mom's dishes: Fu Pei-mei hands down the taste of family happiness], (Taipei: Juzi wenhua shiye youxian gongsi, 2014). All quotes in this paragraph from the same source.
239 **"if you just follow her recipes":** Cheng An-chi, "Mama de weidao tianshang xin fenghua" [Mother's tastes gain a new brilliance], in Wu, *Jingdian*, 4–6.
239 **Jon Tseng:** Jon Tseng, "Pei Mei's Chinese Cookbook by Fu Pei Mei: The Best Chinese Cookbook You've Never Heard of," *More Cookbooks Than Sense*, September 18, 2012, http://morecookbooksthansense.blogspot.com/2012/09/the-best-chinese-cookbook-youve-never.html.
239 **greatest number of new immigrants:** Abby Budiman, "Key Findings about U.S. Immigrants," Pew Research Center, uploaded August 20, 2020, https://www.pewresearch.org/fact-tank/2020/08/20/key-findings-about-u-s-immigrants/.
240 **number of students coming from Taiwan:** "Total Number of Students from Taiwan Studying in the United States from Academic Year 2010/11 to 2020/21," *Statista*, https://www.statista.com/statistics/945323/number-of-taiwan-students-studying-in-the-united-states/#:~:text=This%20statistic%20shows%20the%20total,were%20enrolled%20in%20graduate%20programs.
240 **some of whom may be undocumented:** One estimate from 2016 suggests that there were approximately 362,000 undocumented Chinese immigrants in the United States at the time, about three percent of the total 11.3 million undocumented immigrant population. Carlos Echeverria-Estrada and Jeanne Batalova, "Chinese Immigrants in the United States," Migration Policy Institute, uploaded January 15, 2020, https://www.migrationpolicy.org/article/chinese-immigrants-united-states-2018.
240 **2019 Pew Research Center report:** Abby Budiman, "Chinese in the U.S. Fact Sheet," Pew Research Center, uploaded April 29, 2021, https://www.pewresearch.org/social-trends/fact-sheet/asian-americans-chinese-in-the-u-s/.
240 **"graduate or professional degree":** Echeverria-Estrada and Batalova, "Chinese Immigrants."
240 **Fujianese not only:** Lauren Hilgers, "The Kitchen Network: America's Underground Chinese Restaurant Workers," *The New Yorker*, October 6, 2014; "Chinese Restaurant Workers Face Hurdles," NPR.com, May 8, 2007, https://www.npr.org/transcripts/10069448. See also David Chan's blog post about the Fujianese Chinese restaurant supply company, HF Food Group, a busi-

ness with an annual revenue of $300 million, owned by a Fujianese migrant. "Secrets of Fujianese American Restaurant Industry Go Public," February 19, 2019, http://chandavkl.blogspot.com/2019/02/.

240 **largest subethnic group:** Kenneth J. Guest, *God in Chinatown: Religion and Survival in New York's Evolving Immigrant Community* (New York: NYU Press, 2003), 3.

241 **Hannah Jian:** Hannah Jian, interview by Victoria Tran, "Bamboo House: The Many Perspectives of the New-Ending American Dream," Spring 2020, https://express.adobe.com/page/s9SQaVSfSSzW2/.

241 *Fifth Chinese Daughter:* Jade Snow Wong, *Fifth Chinese Daughter* (Seattle: University of Washington Press, 1989) [orig. 1950].

242 **Jacky Zheng:** Jacky Zheng, interview by Peter Cohen, "Chopstix," Spring 2019, https://mtking.myportfolio.com/chopstix.

242 **"making and remaking of Asian America":** Erika Lee, *The Making of Asian America: A History* (New York: Simon and Schuster, 2015), 3.

243 **"Asian Americans with long roots":** Lee, *Making*, 3.

243 **cook rice properly:** Wong, *Fifth*, 57–58. Notably, the chapter is titled, "Learning to Be a Chinese Housewife."

243 **shop for groceries:** Wong, *Fifth*, 55.

243 **egg foo young and tomato-beef:** Wong, *Fifth*, 157–161.

243 **dean asks her to cook:** Wong, *Fifth*, 170–3.

245 **seven hundred and fifty episodes:** Taiwan Television Official Channel, 傅培梅時間–想起媽媽的好味道 [Fu Pei-mei Time–Thinking of Mom's Great Taste] playlist, YouTube, accessed December 5, 2023, https://www.youtube.com/watch?v=JT49Hvx--xw&list=PLtww_vcpAB8pf-6gUA3_L_H4t39zcOTZT.

245 **dubbed into Tagalog:** Dubbed versions of Fu's program in Tagalog, originally broadcast on ABS-CBN, were uploaded to YouTube by user sandiessss (Jose Bhrix Arabit) and available as of 2015, but have since been taken down.

245 **scallion braised duck:** Episode viewing counts as of June 7, 2022. Taiwan Television Official Channel, "傅培梅時間 -香蔥扒鴨 [Scallion Braised Duck]," uploaded January 15, 2018, YouTube video, 4:59, https://www.youtube.com/watch?v=JT49Hvx--xw; "傅培梅時間—酸辣湯 [Hot and Sour Soup]," uploaded August 8, 2017, YouTube video, 6:04, https://www.youtube.com/watch?v=c3zWtthrf2o; "傅培梅時間—湖南臘肉 [Hunanese Cured Meat]," uploaded July 31, 2017, YouTube video, 4:54, https://www.youtube.com/watch?v=B-dpiUIHfvzA; "傅培梅時間—蔥燒海參 [Scallion Braised Sea Cucumber]," uploaded November 13, 2017, YouTube video, 5:56, https://www.youtube.com/watch?v=Q3feILLYEPI.

245 **"Who? I've never heard of the name":** What She Put on the Table, Episode 3, 16:36.

246 **Harrison Huang:** Harrison Huang, author interview, May 21, 2019. All quotes in this paragraph from the same source.

249 **"I don't dare say":** Fu Pei-mei, *Wuwei bazhen de suiyue* [Years of five flavors and eight treasures] (Zonghe: Juzi chuban youxian gongsi, 2000). 19.

Suggested Readings

FU PEI-MEI'S COOKBOOKS

The original editions of Fu's best-selling bilingual cookbooks are out of print but can occasionally be found through used book sellers. Fu's children have reissued her iconic three-volume series in Taiwan, but under different covers and with all new photos. If you are used to contemporary cookbooks, there is very little in the way of atmospheric discussion or rumination in Fu's cookbooks and the directions are sparse. However, if you pair her cookbooks with some episodes of Fu's iconic Taiwan Television cooking program, *Fu Pei-mei Time* (now uploaded on YouTube, https://www.youtube.com/playlist?list=PLtww_vcpAB8pf-6gUA3_L_H4t39zcOTZT, currently without English subtitles), you can begin to understand her skill and appeal.

Fu Pei-mei. *Peimei shipu diyice /Pei Mei's Chinese Cook Book Vol. I.* Taipei: Self-published, 1969. This is the classic and most popular volume of the series, with recipes arranged regionally by cardinal direction, with eastern, southern, western, and northern dishes.

———. *Peimei shipu dierce / Pei Mei's Chinese Cook Book Vol. II.* Taipei: Self-published, 1974. This volume contains recipes arranged by main ingredient or type.

———. *Peimei shipu disance / Pei Mei's Chinese Cook Book Vol. III.* Taipei: Self-published, 1979. Featuring formal banquet dishes, this volume returns to a regional format, with the addition of Hunanese, Fujianese, Taiwanese, vegetarian, and self-serve buffet dishes.

———. *Peimei shipu jiachangcai / Pei Mei's Home Style Chinese Cooking.* Taipei:

Self-published, 1980. Another popular favorite filled with easy, classic dishes, coauthored by her daughter Cheng An-chi.

CHINESE COOKBOOKS

I love collecting Chinese cookbooks and keep an ever-growing number on my shelf for reference and inspiration. I usually mix and match recipes, techniques, ingredients when I cook, depending on what I happen to have on hand and what I have time for. Here are some of my favorites from Chinese American and Taiwanese American authors. I like these cookbooks because they combine recipes with personal stories.

Anusasananan, Linda Lau. *The Hakka Cookbook: Chinese Soul Food from Around the World*. University of California Press, 2012.

Blonder, Ellen and Annabel Low. *Every Grain of Rice: A Taste of Our Chinese Childhood in America*. Clarkson Potter, 1998.

Chao, Buwei Yang. *How to Cook and Eat in Chinese*, 3rd ed. Vintage, 1963 [orig. 1945].

Erway, Cathy. *The Food of Taiwan: Recipes from the Beautiful Island*. Harvest, 2015.

Kho, Kian Lam. *Phoenix Claws and Jade Tree: Essential Techniques of Authentic Chinese Cooking*. Clarkson Potter, 2015.

Lin, Hsiang Ju and Tsuifeng Lin. *Chinese Gastronomy*. New York: Pyramid Publications, 1972 [orig. pub. 1969].

Lin Tsuifeng and Lin Hsiangju. *Cooking with the Chinese Flavour*. William Heinemann, 1957 [orig. pub. 1956].

Wei, Clarissa, with Ivy Chen. *Made in Taiwan: Recipes and Stories from the Island Nation*. Simon Element, 2023.

Young, Grace. *The Wisdom of the Chinese Kitchen: Chinese Family Recipes for Celebration and Healing*. Simon and Schuster, 1999.

One of my favorite websites for Chinese recipes is *The Woks of Life* (https://thewoksoflife.com/) from Bill, Judy, Sarah, and Kaitlin Leung, which got its start in 2013. I love that the enterprise is a family affair, and the main reason for its inception was for the adult daughters to learn how to cook from their parents. Now also in hardback cookbook form.

Bill, Judy, Sarah, and Kaitlin Leung, *The Woks of Life: Recipes to Know and Love from a Chinese American Family: A Cookbook*. Clarkson Potter, 2022.

CHINESE, TAIWANESE, AND CHINESE AMERICAN FOOD

There have been a growing number of scholarly and popular books about Chinese, Taiwanese, and Chinese American food published recently. Despite the number of titles with "chop suey" in them, there is much more to Chinese American food history than chop suey!

Chen, Yong. *Chop Suey, USA: The Story of Chinese Food in America*. Columbia University Press, 2014.

Coe, Andrew. *Chop Suey: A Cultural History of Chinese Food in the United States*. Oxford University Press, 2009.

Crook, Steven and Katy Hui-wen Hung. *A Culinary History of Taipei: Beyond Pork and Ponlai*. Rowman & Littlefield, 2018.

Dunlop, Fuchsia. *Invitation to a Banquet: The Story of Chinese Food*. W. W. Norton, 2023.

Huang, Eddie. *Fresh Off the Boat: A Memoir*. One World, 2013.

Lee, Jennifer 8. *Fortune Cookie Chronicles: Adventures in the World of Chinese Food*. Twelve, 2009.

Liu, Haiming. *From Canton Restaurant to Panda Express: A History of Chinese Food in the United States*. Rutgers University Press, 2015.

Mendelson, Anne. *Chow Chop Suey: Food and the Chinese American Journey*. Columbia University Press, 2016.

Phillips, Carolyn. *At the Chinese Table: A Memoir with Recipes*. W. W. Norton, 2022.

TAIWANESE AND ASIAN AMERICAN HISTORY

For readers wishing to have a deeper contextual understanding of modern Chinese and Taiwanese relations and history, excellent studies abound. Most books on Taiwan's postwar history focus on the fraught political tension between Taiwan and China, or Taiwan's economic rise, but several of the books listed below focus more on its rich cultural and social history. There are also numerous excellent introductions to Asian American history.

Allen, Joseph R. *Taipei: City of Displacements*. University of Washington Press, 2011.

Hsu, Madeline. *The Good Immigrants: How the Yellow Peril Became the Model Minority*. Princeton University Press, 2017.

Lee, Erika. *The Making of Asian America: A History*. Simon and Schuster, 2015.

Lee, Jessica. *Two Trees Make a Forest: In Search of My Family's Past Among Taiwan's Mountains and Coasts*. Catapult, 2020.

Lin, Hsiao-ting. *Accidental State: Chiang Kai-shek, the United States, and the Making of Taiwan*. Harvard University Press, 2016.

Rigger, Shelley. *Why Taiwan Matters: Small Island, Global Powerhouse*. Rowman & Littlefield, 2011.

Illustration Credits

Frontispiece: Photograph on page ii courtesy of Cheng An-chi.

Introduction: Freezer food list on page xiii courtesy of Ellen Huang King.

Chapters 1, 2, and 3: Photographs on pages 1, 23, and 53 courtesy of Cheng An-chi.

Chapter 4: Photograph on page 77 courtesy of Cheng An-chi. Photographs on pages 81 and 82 by Michelle T. King, with the permission of Cheng Hsien-hao.

Chapter 5: Photograph on page 103 courtesy of Cheng An-chi.

Chapter 6: Photograph on page 131 courtesy of Cheng An-chi. Photograph on page 143 by Michelle T. King, with the permission of Cheng Hsien-hao.

Chapter 7: Photograph on page 155 courtesy of Cheng An-chi.

Chapter 8: Photograph on page 177 reprinted with the permission of Q Place Creative Inc.

Chapter 9: Photograph on page 209 courtesy of Ellen Huang King.

Chapter 10: Photographs on page 229 courtesy of Chris Yang (Piglet & Co., San Francisco), Linda Tay Esposito, Lynn Chang (www.uniqlay.com), and Daphne Wu.

Epilogue: Bar graph on page 251 courtesy of Penelope King.

Index

Page numbers in *italics* refer to illustrations.

dowries, 109–10
DPP (Democratic Progressive Party),
180, 185
Dragon Boat Festival, 69, 220
dragon-phoenix legs, 62–63
Dream of the Red Chamber, The (Cao),
31
Drompp, Michael, 96–99
duck, 44, 92, 93, 133, 135, 171, 234,
238, 245
dumplings, 12, 25–26, 45, 165, *251,*
253–54
Dunlop, Fuchsia, 232
Dynasty Restaurant, 227

E
earthiness, 16
Eastern Han dynasty, 31
*Easy Family Recipes from a Chinese-
American Childhood* (Hom), 224
eel, 44
efficiency, 118
egg rolls, 96
eggplant, *229,* 231, 234, 236
eggs, 49, 63, 71
Election Study Center, 191
elections, 123–24
elementary schools, 115
embroidery, 31
emigration from mainland to Taiwan,
See migration
English language, 94, 205
Erway, Cathy, 192
Esposito, Linda Tay, *229*
Executive Yuan Law and Regulations
Commission, 111
extramarital affairs, 118

F
factory workers, 33
Faist, Ed, 96
families, 18, 29–30, 32–34, 136
Families magazine, 105, 117–18,
165–67

Family (Ba Jin), 33
Family Recipes (TV show), 74
family structures, 17–18, 29–34
family values, 32
fast food, 172–73
February 28 Incident (1947), 18–19,
189
Feminine Mystique, The (Friedan),
111
feminism, 106–7, 111–14, 116–20,
123–24
Fifth Chinese Daughter (Wong), 243
finances, 108–11, 118
Finding Your Roots (TV show), 227
fire-time, 12–13, 55, 141, 172
first wave migration, 223–25
fish, 69, *82,* 92, 133, 189; *See also*
squirreled fish
flexible accommodation, 117
Florida, 147
flour, 12, 16
Flushing, Queens, New York City,
226
Foo, Susanna, 120–23
Foochow regional cuisine, 93
food(s); *See also* frozen foods; industrial food products; specific
foods, e.g. fish
as anchor of Chinese identity, 244
bloggers, 249
canned, 160, 167
cultural significance of, 22
as culture, 255–56
fast, 172–73
history of, 241
ingredients, availability of, 91–93
in matters of state, 136
molded, 84
Western, 63, 64, 69–71, 172–73
Food and Wine magazine, 120
Food Logistics Training Center, 145
food preservation, 159
food shopping, 167–68
food writing, 9–11

gender roles and expectations,
106–25; *See also* feminism; men;
women; working women
and Cheng Shao-ching, 40–41, 116
and cultural shifts, 29, 33–37
and finances, 108–11
and Susanna Foo, 120–23
in meal preparation, 14, 106–8,
114–16, 246, 248
in politics, 123–25
Germany, 6
Getz, Judy, 95, 100
ginger, 21, 25, 56
Girardin, Jaline, 233–34
Global Thai, 150
"Glory's by Blossom Bridge" (Pai), 20
Go Peh-hok (Momofuku Ando), 162
goji berries, 161
gold mines, 223
Gone with the Wind (Mitchell), 227
Gong, Sasha, 139
Good Earth, The (Buck), 214
Google Doodle, 235
goulash, 71
Grace A. Dow Memorial Library, 217
Great Britain, 6, 10–11
Great Hall of the People, 133
Great Leap Forward, 138–39
Great Learning, The (Confucius),
136–37
green beans, 165
Greensboro, N.C., 241
grocery stores, 167–68, 220–21
Guan Renjian, 181
Guangdong, 16, 139
Guangdong Province, 15, 17, 223–24
Guangdong (Cantonese) regional cui-
sine, 16, 68–69, 93, 149, 238
Guilin, 20

H
Hainan Province, 187
Hakka descendants, 15, 184, 203–4
ham, 63, 84, 92

hamburgers, 173
Han descendants, xxii, 194
Hangzhou regional cuisine, 16, 94
Harvard University, 214
Hebei, 16, 17
Henan, 16, 17
Herbert Henry Dow High School, 218
Higgins Lake, 220
Ho, Denise, 232–33
Hokkien descendants, 15, 184, 203
Hom, Ken, 223–24
home cooks, 213, 231–32, 246–47
Hong Kong, 87, 128, 146, 225–26
Honolulu, Hawaii, 223
horsemeat, 20
hotdogs, 127
Houghton Lake, 220
household tasks, 117
housewives, 30, 33, 47–51, 117–19
How to Cook and Eat in Chinese
(Chao), 88, 214
Hsiung, Deh-Ta, 91
Hsu, Alice, 226–27
Hsu, Madeline, 223, 225
Hu Peiqiang, 63, 64, 81
Hu Qingheng, 118
Huang, Eddie, 192
Huang, Elizabeth, 170
Huang, Harrison, 246–47, 254
Huang Su-huei, 90, 94, 183
Huang Yuanshan, 37–40, 42, 63, 71,
81, 83–84, 128, 213
Hubei, 17
humility, 31
Hunan Province, 17, 192
Hunan regional cuisine, 16, 91, 93
Hunanese cuisine, 93, 95, 186
Hung, Katy Hui-wen, 183
hyperinflation, 18

I
I Love Lucy (TV show), 60
Illinois, 100
Immigration and Nationality Act, 225